Ethical Economy. Studies in Economic Ethics and Philosophy

Volume 52

AF738390

Ethical Economy describes the theory of the ethical preconditions of the economy and of business as well as the theory of the ethical foundations of economic systems. It analyzes the impact of rules, virtues, and goods or values on economic action and management. *Ethical Economy* understands ethics as a means to increase trust and to reduce transaction costs. It forms a foundational theory for business ethics and business culture.

The Series *Ethical Economy. Studies in Economic Ethics and Philosophy* is devoted to the investigation of interdisciplinary issues concerning economics, management, ethics, and philosophy. These issues fall in the categories of economic ethics, business ethics, management theory, economic culture, and economic philosophy, the latter including the epistemology and ontology of economics. Economic culture comprises cultural and hermeneutic studies of the economy.

One goal of the series is to extend the discussion of the philosophical, ethical, and cultural foundations of economics and economic systems. The series is intended to serve as an international forum for scholarly publications, such as monographs, conference proceedings, and collections of essays. Primary emphasis is placed on originality, clarity, and interdisciplinary synthesis of elements from economics, management theory, ethics, and philosophy.

More information about this series at http://www.springer.com/series/2881

Josef Wieland
Editor

Creating Shared Value – Concepts, Experience, Criticism

Springer

Editor
Josef Wieland
Leadership Excellence Inst Zeppelin
Zeppelin University Friedrichshafen
Leadership Excellence Inst Zeppelin
Friedrichshafen, Baden-Württemberg,
Germany

ISSN 2211-2707 ISSN 2211-2723 (electronic)
Ethical Economy
ISBN 978-3-319-48801-1 ISBN 978-3-319-48802-8 (eBook)
DOI 10.1007/978-3-319-48802-8

Library of Congress Control Number: 2016963432

Printed on acid-free paper

This Springer imprint is published by Springer Nature
The registered company is Springer International Publishing AG
The registered company address is: Gewerbestrasse 11, 6330 Cham, Switzerland

Contents

About the Authors

Thomas Beschorner is director of the Institute for Business Ethics at the University of St. Gallen. He studied economics at the University of Kassel and the National University of Ireland. In 2001, he realized his PhD at the University of Erfurt and in 2007 his habilitation at the University of Oldenburg. He was visiting professor at McGill University and DAAD professor at the Université de Montréal. He is professor for business ethics at the University of St. Gallen since 2011.

Michael Fürst has responsibilities for the Novartis CR strategy that has a focus on inclusive business solutions and innovations that are scalable in nature and pursue the ultimate objective to increase access to healthcare. He is the secretary of the Novartis CR Board. Michael was appointed as a social entrepreneur in residence by INSEAD and holds lectures at leading universities and business schools. His PhD is from the University of Oldenburg (summa cum laude). In 2006, he was awarded with the German Max Weber Prize for Business Ethics.

Thomas Hajduk is CSR policy advisor at the Economics Ministry of North Rhine-Westphalia and visiting lecturer at the Institute for Business Ethics. Thomas studied history, political science, and philosophy in Münster, Potsdam, and Berlin and received his master's degree in modern history from the University of Durham. He is working on his PhD thesis (working title: "Multinational enterprises and international codes of conduct") at Viadrina European University.

Matthias Kettner is professor of practical philosophy at the Faculty of Humanities and Arts at Witten/Herdecke University (www.uni-wh.de) in Germany. He was faculty dean between 2003 and 2006, and he is now research dean. From 1994 to 2000, he was a fellow at the Institute for Advanced Studies in the Faculty of Humanities at Essen University (www.kwi-nrw.de) where his research focused on clinical ethics committees in Germany, communicative ethics, and the relations amidst applied ethics, biopolitics, and democracy. In 1987–1993, he collaborated with Karl-Otto Apel in his research on discourse ethics at Frankfurt University where he had earned a PhD in philosophy (thesis advisors: K.-O. Apel and J. Habermas), a diploma in psychology, and his postdoctoral lecture qualification (habilitation).

Aloys Leo Prinz is full professor of economics at Westfälische Wilhelms-University Münster, Institute of Public Economics. He holds a doctoral degree in economics from Free University of Berlin. Before coming to Münster, he was full professor of economics at Johannes Gutenberg University Mainz. His work focuses primarily on public economics. In addition to publishing intensively in scientific journals, he has also co-authored economic books for general readers.

Jacob Dahl Rendtorff is senior associate professor of responsibility, ethics, and legitimacy of corporations at Roskilde University, Denmark, and he is also visiting professor in philosophy of management and ethical judgment at Copenhagen Business School. Rendtorff has a background in research in ethics, business ethics, bioethics, information ethics, political theory, and philosophy of law. Rendtorff has written many articles and more than ten books on issues of existentialism and hermeneutics, French philosophy, ethics, bioethics and business ethics, as well as philosophy of law, and he has been co-author and editor on more than ten other books. In particular, these are *Responsibility, Ethics and Legitimacy of Corporations* (Copenhagen Business School Press 2009) and *French Philosophy and Social Theory: A Perspective for Ethics and Philosophy of Management* (Springer International Publisher 2014).

Ford Shanahan is the general counsel for a multinational group of companies in the healthcare sector. He also serves as an adjunct professor at Franklin University in Lugano, Switzerland, where he teaches courses in business ethics and business law. He obtained his law degree and MBA from the University of Denver and is completing a PhD in business ethics at the Università della Svizzera italiana in Lugano.

Michael Schramm is professor of Catholic theology and business ethics at the Faculty of Business, Economics and Social Sciences at the University of Hohenheim since 2001. Prior to this, he held the chair of Christian social sciences at the Faculty of Catholic Theology in Erfurt (1995–2001). He was speaker of the Association for Social Ethics (2006–2009) and is a member of the German Economic Association and the German Whitehead Society. His main research topics include business metaphysics, transaction ethics, process theology, and the metaphysics of money.

Peter Seele is associate professor of corporate social responsibility and business ethics at the Università della Svizzera italiana in Lugano, Switzerland, where he also directs the Ethics and Communication Law Center. Peter has studied philosophy, economics, and theology in Germany at the Universities of Oldenburg, Düsseldorf, and Witten/Herdecke as well as the Delhi School of Economics.

Josef Wieland is professor of institutional economics, organizational governance, integrity management, and transcultural leadership at the Zeppelin University in Friedrichshafen and director of the Leadership Excellence Institute Zeppelin (LEIZ). Prior to this, he was the professor for business administration and economics with an emphasis on business ethics at the University of Applied Sciences, Konstanz, and continues to be the director of the cooperative doctoral program there. He is the initiator and president of the Forum Compliance & Integrity (FCI), as well as chairman of the German Network of Business Ethics (DNWE). He is a member of the national CSR Forum of the BMAS (German Federal Ministry of Labor and Social Affairs) and serves on the jury board for the "CSR Prize" of the German government.

Over the last years, "Creating Shared Value" has become a much discussed concept in business practice as well as in management theory and especially in the context of corporate social responsibility. This book offers a contribution to the current academic discussions on the well-received article of Michael Porter and Marc Kramer in *Harvard Business Review* in 2011. In the light of the increasing references to the shared value concept, it develops a critical discussion on its fundamentals and its implications for the relationship between economy and society. By that, the book seeks to shed light on the understanding of the role and the nature of the firm in a globalized economy. The result is a collection of interdisciplinary academic reviews which offer interdisciplinary reflections on "Creating Shared Value" to illuminate theoretical, conceptual, and practical challenges of the topic. Within the fields of business ethics, theory of the firm, management, and philosophy, researcher, students, and practitioners will be given a deeper insight on how to approach the concept in a conceptional and philosophical way.

Chapter 1
Introduction

Josef Wieland

Abstract The present issue is based on contributions to the annual meeting of the German Philosophical Society's Research Group on Economics and Ethics. The conference took place in May 2015 at the Leadership Excellence Institute Zeppelin | LEIZ at Zeppelin University Friedrichshafen and focused on the topic of "Creating Shared Value".

The present issue is based on contributions to the annual meeting of the German Philosophical Society's Research Group on Economics and Ethics. The conference took place in May 2015 at the Leadership Excellence Institute Zeppelin | LEIZ at Zeppelin University Friedrichshafen and focused on the topic of "Creating Shared Value".

Over the last years, "Creating Shared Value" has become a much discussed concept in business practice as well as in management theory and especially in the context of corporate social responsibility. This book offers a contribution to the current academic discussions on the well-received article of Michael Porter and Marc Kramer in Harvard Business Review in 2011. In the light of the increasing references to the shared value concept, the book develops a critical discussion on its fundamentals and its implications for the relationship between economy and society. In this way, the book seeks to shed light on the understanding of the role and the nature of the firm in a globalized economy. The result is a colorful collection of interdisciplinary academic reviews which offer interdisciplinary reflections on "Creating Shared Value" to illuminate theoretical, conceptual and practical challenges of the topic.

Notably regarding the debate on corporate social responsibility the concept of "Creating Shared Value" gained much interest (Porter and Kramer 2006, 2011; Beschorner 2013; Hartmann and Werhane 2013; Wieland and Heck 2013; Crane et al. 2014). Porter/Kramer use the concept to contest their understanding of CSR. Shared value in this sense could be characterized as a driver for market development, innovation and economic growth (Porter and Kramer 2006: 65). By

J. Wieland (✉)
Leadership Excellence Inst Zeppelin, Zeppelin University Friedrichshafen Leadership Excellence Inst Zeppelin, Friedrichshafen, Baden-Württemberg, Germany
e-mail: josef.wieland@zu.de

J. Wieland (ed.), *Creating Shared Value – Concepts, Experience, Criticism*, Ethical Economy 52, DOI 10.1007/978-3-319-48802-8_1

"reconceiving products and markets", by "redefining productivity in the value chain", and by "enabling local cluster development" companies are seen to be able to "create shared value opportunities" (Porter and Kramer 2006: 65). The European Commission likewise asks companies to maximize the "creation of shared value for their owners/shareholders and for their other stakeholders and society at large" (EU 2011: 6). Companies shall integrate "social, environmental, ethical, human rights and consumer concerns into their business operations" (EU 2011: 6) to fully meet their corporate social responsibility. Critics for example stress that the concept of creating shared value, as development by Porter/Kramer, implies a shallow view on the role of the corporation in society (Crane et al. 2014: 139), that their understanding of CSR is too narrow (Beschorner 2013: 109; Crane et al. 2014: 134), or that they focus too much on purely economic logic (Beschorner 2013: 109).

Nevertheless "Shared Value" increasingly becomes both a subject of the broad field of CSR research and a central term in dealing with the universal challenges of the present world. In 2015, United Nations passed "The 2030 Agenda for sustainable development" building upon "The Road to Dignity by 2030" (United Nations 2014) wherein the Secretary-General calls for "shared responsibilities to embark on a path to inclusive and shared prosperity" (United Nations 2014: 3). Multilateral action is demanded that is "build on shared values, principles, and priorities for a common destiny." (United Nations 2014: 5) People have "to think in terms of shared responsibilities for a shared future" (United Nations 2014: 14). Furthermore, the paper provides six essential elements to frame and reinforce Sustainable Development Goals. One of these goals claims that "Economic growth should lead to shared prosperity" (United Nations 2014: 22), that it is "vital for growing inclusive and sustainable economies" that business models are to be transformed to the creation of shared value (United Nations 2014: 22). Furthermore, this will necessitate a broader, deeper, and more precise "understanding of economic performance, and our metrics for gauging it" (United Nations 2014: 37).

In the light of the increasing references to the shared value concept, a critical discussion on its fundamentals and its implications for the relationship between economy and society could shed light on our understanding of the role and the nature of the firm in a globalized economy.

The following contributions all examine the issues which are outlined here in brief:

Part I deals with the *fundamental conceptions of "Shared Value"* as caught in a tension between society and economy. The chapter is structured with a more conceptual and theoretical frame and includes contributions to the critical debate on "Creating Shared Value". In addition, the contributions serve to further the discussion regarding the perception of "Corporate Social Responsibility" either in a contrary, complementary or novel way.

My own contribution opens with a critical reflection on the different ways of interpreting "Creating Shared Value" (CSV) and argues that it was conceived of primarily as a concept for development and growth in a globalised world. In this context, it is the task of companies and their strategic management teams to contribute to the latter by activating the potential for value creation. In my view, Porter/

Kramer fail to devote sufficient attention to the question of whether it is possible under these conditions for a company-specific internal CSV strategy to emerge. The uncertainty regarding information and expectations that goes hand in hand with a CSV strategy therefore necessitates intersectoral cooperation and the integration of stakeholders using corporate governance mechanisms. The approach taken in this contribution is based on a debate which is rooted in economic philosophy and which places the social dimension of the SV concept into the dimensions of management theory and morality within an economic discussion.

Thomas Beschorner/Thomas Hajduk use their contribution to express fundamental criticism of the "Creating Shared Value" (CSV) approach. In this contribution, CSV falls short of what can be understood as a modern form of corporate responsibility. As a "one-trick pony", CSV fails to adequately address all social issues, especially in cases where no economic opportunities are to be found. Essentially, the authors address the reductionist perspective of Porter/Kramer towards companies and society. Instead, they call for a more balanced relationship to be defined in order to reposition the concept's economic value and use connotation against a background of rising societal demands. The contribution ends with some critical remarks on the role of academic scholarship and how it relates to practice.

The contribution by *Aloys Leo Prinz* examines the discussion surrounding "*Corporate Social Responsibility (CSR). Cui bono?*" from the viewpoint of political economics. People and groups that are not directly associated with the company engage in rent-seeking by using a logic based on moral justification to articulate their claims against the company. The author makes a distinction between productive and unproductive forms of rent-seeking, based on whether a moral dimension has been satisfied with respect to demand for the product. At best, the conditions of productivity and competition generate economic and social value for the company stakeholder, which nevertheless results in distribution issues and conflicts – so-called "justification conflicts". CSR can therefore have a negative as well as redistributing effect. The trade-off between the profit-orientated goals of the shareholder and the social and ethical goals of the stakeholder is described by the author using the "Profits-Ethics-Possibility Frontier (PEPF)" utility curve. By doing so, it is possible to derive an optimum for CSR as well as CSV.

Michael Fürst uses his deliberations to address traditional readings of corporate responsibility. He discusses Milton Friedman's economic-libertarian understanding of a company together with its purpose and legitimising function, and the management view of corporate responsibility developed by Peter Drucker. The latter focuses on the avoidance of negative external effects as well as opportunities for creating social well-being. In doing so, *Fürst* works on the level of a targeted perspective in order to sketch out ways of arriving at a constructive critical appreciation of the "Creating Shared Value" (CSV) approach and to develop it further. In this respect, Fürst understands CSV to be a strategic, competition-orientated intervention element in the "Corporate Social Responsibility" (CSR) portfolio, not least because the theoretical and practically established maturity of CSR allows for such differentiations to be made.

Part II is devoted to the *Philosophical Debate and Critical Reflections* on "Creating Shared Value".

The contribution by *Michael Schramm "How the (Business) World Really Works. Business Metaphysics & 'Creating Shared Value'"* is a discussion which addresses business ethics, and how the connection between corporate value-addition and the demands of society is constructed. Having established that Porter/Kramer lack a systematic method for examining this connection, *Schramm* then arrives at the conclusion that the "Creating Shared Value" (CSV) approach does indeed do justice to its own conceptual ambitions. Far more than being a purely pragmatic approach to saving the capitalist model, companies are, by way of their legitimation, agents of added social value and the common good. That CSV in this case merely marks the starting point for addressing how additional economic value can be created through added social value essentially encapsulates the long-lasting need to establish a synthesis between economics and ethics.

The essay written by *Jacob Dahl Rendtorff* addresses "*Corporate Philanthropy, CSR and CSV. Limits and Possibilities.*" He begins with considering the outcome of a detailed examination of Milton Friedman's profit-maximising position. To this end, he uses the results of a literature analysis which indicate that Friedman's lines of argument in "Capitalism and Freedom" and "The Social Responsibility of Business is to Increase its Profits" are inconsistent in their treatment of ethical practice. *Rendtorff* believes that the problematic nature of such a theoretically simplistic view – which is also to be found in Porter/Kramer – is apparent in the narrow understanding of concepts such as corporate philanthropy and CSR. He argues in favor of a more pertinent inclusion of issues relating to business ethics as a way of pursuing a more appropriate understanding of the role companies play in society.

The contribution written by *Ford Shanahan/Peter Seele* continues the philosophical discussion of Aristotelian virtue and transfers it to economic organisations using the term "corporate virtue". In their discussion, the authors posit the view that the pursuit of corporate value-addition is founded on an understanding of virtue which is inadequately reflected in the mere functional pursuit of profit. This is expressed in the "Creating Shared Value" approach put forward by Porter/Kramer. As a consequence, social and economic processes of value- addition encourage an understanding of corporate virtue which strives for moral excellence, and which is reflected in the decision-making and actions of the management and in commercial processes.

Closing the book is an article by *Matthias Kettner "Between Enthusiasm and Overkill. Assessing Michael Porter's Conceptual Management Frame of Creating Shared Value"*. Kettner outlines the influence of the CSV concept of Porter/Kramer, presents the critical aspects suggested in the discussion and expands on them from the viewpoint of discourse ethics. Unlike many scholars he makes the point that impact on and popularity among practitioners are not necessarily de-pendent on scientific theory quality but rather on communicability via clear and applicable conceptual management frames and other factors. In his final analysis, *Kettner* argues that the valuable lessons of CVS should be handled more productively, and uses discourse ethics to offer an alternative solution to the crisis of legitimacy affecting modern capitalism.

I would like to thank all the authors sincerely – not only for their contributions to this book, but also for the lively, critical and valuable discussion which took place at the "Annual meeting of the German Philosophical Society's Research Group on Economics and Ethics" in early summer last year.

Moreover I would particularly like to thank Isabel Jandeisek, and furthermore Marcus Ehrenberger and Anika Rehder for their support in creating this book.

Friedrichshafen, July 2016 Josef Wieland

References

Beschorner, Thomas. 2013. Creating shared value: The one-trick Pony approach – A comment on Michael Porter and Mark Kramer. *Business Ethics Journal Review* 1(17): 106–112. doi:10.12747/bejr2013.01.17.

Crane, Andrew, Guido Palazzo, Laura J. Spence, and Dirk Matten. 2014. Contesting the value of the shared value concept. *California Management Review* 56(2): 130–153.

Europäische Kommission. 2011. A renewed EU strategy 2011-14 for Corporate Social Responsibility. COM (2011) 681 final.

Hartman, L.P., and P.H. Werhane. 2013. Proposition: Shared Value as an Incomplete Mental Model. *Business Ethics Journal Review* 1(6): 36–43. doi:10.12747/bejr2013.01.06.

Porter, M.E., and M.R. Kramer. 2006. Strategy and society. The link between competitive advantage and corporate social responsibility. *Harvard Business Review* 84(12): 78–92.

———. 2011. Creating shared value. How to reinvent capitalism – and Unleash a wave of innovation and growth. *Harvard Business Review* 89(1): 62–77.

United Nations. 2014. A/69/700 – The road to dignity by 2030: Ending poverty, transforming all lives and protecting the planet. UN Sustainable Development Knowledge Platform. http://sustainabledevelopment.un.org/content/documents/5527SR_advance%20unedited_final.pdf. Accessed Mar 2016.

Wieland, Josef, and Andreas E.H. Heck. 2013. *Shared value durch stakeholder governance*. Marburg: Metropolis.

Part I
Creating Shared Value: Concept and Discussion

Chapter 2
Shared Value – Theoretical Implications, Practical Challenges

Josef Wieland

Abstract Academic and public debate on Michael Porter and Mark Kramer's concept of "Shared Value Creation" (SVC) as a strategic orientation for business models reflects a fundamental and significant debate in society about reconfiguring the relationship between business and society. (Porter and Kramer, Creating shared value. Harv Business Rev 89(1/2): 62–77, 2011) The demand made by the Secretary General of the UN to ask and answer, as part of this debate, questions to do with "understanding economic performance, and our metrics for gauging it" (United Nations, The road to dignity by 2030: ending poverty, Transforming all lives and protecting the planet. Synthesis report of the secretary-general on the post-2015 Agenda. UN. http://www.un.org/disabilities/documents/reports/SG_Synthesis_Report_Road_to_Dignity_by_2030.pdf. Accessed 13 Jan 2016, 2014: 37) is therefore fundamental. The dominance of "shareholder value creation" as a strategic orientation has been subjected to radical questioning. The times are over when it was sufficient to answer questions about corporate social responsibility with the terse statement "the business of business is business". This debate is about social-theoretical and philosophical questions, but also about the long-standing discussion in economic theory about the nature of the firm. At the same time, though, practical issues regarding the strategic and operative management of companies are being discussed. This is not only legitimate, but also inevitable, if the CSR debate is to assume a practical and leading role in the business models of firms. The Porter/Kramer concept for a strategy of SVC is relevant here, since it is an essential, and currently the most important, contribution to an economic discussion that is necessary in, not least, a socio-theoretical and philosophical sense.

J. Wieland (✉)
Leadership Excellence Inst Zeppelin, Zeppelin University Friedrichshafen Leadership Excellence Inst Zeppelin, Friedrichshafen, Baden-Württemberg, Germany
e-mail: josef.wieland@zu.de

J. Wieland (ed.), *Creating Shared Value – Concepts, Experience, Criticism*, Ethical Economy 52, DOI 10.1007/978-3-319-48802-8_2

2.1 Theoretical Concepts

2.1.1 Shared Value – Society and Business

1. The concept of "Shared Value Creation" (SVC) put on the agenda of economic, political, and civil-society debates by Michael Porter and Mark Kramer in their Harvard Business Review article of 2011 has attracted different interpretations. The diverse reception of this concept, which goes far beyond its discussion in the economic discipline, is not always understood by its critics. This can lead to distortions when it comes to assessing its theoretical and practical importance. We therefore wish to begin by investigating these different variants of interpretation.

In essence, the concept itself, and all the different concepts of "shared value" related to it, focus on the relationship between "business and society". That is their common denominator. It is frequently overlooked that this includes not only the economic and business dimension of this relationship, but also its socio-political dimension. As Porter and Kramer write:

> The concept of shared value – which focuses on the connections between societal and economic progress – has the power to unleash the next wave of global growth. (Porter/Kramer 2011: 65)

We should distinguish this overarching economic dimension from the strategic management of a company on the one hand, and from the moral coding of the concept on the other. Both perspectives believe that creating a parallelism and win-win situation of private and public wealth is feasible. Unlike Adam Smith,[1] though, wealth is understood here not as the automatic result of the market's invisible hand, but as something that requires appropriate structures of corporate governance.

> More and more, companies are creating shared value by developing profitable business strategies that deliver tangible social benefits. The thing is creating major new opportunities for profit and competitive advantage at the same time as it benefits society by unleashing the power of business to help solve fundamental global problems. (Porter et al. 2012: 1)

Among other things, SVC is essentially about "creating", "developing", "opportunities", "to help", with the cooperation of organizations, i.e., about a common learning process involving business, politics and society, that includes the possibility of failure. The common criticism of this concept – that the trade-off between private and public wealth is not automatically given (and can in fact even be negative) – is undoubtedly true, although it fails to apply to the challenges the concept of SVC seeks to meet. The criticism also lacks specificity, since this applies to all human practice.

2. The possible consequences of this multi-dimensional debate on the theoretical and practical content of the Porter/Kramer concept, which we will explore in more detail later, are difficult to foresee at present. Professional investors and business ethicists are, albeit for different reasons, united in their critical scepticism when it

[1] Cf. Smith (1991).

comes to the practical usefulness of the concept. What seems to be indisputable, however, is that mainstream theory-formation in economics reflects the narrowing of perspective to the economic responsibility of business, but not the formative developmental dynamics in the emergence of a global economic space and a global society. On the one hand, there is the question of how the economic and social responsibility of companies can be redefined jointly with government and civil society in consideration of social and environmental arguments in order to be able to deal with the consequences and challenges of global value chains that have long been visible. On the other, this presupposes for exactly these consequences and challenges to be understood and accepted as those of a common world shared by many nations and stakeholders. After all, the "Sustainable Development Goals"[2] adopted by the UN in 2015 as part of its Agenda 2030 not only include 17 targets with more than 700 subtargets, but can only be achieved by politics, business and civil society through collective action that has a global reach. In a sense, they require awareness of the fact that the global world is not simply a world, but the shared world of present and future generations. This is reflected not least in the title given to this agenda: "Transforming our world – the Agenda 2030", which the UN Global Compact accurately interprets:

> The Sustainable Development Goals provide a powerful aspiration for improving our world – laying out where we collectively need to go and how to get there.[3]

The heated debate on a strategic orientation of the economy and its businesses towards "shared value" should therefore, and can only, be seen against this background, which, ultimately, it reflects. The European Commission already called for business to be aware of its social responsibility in its CSR communication of 2011:

> [...] maximizing the creation of shared value for their owners/shareholders and for their other stakeholders and society at large [...] enterprises are encouraged to adopt a long-term, strategic approach to CSR [...] (European Commission 2011: 6)

In preparation for "Agenda 2030", the UN circulated in December 2014 a working paper by the Secretary-General entitled "The Road to Dignity by 2030". In it, he made explicit the connection between social responsibility, "shared value creation", and inclusive societies. The demand for "shared responsibilities to embark on a path to inclusive and shared prosperity" (United Nations 2014: 3) builds in turn on "shared values, principles, and priorities for a common destiny", (United Nations 2014: 5) and requires a global, rather than a local or national, perspective, a perspective that is to be thought of "in terms of shared responsibilities for a shared future" (United Nations 2014: 14). He then argues from an economic angle that "economic growth should lead to shared prosperity" (United Nations 2014: 22), and that conventional "business models [are to be transformed] for creating shared value" (United Nations 2014: 22). But this necessarily requires a wider and deeper

---

[2] Cf. United Nations 2014. http://www.un.org/disabilities/documents/reports/SG_Synthesis_Report_Road_to_Dignity_by_2030.pdf (accessed 16.02.2016).

[3] United Nations Global Compact 2015. https://www.unglobalcompact.org/what-is-gc/our-work/sustainable-development/sdgs (accessed 16.02.2016).

"understanding of economic performance, and our metrics for gauging it" (United Nations 2014: 37). This will be the focus of our analysis here.

2.1.2 *Shared Value Creation (SVC) – The Porter/Kramer Concept*

1. It is essential to point out here that the debate on "shared value" as a task for the strategic management of companies as launched and since dominated by Porter and Kramer (2006, 2011, 2012), relates to the discussion in politics and society sketched above, which it reflects and productively implements this discussion through a proposal for corporate management. It is important to understand here that both concepts – Porter and Kramer's, as well as that arising from the political and civil-societal discussion – are not identical in terms of content.

We have already noted that "shared value" is first and foremost economic concept of development and growth for a globalized world, a concept based on the ideas of strategic philanthropy developed by Porter and Kramer (1999, 2002) and on the "bottom-of-the-pyramid" approach of Prahalad and Hart (2002). Companies can then participate in this global economic process of development and growth, which, according to Porter and Kramer, could lead to a reinvention of capitalism:

> Every firm should look at decisions and opportunities through the lens of shared value. This will lead to new approaches that generate greater innovation and growth for companies – and also greater benefits for society. (Porter/Kramer 2011: 65)

For Porter and Kramer, "shared value" should therefore be understood not as a "redistribution approach", (2011: 65) but rather as a parallel process of value creation through new products and markets, through increases in productivity in the value chain, and through the development of supporting, local business clusters (Ibid: 67). Porter and Kramer's division of an appropriate strategic win-win management model can therefore, at least according to the authors, reconcile social progress and profit maximization as a corporate goal (Ibid: 76), just as much as it can reconcile claims that, while the model is concerned with solving social problems, its "agenda [is] company specific and internally generated" (Ibid: 76). We will have to return to the question of how this duality leads to theoretical inconsistencies in the Porter/Kramer approach, which, in this form, renders it somewhat hazardous.

2. Unlike Porter and Kramer's innovation, competition, and market-growth-focused approach which, in my view, rashly, declares "Creating Shared Value" (Porter and Kramer 2011: 64) to be an alternative to CSR (Ibid: 76), the European Commission understands "shared value" as a consequence of a long-term and strategic concept of CSR placing social and ecological alongside the economic components within the core business of companies and, thereby, taking account of the interests of the relevant stakeholders (European Commission 2011: 7f). Unlike Porter and Kramer, the EU communication understands the "agenda" of the "shared

value" concept not as "company specific and internally generated" (Porter and Kramer 2011: 76), but rather as value creation driven by the integration of stakeholder interests and stakeholder resources, which results in anchoring CSR in the core business.[4] In this integrative and strategic understanding of CSR, the EU Commission answers the question of whether CSR should be an element of the business model of a company positively; this is in contrast to Porter and Kramer. The impetus behind this business model is therefore not a company's strategy of innovation and growth, but the negative external effects of economic value creation as perceived and defined by society. Only their internalization in the core business of companies can lead to innovations and new business opportunities, which may then require legitimation by society as not only technically and economically attractive, but also as a socially accepted solution of internalization. "Open Innovation" (cf. Chesbrough 2006) and "Social Innovation" (cf. Mulgan 2006) are the relevant strategic elements here. If a company cannot achieve this social and political acceptance both of strategic decisions and of the products or services that result, then a SVC strategy in Porter and Kramer's sense is not feasible. In other words, if the SVC agenda really were only generated internally and company-specific, then it would be doomed to failure. And what is more: we have to distinguish between CSR as a component of the core business, as an expression of a "shared value" strategy, and the configuration of CSR actions to address specific stakeholder interests (Maltz et al. 2011: 344), both of which together constitute the essence of companies' awareness of social responsibility. CSR is therefore not absorbed into SVC. Social commitment at the company's location, in the global value chain, or with regard to employees – these cannot simply be subsumed to an SVC strategy. Later we will see that both CSR types (or, in the diction of Porter and Kramer, three types) can be related to each other. Porter and Kramer (2006) too accept this social differentiation and distinguish between "Generic social issues", "Value chain social impact", and "Social dimensions of competitive context" (Porter and Kramer 2006: 85). For them, this poses the problem of prioritizing between those three areas, depending on the company, although their concept of SVC refers only to the latter area.

3. The Porter/Kramer concept of "Creating Shared Value" has often been criticized for various sound reasons and by different groups of actors.[5] But this need not mean abandoning the concept itself, since it reflects and condenses a debate in society that is and will be of fundamental importance for the further theoretical generalization and practical development of the CSR debate – for example, for the debate on the "Theory of the Firm" or on "Corporate Governance". Above I tried to develop the reasons for this view:

(i) The concept of an economy to create "shared value", as demanded by society, is deliberately opposed to the concept of "shareholder value" as the dominant

[4] On this argument, see also Wieland and Heck (2013: 14ff.).

[5] For the discussion on business ethics, cf. Hartmann and Werhane (2013); Beschorner (2013); Crane et al. (2014). For the German discussion of business ethics, cf. the articles on the theme in zfwu, vol. 16 (2), 2015.

and exclusive objective of economic activity. It ultimately comes down to regulatory policy and corporate governance, issues that are of the greatest practical and theoretical interest – not least because they are the result of a long-lasting and far-reaching debate in society.

(ii) However, the discursive proliferation of terms containing the adjective "shared" (such as "shared value", "shared values", "shared principles", "shared prosperity", "shared responsibility") also points to an implicit, yet differently approached, moral discussion about social justice. This discussion (on issues such as, inter alia win-win situations, distributive justice, inclusion, welfare, and fairness) including its philosophical presuppositions and relevant practical consequences, has barely yet been addresses and fed into public discourses.

(iii) The containment of the concept of shareholder value by societal interests that we perceive today feeds on the globalization of economic and political development, whose challenges are specified in the Agenda 2030 as, inter alia, tasks facing business and the management of its companies. Thus, both the economic and the moral meaning of the terms "shared" and "value" should be understood along global and thus transcultural lines. Sharing, commonality, value – these are fundamental societal categories whose connotation draws on the respective cultures and whose development into transcultural categories is still very much in its infancy. Porter's and Kramer's approach fails to acknowledge this issue of intercultural difference in the local meaning of values, which is a further theoretical inconsistency that calls into question whether this concept is feasible for companies that operate globally. For, if different views prevail as to what sharing, commonality and value mean with regard to a concrete transaction, then we cannot talk either logically or practically of creating them globally.

I would therefore argue that we need a debate in the philosophy of business not least to sharpen further the corporate and social, the economic and moral, content of the concept of "shared value". For, a particular flaw in the Porter/Kramer concept is precisely that it reduces social debate to one of management theory, and moral debate to one of economics. But reducing complexity is the lifeblood of any science and would therefore be inappropriate as a criticism of this concept. My point, rather, is the question of how different sectoral logics (which Porter and Kramer also acknowledge) can be linked theoretically and practically without thereby dissolving society into business and morality into economics (or *vice versa*).

2.1.3 Shared Value Through Stakeholder Governance

1. As far as I can tell from the literature and academic debate, the Porter/Kramer concept has not yet led to the further evolution in our "understanding of economic performance, and our metrics of gauging it" (United Nations 2014: 37), that the UN mentions in the context of its Sustainable Development Goals (SDGs) agenda.

Porter et al. (2012) have already addressed this challenge in their (as yet) unpublished article "Measuring Shared Value – How to Unlock Value by Linking Social and Business Results":

> Even the companies that are most advanced in pursuing shared value today lack the data they need to optimize its results. [...] To develop such a strategy, companies must identify key social issues to focus on, plan the relevant business activities involved, and model anticipated business and social benefits relative to projected costs. (Porter et al. 2012: 2)

Porter et al. (2012) are primarily concerned here with emphasizing the economic quantification and measurability of the "benefits" and "costs" of the social involvement of businesses so as to convince the capital market of the validity of this strategic orientation.

> Data and insights from measuring shared value enable companies to scale shared value initiatives while also providing an indispensable basis for effective communication with the investment community. [...] In other words, measurement makes shared value strategies tangible for investors. (Ibid)

And further:

> [...] the aim is to establish a direct linkage between social outcomes and actual financial results. (Ibid: 13)

From an economic perspective, then, this is about the areas of controlling and investor relations, which would have to provide the relevant figures for a company's CSR or SVC strategy. However, the "Shared Value Measurement Process" (Ibid: 4) developed by Porter et al. (2012), and its verification in case studies,[6] shows that this is more about a challenge to be resolved in the future than about an empirically sound corporate-management tool.

It remains ambiguous both in the case studies cited by Porter et al. (2012) and in the academic literature[7] whether there exists a direct causal and directional link between the social commitment of a company and its financial success, besides goodwill and considerations of plausibility. Contrary to what is often suggested in the literature, this is by no means due only to non-valid methods used to calculate the social performance of a company, but rather due to the fact that the costs of corporate social engagement are still not calculated systematically and empirically. If we do not fundamentally revise the controlling instruments currently available, it will remain impossible to calculate empirically the input-output of social commitment (cf. Wieland 2015a). I will discuss this at greater detail in the next section. At any rate, Porter et al. (2012) do see these problems very clearly when they specify, albeit only towards the end of their discussions, a future objective of the SVC concept as follows:

> [...] measurement must assess the extent of value creation – tracking social and business results relative to the costs [...] (Porter et al. 2012: 18)

[6] Coca-Cola, Novo Nordisk, Intel, Nestlé, InterContinental Hotels Group.

[7] Cf., for example, Wieland and Heck (2013); Jhunjhunwala (2014); Spitzeck and Chapman (2012).

2. Without legitimation from society, neither (i) identifying the issues of social responsibility, nor (ii) planning appropriate processes and products in a company, can lead to a consistent and successful strategy of private and social value creation. In the neo-classical theory of the market economy, this normally occurs *ex post* through the market as a governance mechanism to allocate supply and demand. However, identifying and planning socially legitimated opportunities do not take place *ex post* in the medium of the market but *ex ante* in the medium of the organization –through appropriate mechanisms of corporate governance. This is perceived and acknowledged also by Porter et al. (2012), albeit solely with regard to the process of implementing, and measuring the success of, SVC strategies.

> Cross-sector partnerships are becoming increasingly important for executing and measuring shared value strategies. [...] In partnering with companies to achieve shared value objectives, they become co-creators of social and business value. (Porter et al. 2012: 17)

In their quest for social change, NGOs and other political and civil-social actors can become involved as "external evaluation partners", improve the performance of the company by using their "social sector expertise", and "add credibility to the results" (Ibid: 18). Porter et al. are assuming here that a fundamental congruence or parallelism between the objectives pursued (profit/social change) already exists as a basis for cooperation between business and other sectors of society. In reality, however, this needs to be created in the everyday life of the company.

Companies must, in the first place, build the capability of feeding the "Stakeholder View"[8] of their current and future transactions into their business decisions as part of a "shared value" strategy. This does not aim at somehow linking together different interests in a dyadic relationship, as in the Porter model (company interests/ stakeholder interests), but rather at creating a stakeholder network that is the condition of possibility of a common recognition of the "agenda" of corporate social responsibility, and to collectively define the business models, innovations and transactions that might arise from this (cf. ibid: 149). To this end, Sachs, Groth and Schmitt propose a five-stage model that describes a "process of the 'Stakeholder View' to tap stakeholder potential" (Ibid: 150).

Also pointing in the same direction are empirical studies and theoretical debates in the field of corporate governance[9] on "Stakeholder Advisory Boards" and "Stakeholder Advisory Committees", whose influence lies essentially in improving the quality of senior-management decisions, in the field of organizational learning, and, to a lesser extent, in the direct participation in individual decisions. Cooperation can relate to a company's operations, management, and strategic development. These are to be distinguished from "Joint Management-Stakeholder Committees"[10], which aim at the active involvement of stakeholders in the management of companies. In practice, this is often less about dealing with "shared societal concerns", and more

---

[8] For a discussion of the literature, cf. Sachs/Groth/Schmitt (2010).

[9] Cf. Spitzeck and Hansen (2010: 384). Their empirical findings mainly characterize the influence of these forms of cooperation as "low power/low scope".

[10] Cf. Spitzeck/Hansen/Grayson (2011). For the forms of CSR governance, cf. Lock and Seele (2016).

about balancing different stakeholder interests (cf. Lee 2011). But where is the incentive for NGOs and other civil-social organizations to become involved in a company's SVC strategy? Porter and Kramer's answer is: the parallelism of the objectives of cooperation. However, the literature on the intersectoral governance of cooperation clearly shows that this is not enough.[11] It is the task of intersectoral governance and management to provide an accurate analysis of the interests, objectives and motivations of the stakeholders involved so as to make these commonalities visible and then also effective in the cooperation (cf. Wieland 2016).

An SVC strategy as a process that creates (through common awareness and common learning) socially accepted descriptions of problems of economic and social development, and preferences in how to deal with these problems, therefore goes far beyond Porter and Kramer's idea of accompanying and monitoring an agenda that is "company specific and internally generated" (Porter and Kramer 2011: 76). At the same time, "Stakeholder View" processes and "Stakeholder Advisory Groups" are corporate governance mechanisms with low transaction costs, which can deal with, and (at least that is the intention) reduce, the innovation- and investment risks arising from the massive uncertainties regarding information and expectations implicit in an SVC strategy.

This also shows once again the theoretical and practical inconsistency of their concept, since it assumes something that first needs to be created through integrating stakeholders into strategy development and thus into the definition of a network relationship comprising the company and its stakeholders. But such a procedure is not the intention of the SVC approach, which – perhaps not least for this reason – limits stakeholder management to the "execution" and "evaluation" of the company's strategy of social responsibility. I have argued in detail elsewhere[12] that, from the perspective of a stakeholder theory of the firm, all this is about creating governance structures that facilitate (i) the integration of all relevant stakeholder interests into the processes of a company, and (ii) generating and sharing a cooperation rent for all stakeholders involved. In other words, it is about developing governance structures that allow us to simultaneously put into practice business demands vis-à-vis society and society's demands vis-à-vis business.

2.2 Practical Challenges of Strategic Management

2.2.1 SVC – Strategy Development and Measurement

1. The strategic toolkit developed by Porter and Kramer is intended to link the strategy development and the performance measurement of SVC from the perspective of the company.

[11] For an overview, cf. Wieland (2016).

[12] Cf. Wieland (2014: chapter 8), (2016); Heck and Wieland (2013).

The first step is to identify and prioritize those social challenges "that represent opportunities to increase revenue or reduce costs" (Porter/Kramer et al. 2012: 4). The sole criterion for prioritization is the company's competitiveness. Societal relevance and priority – as documented, for example, in various standards, such as the ILO Core Norms (cf. ILO 1998, 2006), the OECD Guidelines for Multinational Enterprises (cf. OECD 2001), the ISO 26000 Social Responsibility (cf. ISO 2011), the UN Guiding Principles for Business and Human Rights[13], the Millenium or Sustainable Development Goals (SDGs)[14] – remains systematically beyond the scope of consideration. The participation of business in the social discourse, which is the source of legitimacy of the business model selected, is therefore severed at a systematic level. This does not preclude for business and societal priorities to correspond occasionally, but this cannot be a systematic basis of successful strategic management.

The second step, "Making the business case", specifies the potential of value creation of the field of activity chosen by the company, "modeling the potential business and social results relative to cost" (Porter/Kramer et al. 2012: 4).

The third step calculates "inputs and business activities, outputs and financial perfomance (revenues and costs) relative to projections" (Ibid). The fourth and final step measures the results from the perspectives of business and society. This requires not only an adequate controlling instrument to measure the company's economic performance, but also the ability to understand "the social results from business investments". For the strategy area of products and markets, for example, that might be "increased revenue" and "improved patient care"; for the area of productivity, "reduced logistical and operating cost" and "reduced energy use"; and, for the area of cluster formation, "reduced costs" and "improved job creation" (Ibid: 3).

2. From a purely managerial perspective, the essential problem of the scheme underlying the process of strategy development sketched above lies in the absence of is that the cost accounting systems do not yet exist that could capture and delineate the relevant "revenues" and "cost" for individual measures. According to the current state of research, to introduce such a scheme one might draw upon qualitative case descriptions and plausibility assumptions about costs and earnings. If we include in our evaluation of the Porter/Kramer concept the insufficient social legitimacy of a definition of social responsibility purely immanent to the business, then a mixed picture emerges. On the one hand, the concept implies an understanding of CSR as a challenge and a mission for corporate strategy and management – this is definitely a step forward in the debate on the social responsibility of business. On the other hand, though, it restricts the integration of social discourse into strategy development to the *ex post* evaluation of each individual project, which results in a potential loss of legitimacy and in an increase of informational and expectational uncertainty concerning the possible quality of future markets. In short, the innovation potential of the company is not exploited to the full while, simultaneously, the

[13] United Nations Human Rights Council (2011); UN Global Compact www.unglobalcompact.org (accessed 15.01.2016). www.unglobalcompact.org (accessed 15.01.2016).

[14] Cf. United Nations (2000; 2015).

risk to investment increases. The authors' explicit objective – namely, "Integrating inside-out and outside-in practices" (Porter and Kramer 2006: 89) – is therefore feasible only to a very limited extent.

2.2.2 CSR Evaluator – Dual Evaluation

1. The "CSR evaluator" has been designed in order for this link between social and corporate practice to become visible and manageable.[15] With a view to corporate social responsibility, the evaluator integrates and gives equal weight to both the perspective of society (outside-in) and also that of business (inside-out) in a mutual learning process. Consequently, not only can the company evaluate its CSR commitment in relation to its business strategy, but society too may access the evaluation of the company's CSR activities in relation to the accepted social, environmental and humanitarian norms.[16] In accordance with this dual objective, the "CSR evaluator" has three components.

Component I: Catalogue of Measures for Five Stakeholder Groups This provides a condensed form of the material content and requirements of generally accepted social, environmental and human-rights norms that can then serve as a basis to analyze the CSR measures already practiced in the company, which may then be assigned to the stakeholder interests thus addressed (employees, partners, customers, society, investors). In a third step, the costs of the measures are calculated and assigned to the measure/stakeholder relation. On the basis of this measure/stakeholder calculation of the operating expenses, the company's CSR commitment can be made visible and eventually manageable. At the same time component I allows the CSR evaluator for affiliating to a company's strategic stakeholder management (identification, prioritization, distribution of cooperation rent). Thus, it is not only shown whether the "catalogue of measures" reflects identification and prioritization of stakeholders, but whether the distribution of cooperation rent (CSR costs) corresponds to strategic corporate management soever. Hereby, a feedback loop comes into being which connects stakeholder management to the CSR program of a company.

Component II: Performance Indicators The sum of expenses of all CSR measures across all five stakeholder groups provides an initial indication of the overall level of CSR commitment. The key figure "CSR rate" relates CSR expenses to turnover as a measurement of a company's economic success. For Wieland and Heck (2013), the turnover of a company is a useful indicator to measure the performance and competitiveness of a company, since it depicts all stakeholder contribu-

[15] Cf. Wieland and Heck (2013); Wieland (2015a).

[16] Cf. Wieland (2015a, b).

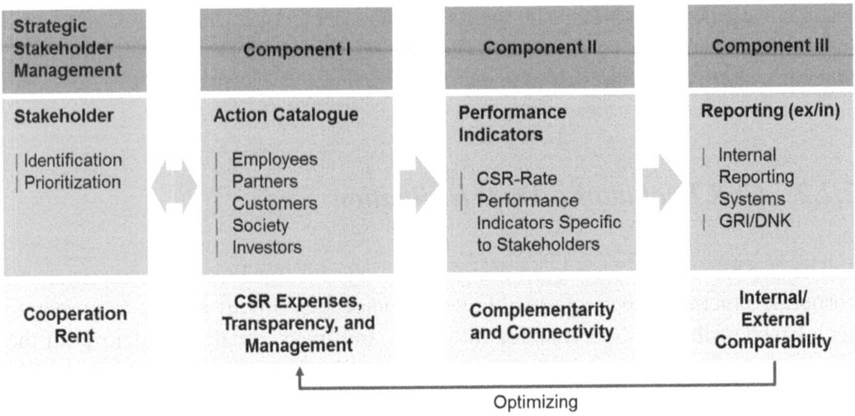

Fig. 2.1 CSR evaluator – evaluating and operating stakeholder management as a learning process

tions to the company's success. At the same time, a comparison with the strategy and performance of other companies will in principle be possible.

Component III: Integration Into Existing Standards This component combines CSR management with CSR reporting frameworks in business or society (for example, Global Reporting Initiative), and with the company's own controlling system. In this way, as in component I, the internal steering of CSR resource allocation (identification and relevance of stakeholders, amount of funds expended, deficits in CSR commitment in relation to social norms and corporate stakeholder identification and prioritization) is linked to transparency regarding the corporate-strategy-driven implementation of social responsibility. The results of component III can then, in turn, be fed into component I as potential for improvement. The following figure illustrates this process (Fig. 2.1):

In a research project carried out at the Leadership Excellence Institute of Zeppelin University in 2014,[17] we examined the applicability of this instrument in corporate practice in Germany.

Of the 238 companies from all sectors that we contacted, 51 participated as "practice partners", 28 as "workshop participants" (they were presented with and discussed the CSR evaluator in workshops), 13 as "users" (they carried out their own data collection using component I), 22 as "commentators" (they examined the evaluator and evaluated it in writing), and 20 as "evaluators" (they participated in the evaluation of the research results obtained). We can present only some of the results of this study here, but the below chart "Average CSR expenses according to stakeholders" (Wieland 2015a: 36), shows that nearly 80% of the CSR expenditure calculated is accounted for by the stakeholders *employees* and *society* (Fig. 2.2).

[17] Cf. in more detail and for the full study Wieland (2015a, b).

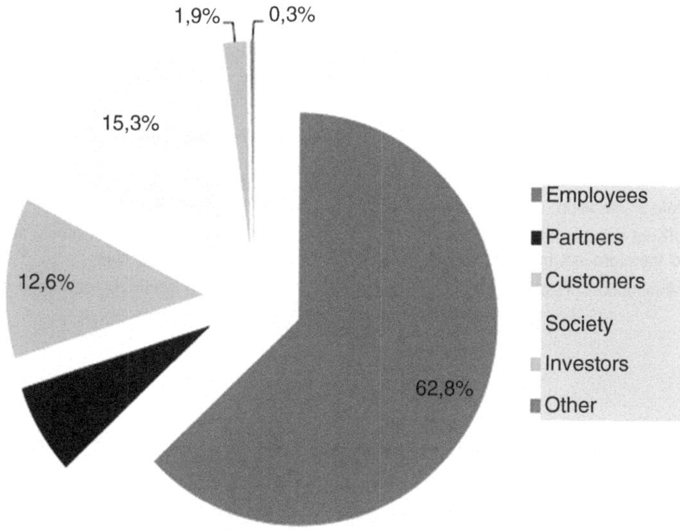

Fig. 2.2 Average CSR expenses by stakeholders

This ought certainly to be seen against the backdrop of the German tradition of the social-market-economy tradition; however, it also shows that precisely for this reason expenditure is captured, for example, in social reports. 95% of participants in the evaluation study said the high availability of data showing the costs of CSR measures for the stakeholder "employees" was high. For the stakeholder "society", that figure was 86%, while, for "partners" (33%), "customers" (52%) and "investors" (38%), the data availability was inadequate. This is especially true for CSR commitment in global value chains, where, with a mere 40%, there existed huge difficulties in demarcating and allocating expenses the capacity to provide detailed data of CSR measures, too, was identified as being insufficient. As for availability of data, this stakeholder group posed greatest challenge, not least because there are no specific cost accounting systems for the CSR area (Wieland 2015a: 22f, b: 12ff.).

2. n nearly all cases, the "practice partners" pointed to the difficulties of delimiting "voluntary" CSR actions from actions in the context of the core business. In principle, this is to do with the problem of whether a specific CSR expenditure can be assigned to the area "CSR" or to individual stakeholder groups, or whether the expenditure should be considered an investment as part of the company's standardized business activity. Bearing in mind the discussion about SVC presented here, we therefore have two dimensions. "CSR in the core business" refers to investments, particularly in research and development that relate to the standardized business activity of companies. It is in this world that the Porter/Kramer concept is situated. Here there occurs a successive merging of "CSR" and core business, with a technical isolation of CSR and core business being ultimately neither possible nor necessary. The assessment of whether an investment is to be made, and whether it is successful, is not carried out hereby talking to stakeholders, but by comparison to

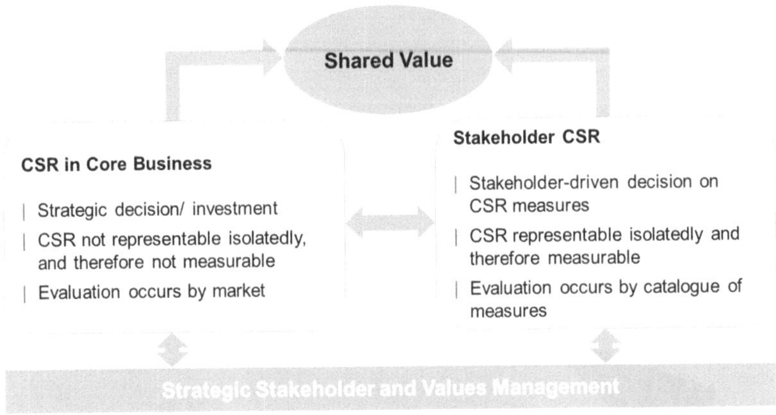

Fig. 2.3 Shared value, core business and stakeholder-CSR

other possible investments and on the basis of consumer behavior, i.e., through the market. The "stakeholder-CSR" is the second dimension of SVC. This reflects the constantly changing debate on social responsibility and imitates learning processes that can, but need not, lead eventually to innovations (product, service, management) in the company. The catalogues of component I in the CSR evaluator, assigning specific measures to specific stakeholders make this debate dynamically visible both inside and outside the company. This can lead to movements in both directions: "stakeholder-CSR" can condense into a regular component of the core business, while "CSR in the core business" can be scrutinized and developed further through stakeholder dialogues. Thus, the integration of a shared value policy occurs via strategic management, more precise via the stakeholder and values management of a company. Figure 2.3 illustrates this:

The CSR evaluator is a tool that makes the stakeholder management of a company visible, and helps to integrate it into the strategic management of the company as a steering mechanism. Component I serves the identification and the actual-target prioritization of stakeholders of the company and of its transactions, as well as the capture and actual-target allocation of cooperation rents (expenditure) to the various stakeholders. Component II captures the proportion of the cooperation rent against the company's entire added value (turnover). Finally, component III serves the documentation, and internal and external communication, of the CSR strategy of a company, i.e., its priorities, development perspectives, and the organizational learning processes required.

The following figure illustrates initial starting points and possible linkages for these learning processes (Fig. 2.4):

In the following section, I will deal with these relationships in greater theoretical detail, including in distinction from the concept of SVC.

CSR Evaluator	Catalogues of measures	Performance indicators
Focus on stakeholder CSR, learning processes and processes of internalization	Specification of CSR issues in underrepresented stakeholder groups	Creation of stakeholder-related performance indicators
Distinction from normal core business	Further sharpening of CSR categories and CSR measures; sector-based specifications	Determination of suitable operational benchmarks
Link to existing reporting standards	Adjustment of terminology, relative relevance and granulation	Comparison of performance indicators over several business periods

Fig. 2.4 "CSR evaluator" and modification

3. The model of the "CSR evaluator" is based on a governance-economic "theory of the firm as a nexus of stakeholders",[18] and further develops this theory. At its core lies the idea that the company can be understood as a set of material (capital, loans) and immaterial (knowledge, morality) resources with which an organization carries out its transactions and reproduces itself. Stakeholders are then not defined by their "demands" on, or the degree to which they are affected by, business models, but are owners of the very resources that the company uses for these business models and its survival. Stakeholders therefore also have no stake in the "company", but instead in the specific transactions of the company and, through their implementation, in the process of value creation and the reproduction of the organization (which is, at least in principle, infinite). In return for contributing their resources to these processes, all stakeholders acquire either a right to compensation[19] and/or, according to the mode of their resource investment, a share of the cooperation rent of the firm.[20]

For the strategic management of a company, this means that the latter can and must be led with the help of various, non-substitutive, performance indicators. While, for example, the "shareholder value" expresses future expectations of added value of the equity provider (or the capital market), the indicator "profit" is a measurement related to the past for return on investment. In contrast, "shared value" in the context of stakeholder management developed here is an indicator of the cooperation rent generated by the company, which only becomes possible as an additional yield beyond the factor income through the cooperation of all resource owners involved. The size of this income results from the transactional and organizational specificity of the resources invested by the stakeholders, and from the ability of management to gain these resources for the organization and to combine them so

[18] Wieland (2008: 17; 2014: chs.7/8); Wieland and Heck (2013: 36ff.).

[19] For example, profit, payment, interest, taxes. For a detailed list, see Wieland (2014: 137).

[20] For example, voluntary training of staff, implementation of social and humanitarian norms, social and environmental commitment to the immediate vicinity.

that a competitive advantage is won.[21] "Shareholder value", profit and "shared value" are therefore not substitutive, but complementary. They are indicators that illuminate different sides of the performance of a company, and therefore satisfy the justified demands of different stakeholder groups for information and monitoring. While the finance community will probably have the greatest interest in the expected "shareholder value", profit is an indicator that interests especially, but not exclusively, investors. Statements on the generation of shared value, however, are important for all stakeholder groups involved in the transaction of the company, and not least for civil-societal groups. The fact that modern companies have been creatures of society and its discourse since their beginnings in the nineteenth century and up to the present day manifests itself in "shared value". Their societal character comes to light within it.

Therefore, the CSR evaluator is in both senses a dual indicator (inside-out: management and evaluation; and outside-in: business and society) to measure the success of strategic and operational stakeholder management as a prerequisite for any kind of corporate and social value creation. The Porter/Kramer model of SVC, in contrast, is aimed at the competition- and market-driven internalization of the negative external effects of economic development (cf. Kitzmueller and Shimshack 2012) through innovations of product, process and organization of a company defined fundamentally by the interests of investors and outside creditors. Thus, while the "CSR evaluator" derives a company's capacity for innovation from the quality of its strategic stakeholder management, the "SVC" model works in exactly the opposite way – by deriving the quality of its stakeholder management (societal benefits) as a residual amount from the company's ability to innovate. Hence also the fundamental inconsistency of the SVC model to which I have already drawn attention: the model has to presuppose the availability and appropriate assessment of stakeholder resources to develop and implement successful innovations for business and society, while at the same time claiming that this agenda of innovation management is purely "company specific" and "internally generated".

2.2.3 Outlook

Without instrumentation (not instrumentalization) of moral and social claims on the leadership, management and monitoring of economic organizations, such claims cannot be systematically and sustainably realized in everyday business. To do so, SVC, CSR and SDGs must find expression in effective and adaptive structures of corporate governance. These are the basic ideas and the logic of the SVC model developed by Porter and Kramer. They are correct. One has to ask, though, how they will be shaped and on which premises they will be based: dominance of the economic paradigm of competition *vs.* integration of stakeholders from business and society. In this essay I tried to elucidate this by discussing and comparing the

[21] Cf. in more detail Wieland and Heck (2013: 38f).

strategy concepts of SVC and the CSR evaluator. Neither concept has yet gone beyond the idea stage. Both will also remain at this stage if we fail to further develop the cost accounting and the controlling of companies in a way that is compatible with CSR. The ultimate aim is to raise the quality and reliability of non-financial reporting to the level of the financial report. The development of the latter to its present state has taken, if we accept Luca Pacioli and therefore the year 1494 as our starting point, more than 500 years. The history of its evolution shows the legal, economic, technical and moral challenges that also face, to a greater or lesser extent, non-financial reporting, inside-out and outside-in. If, therefore, some critics want to declare the debate over, that is not a good idea.

References

Beschorner, Thomas. 2013. Creating shared value: The one-trick pony approach – a comment on Michael Porter and Mark Kramer. *Business Ethics Journal Review* 1(17): 106–112.

Chesbrough, H.W., and M.M. Appleyard. 2007. Open innovation and strategy. *California Management Review* 50(1): 57–76.

Crane, Andrew, Guido Palazzo, Laura J. Spence, and Dirk Matten. 2014. Contesting the value of "Creating Shared Value". *California Management Review* 56(2): 130–153.

European Commission. 2011. A renewed EU strategy 2011–2014 for corporate social responsibility. Access to European Union Law. http://eur-lex.europa.eu/LEXUriServ/LexUriServ.do?uri=COM:2011:0681:FIN:EN:PDF. Accessed 13 Jan 2016.

International Labour Organization (ILO). 2006. Tripartite declaration of principles concerning multinational enterprises and social policy. ILO. http://www.ilo.org/wcmsp5/groups/public/---ed_emp/---emp_ent/--multi/documents/publication/wcms_094386.pdf. Accessed 15 Jan 2016.

———. 1998. International labour standards. ILO. http://www.ilo.org/global/standards/introduction-to-international-labour-standards/lang--en/index.htm. Accessed 15 Jan 2016.

International Organization for Standardization (ISO). 2011. ISO 26000 Social Responsibility. ISO. http://www.iso.org/iso/catalogue_detail?csnumber=42546. Accessed 15 Jan 2016.

Jhounjhounwala, Shital. 2014. Intertwining CSR with strategy – The way ahead. *Corporate Governance* 14(1): 211–219.

Kitzmueller, Markus, and Jay Shimshack. 2012. Economic perspectives on corporate social responsibility. *Journal of Economic Literature* 50(1): 51–84.

Hartmann, L.P., and P.H. Werhane. 2013. Proposition: Shared value as an incomplete mental model. *Business Ethics Journal Review* 1(6): 36–43.

Lee, Louise. 2011. Business-community partnerships: Understanding the nature of partnership. *Corporate Governance: The International Journal of Business in Society* 11(1): 29–40.

Lock, Irina, and Peter Seele. 2016. CSR governance and departmental organization: A typology of best Practices. *Corporate Governance* 16(1): 211–230.

Maltz, Elliot, Debra J. Ringold, and Fred Thompson. 2011. Assessing and optimizing corporate social initiatives: A strategic view of corporate social responsibility. *Journal of Public Affairs* 2: 384–395.

Mulgan, Geoff. 2006. The process of social innovation. *Innovations* 1(2): 145–162.

Organisation for Economic Co-operation and Development (OECD). 2001. OECD guidelines for multinational enterprises: Annual Report. Paris. OECD. http://www.oecd.org/department/0,3355,en_2649_34889_1_1_1_1_1,00.html. Accessed 15 Jan 2016.

Porter, M.E., and M.R. Kramer. 1999. Philanthropy's New Agenda: creating value. *Harvard Business Review* 77(6): 121–131.

———. 2002. The competitive advantage of corporate philosophy. *Harvard Business Review* 80(12): 56–68.
———. 2006. Strategy & society: The link between competitive advantage and corporate social responsibility. *Harvard Business Review* 85(12): 78–92.
———. 2011. Creating shared value. *Harvard Business Review* 89(1/2): 62–77.
Porter, Michael E., Greg Hills, Marc Pfitzer, Sonja Patscheke, and Elisabeth Hawkings. 2012. *Measuring shared value: How to unlock value by linking business and social results*. Unpublished work. FSG. http://www.fsg.org/publications/measuring-shared-value. Accessed 13 Jan 2016.
Prahalad, C.K., and S.L. Hart. 2002. *The Fortune at the bottom of the pyramid*. Strategy + Business 26: 1–14.
Sachs, Sybille, Hans Groth, and Ruth Schmitt. 2010. The stakeholder view approach: An untapped opportunity to manage corporate performance and wealth. *Strategic Change* 19: 147–162.
Smith, Adam. 1991. In *The Wealth of Nations*, vol 3, ed. Andrew S. Skinner. New York: Prometheus Books.
Spitzeck, Heiko, and Erik G. Hansen. 2010. Stakeholder governance: How stakeholders influence corporate decision-making. *Corporate Governance* 10(4): 378–391.
Spitzeck, Heiko, Erik G. Hansen, and David Grayson. 2011. Joint management – stakeholder committees: A new path to stakeholder governance? *Corporate Governance: The International Journal of Business in Society* 11(5): 560–568.
Spitzeck, Heiko, and Sonja Chapman. 2012. Creating shared value as a differentiation strategy – The example of BASF in Brazil. *Corporate Governance: The International Journal of Business in Society* 12(4): 499–513.
United Nations (UN). 2000. *Millennium development goals. United Nations Development Program*. Retrieved 25 Sept 2015. UN. http://www.undp.org/content/undp/en/home/sdgoverview/mdg_goals.html. Accessed 15 Jan 2016.
United Nations Human Rights Council. 2011. *Guiding principles on business and human rights: Implementing the United Nations "Protect, Respect and Remedy" Framework*. http://www.business-humanrights.org/media/documents/ruggie/ruggie-guiding-principles-21-mar-2011.pdf. Accessed 15 Jan 2016.
United Nations. 2014. *The road to dignity by 2030: Ending poverty, Transform-ing all lives and protecting the planet*. Synthesis report of the secretary-general on the post-2015 Agenda. UN. http://www.un.org/disabilities/documents/reports/SG_Synthesis_Report_Road_to_Dignity_by_2030.pdf. Accessed 13 Jan 2016.
United Nations Global Compact. www.unglobalcompact.org. Accessed 13 Jan 2016.
Wieland, Josef. 2008. *Die Stakeholder-Gesellschaft und ihre Governance. Management, Netzwerke, Diskurse*. Marburg: Metropolis-Verlag.
Wieland, Josef, and Andreas Heck. 2013. *Shared value durch stakeholder governance*. Marburg: Metropolis-Verlag.
Wieland, Josef. 2014. *Governance ethics: Global value creation, economic Or-ganization and normativity*. New York et al.: Springer.
———. 2015a. Forschungsstudie zur Konzeption und Durchführung einer empirischen Untersuchung über die Validität und Wirksamkeit eines CSR- Evaluierungs- und Steuerungsinstruments. *BMAS-Forschungsbericht* 454.
———. 2015b. Forschungsstudie zur Konzeption und Durchführung einer empirischen Untersuchung über die Validität und Wirksamkeit eines CSR-Evaluierungs- und Steuerungsinstruments. Auswertung der Evaluierungsstudie. Unpublished working paper.
———. 2016. CSR – Shared value creation through intersectoral governance. In *Handbook on the economics of social responsibility: Individuals, corporations and institutions*, ed. L. Sacconi, and G. Degli Antoni. Cheltenham: Edward Elgar (in press).

Chapter 3
Creating Shared Value. A Fundamental Critique

Thomas Beschorner and Thomas Hajduk

Abstract This article offers a fundamental critique of Michael Porter's and Marc Kramer's "Creating Shared Value" (CSV) concept. First, the authors summarise the positive and negative criticism which CSV has received since 2011. They then show that CSV falls short of a modern understanding of corporate responsibility which is centred on more adequate ideas about the relationship between business and society. The article concludes with critical comments on the role of scholars in their interaction with practitioners.

3.1 Introduction

"Creating Shared Value" (CSV) – that is what Harvard professors Michael Porter and Mark Kramer (2011) propose. In a well-received article in the Harvard Business Review they recommend a type of value-based management which promises nothing less than the reinvention of capitalism. According to the authors the creation of "shared value" is meant to replace a narrow understanding of management with its rigid fixation on short-term profits. Thus business is thought to regain trust which was lost in the wake of the financial crisis and business scandals. For Porter and Kramer, the objective is to re-integrate and re-embed business into society.

Creating Shared Value has become a buzzword in recent years, in business practice as well as in management theory. Some of its appeal probably owes to its authors' celebrity – and the use of the economic notion of "value". With about 2800 citations in Google Scholar within nearly 5 years, the publication can be classified as highly influential. Although there is no information with regard to the reception of the article, it is fair to assume the reaction to it as mostly positive and approving. The CSV-articles in the Zeitschrift für Wirtschafts- und Unternehmensethik (Vol.

This article is based on our contribution „Creating Shared Value: Eine Grundsatzkritik" (2015), published in the Zeitschrift für Wirtschafts- und Unternehmensethik (zfwu) 16 (2): 219–230.

T. Beschorner (✉) • T. Hajduk
University of St. Gallen, St. Gallen, Switzerland
e-mail: thomas.beschorner@unisg.ch; thomas.hajduk@unisg.ch

J. Wieland (ed.), *Creating Shared Value – Concepts, Experience, Criticism*,
Ethical Economy 52, DOI 10.1007/978-3-319-48802-8_3

16/No. 2), in which this paper was originally published, also indicate a tendency towards a positive reception of CSV.

However, the approach did receive some criticism as well. One of the first critical reviews was published in The Economist. The commentary was entitled "Oh, Mr Porter" and stated: "[t]he new big idea from business's greatest living guru seems a bit undercooked" (Economist 2011) – and that is a rather favourable appraisal of CSV, as we will show. However, virtually no critical voices were heard during the first 2 years after the publication of the CSV-paper. This is quite remarkable. It was only in 2013 and 2014 that a number of academic articles criticising CSV were published (cf. Beschorner 2013a; Hartman and Werhane 2013; Crane et al. 2014).

We do not want to review these critical positions in detail, but rather focus on some selected aspects of the discussion. On the basis of this critique, we contrast CSV with a modern understanding of corporate responsibility. We close this article with reflections on the relationship between business and society on the one hand, and the role of social sciences on the other.

3.2 CSV: Positive and Negative Criticism

Creating Shared Value aims to re-invent capitalism and thereby to unleash a wave of innovation and growth, from which both businesses and society would profit. Does CSV really live up to this promise? Do Porter and Kramer herald a turnaround in the discussion on business and society? Does their concept obviate Corporate Social Responsibility (CSR)?

Indeed, CSV touches on some progressive ideas. For instance, the authors stress potentially positive contributions of business and focus on them. They hence reject a mere (reputation-based) risk-avoiding, defensive concept. Companies are instead encouraged to "utilize their skills, resources, and management capability to lead social progress" (Porter and Kramer 2011: 77). Even though the understanding of business as a proactive actor has been discussed in the academic literature for some time (cf. Zadek 2001; Beschorner 2004; Matten and Crane 2005; Palazzo and Scherer 2007), this aspect of the article indeed points in a right and important direction.

Furthermore, Porter and Kramer suggest thinking in terms of societal needs – instead of "products" and "services" – and take them as a starting point for innovations. This differentiation is of great importance for companies and their business models, in theory as well as in practice: if you take the need for mobility, then the production and the selling of motor vehicles, for instance, is a means to an end. However, mobility could be provided by other products and services as well (e.g. car sharing, mobility subscription models, etc.). Thus car manufacturers catering to the need for mobility could turn into mobility businesses and develop new, sustainable markets.

While Porter and Kramer seem to be quite progressive regarding these ideas, their orthodox creed becomes apparent in their economic line of argumentation. It is no coincidence that they published their article in the Harvard Business Review and thereby framed it for an audience of business administrators and managers. At the beginning of their paper, they spell out that CSV is neither associated with unwieldy normative terms such as justice, responsibility or the common good, nor related to the known CSR debates, but is rather about a new understanding of the creation of value. With this terminological transition from *responsibility* to creating *value*, Porter and Kramer (2014: 150) want to reach a so far sceptical mainstream which otherwise would have continued keeping its distance. The "Shared Value Initiative" booted by their business consultancy "Foundation Strategy Group" invites businesses, civil society and politics to implement the concept in practice.

The attempt to win over CSR sceptics proves to be highly problematic on second thought, though. In particular, Porter and Kramer contrast their CSV with an outdated understanding of CSR by equating CSR with mere philanthropy that is disconnected from the company's core businesses, while CSV is claimed to be integrated into the core business activities (Porter and Kramer 2011: 76). However, today there is practically nobody who would advocate such a simplistic understanding of CSR, neither in theory, nor in practice (cf. Beschorner 2013a). Despite the great multiplicity of CSR definitions in the field, there is a broad consensus about the fact that CSR is not a supplement to business activities but rather an incremental element of a company's core business. Indeed, CSR is not about how businesses spend their profits, but rather about how they make them in the first place. This should have become common currency by now, even in Boston.

Instead, Porter and Kramer re-imagine Corporate Social Responsibility as philanthropy or, in other words, as a straw man (cf. Beschorner 2013a: 109) in order to make their "big idea" plausible. In a special issue on CSV, Crane et al. (2014: 134) criticise the authors for this peculiar notion of CSR. Although Porter and Kramer (2014) give a response to their critics, they do not bother replying on that particular criticism. To make it perfectly clear: we think that this approach is inappropriate in terms of research integrity. If students ignored criticism in similar fashion, they would risk a poor grade. In fact, Porter's and Kramer's critique of CSR hints at how limited the understanding of corporate responsibility still is in mainstream economics. It seems that not much has changed since Milton Friedman's famous New York Times Magazine, according to which CSR is nothing more than philanthropy at the expense of the shareholders (cf. Friedman 1970; for a historical analysis of the article: Hajduk 2015).

Likewise, the authors remain trapped in their neoclassical paradigm when it comes to the remainder of their argumentation. For instance, one-dimensional profit maximization, which CSV has apparently left behind, remains the normative reference point. It is not only presumed that profit maximization is empirically given – business needs to maximize profits in a competitive environment – but it is also considered as morally good. CSV reinforces this normative predefinition by assuming that businesses meet "societal needs" while they are generating profits. However, the profit motive alone is questionable, because social needs are seen as a mere means to an end, allowing businesses to discover new market opportunities, to calculate the business case and to invest profitably. Such businesses would be good rational agents, but this behaviour would have nothing to do with genuinely responsible, ethical behaviour.[1]

Even in those cases in which a "shared value" for businesses and society is created, in so called "A-Cases" (cf. Scholz 2014), CSV neither reveals anything new nor can it abandon its purely economic perspective. Crane et al. (2014: 143) and Beschorner (2013a: 110) remind their readers of well-established approaches in management theory (such as stakeholder theory) that consider businesses to be more than just economic agents. They refer to stakeholder theory as a case in point. It had been successful because two of its central premises – business is influenced by society, which is why good management interacts with social groups – were compatible with a business-centred economic point of view. CSV takes a similar approach when it responds to societal claims in a purely economic manner. CSV shares a weakness with the stakeholder approach (Beschorner 2013a: 110): business only caters to "relevant" – i.e. influential and powerful – stakeholders, but not to other ethically justified claims of "claimholders" (cf. Waxenberger and Spence 2003). It therefore fails to achieve true legitimacy.

The economic rationale of the "A-Cases" reaches its limits when a corporation cannot generate any value because business and social interests either do not go hand in hand or are even opposed to each other. In those "B-Cases" CSV does not apply, as Scholz (2014) emphasises (cf. Scholz and des los Reyes 2015). Instead, Porter and Kramer refer to compliance with "laws and ethical standards" (2011: 76) without explicating these standards. This neoclassical idea of rational and profit-driven businesses within a (certainly not too extensively regulated) legal framework points to their limited, rather orthodox understanding of business.

It is correct that businesses are profit-orientated actors and that they operate based on an economic rationality. However, they are also societal actors and as such they understand how to interact with their environment through different rationalities (cf. Matten and Crane 2005). They are, for instance, not merely objects of law and order, but also political actors which actively participate in the political decision-making process through lobbying and campaign donations or by engaging in public discourse (cf. Curbach 2009). Businesses can get involved in their communities by acting as "corporate citizens" and thus shaping their social environment. These activities are not about generating an economic added value for the company; they illustrate rather how businesses assume different roles within society. What we can observe here is that companies follow different rationales or, in other words, speak different languages depending on the context. Pretending that businesses and managers speak only the language of creating (economic) value all the time, Porter and Kramer misconceive business profoundly.

Instead of the functional concept of CSV, businesses need an ethical mission statement on the basis of which they understand themselves not only as economic, but also as societal actors. This touches upon aspects like their fundamental values or their contribution to society. Such a mission statement lays the normative

[1] We therefore characterized CSV in a different publication as a "One-Trick Pony Approach" (cf. Beschorner 2013a).

foundation on which businesses can act responsibly. This does not exclude profit maximization. On the contrary, it is the normative foundation that renders profits legitimate in the first place. This legitimacy, and with it the recovery of public trust, is essential for the promised reinvention of capitalism. For this cause though, it is not enough to re-tell the old story of economic rationality, innovation and growth. A real paradigmatic shift requires better ideas and bolder propositions which recognise businesses as a part of society.

3.3 Modern Corporate Responsibility Is Different

It should have become quite clear by now that CSV is not a convincing alternative to CSR. On the contrary, it falls short of modern corporate responsibility. But what is meant by "modern corporate responsibility"? First of all, it means to view its supposed weakness – the diversity and at times ambiguity – as a strength. CSR is the conceptual bracket for the discourse on and practice of corporate responsibility. As such, the notion is subject to (historical) change in the same way as other basic terms like "freedom", "democracy" or "public" and necessitates constant (re)definition by discourse. CSR is less about one specific understanding or definition, but rather about a reflection on different ideas and visions of corporate responsibility as well as empirical practices. In our view, the following aspects belong to such a conception of CSR:

First, institutional rules and structures are required in business as well as in society (cf. Wieland 1999). In a liberal, pluralistic society, individual ethics reaches its limits, for example in form of the "honourable merchant".[2] Today's societies are too diverse to be guided only by honour or virtues. Individual ethics therefore has to be complemented by institutional ethics (though not to be replaced by it) (cf. Hajduk and Schank 2015). These institutions, for example in the form of a code of conduct or an advanced value management system, have three functions:

- they relieve individuals of the burden of permanent moral decision-making, which otherwise could overwhelm them;
- clearly defined and transparent rules protect employees against whimsical patriarchs (a potential downside of "honourable merchants"); and
- they signal and communicate both within and outside the company reliable values (e.g. through a corporate philosophy) (cf. Wieland 1999; Gelbman and Baumgartner 2012; Lorentschitsch and Walker 2012).

Second, purely functionalistic and value-free concepts like CSV are neither normatively appropriate nor empirically accurate. We can observe diverse value orientations in businesses which significantly determine the identity of the respective

[2] Cf. description and examples of the concept in Hajduk (2014) and a fundamental critique in Beschorner and Hajduk (2012).

business. Corporate responsibility needs both to determine these basic values, and to reflect them in a critical and constructive manner.

Implementing such values within the organisation depends on certain capabilities which have to be considered in the empirical analysis and the normative reflection:

- Individual capabilities like (self-) critical thinking, sense of responsibility and (technical) knowledge.
- Organisational capabilities allow for and promote value-oriented behaviour, for example in the form of long-term remuneration models, awareness-building CSR programs, grievance mechanism (e.g. through whistleblowing-systems) or innovation processes which integrate social and ecological considerations.
- Language capabilities for the dialogue with stakeholders are a necessary requirement for creating legitimacy of business activities. The name of the concept "responsibility" points towards such a dialogue that goes beyond strategic stakeholder management and the mere recognition of powerful stakeholders (to which CSV seems to be primarily addressed) (cf. Beschorner 2013a: 110; Crane et al. 2014: 137).

The language-aspect is, *thirdly*, accompanied by new roles and responsibilities for businesses. Business is not only part of the production system, but rather participates in a wide spectrum of social governance processes which are about the distribution and management of public (global) goods (cf. Wolf and Schwindenhammer 2011). Market transactions and negotiation are only one possible mode of these processes which are already familiar to businesses. There are, however, also other modes such as taking part in societal discourse and deliberative processes.

In this regard, we can observe ever more companies embracing the (political) role as equal partners in public-private-partnerships and in co-regulatory initiatives (cf. Beschorner et al. 2013). As a consequence, the relationship between businesses and public actors is changing and growing more complex (cf. Schmiedeknecht and Wieland 2012). It is no longer only limited to business compliance with government rules, but also includes co-governance and shared responsibility, for example by creating and implementing soft law.

3.4 Business and Society

Against the background of our understanding of modern CSR and in line with Crane et al. (2014) we arrive at some fundamental conclusions about business and society. They go beyond the critique of CSV and are essential for a theory of the firm and for business ethics as a whole. To determine the relationship between business and society, it is necessary to develop an appropriate understanding of business and society at first. As for business, neither "as if" constructs, nor theories of normative ethics seem suitable. On the contrary, we need empirical perspectives true to the motto "Corporations ARE what they DO" (Post et al. 2012: 8). With regard to society, we need to develop (from empirical perspectives) a picture of societal contexts that is both a useful theoretical abstraction and sufficiently complex. Preston stated as early as 40 years ago:

> serious analysis of the corporation-society relationship requires rigorous and comprehensive conceptions of both the corporation and society; and these conceptions must be articulated in comparable, or at least translatable, terms (Preston 1975: 446).

This is important because:

> (…) society at large might be interested in performance features of the economic system other than the amount of total current output and its distribution (Preston 1975: 446).

Comparing these paradigmatic observations with Porter's and Kramer's CSV-concept, we see that, *firstly*, their understanding of business is too reductionist (one-trick pony). *Secondly*, even though they claim that CSV is oriented towards social questions and they refer to terms such as civil society and regulations, they have an inadequate and theoretically underdeveloped understanding of society. *Thirdly*, the "translatable terms" (Preston) of CSV are strictly limited to categories of utility, evincing "a very narrow dated notion of what the corporation is" (Crane et al. 2014: 143). The relationship between business and society is thus guided by a purely economic perspective. This economic focus is reflected in the terminology of CSV: "(creating) value" is an economic term that is supposed to replace other – non-economic – business ethics terms such as corporate *responsibility* or corporate *citizen* (in the sense of *citoyen*). Crane et al. pointed out the business-centred perspective of CSV:

> to study CSR properly, or for that matter CSV, we cannot start with a notion of what a business is and let its role in society just follow from this (Crane et al. 2014: 143).

Against this backdrop, we hence argued elsewhere:

> Porter and Kramer basically tell the old story of economic rationality as the one and only tool of smart management, with faith in innovation and growth, and they celebrate a capitalism that now needs to adjust a little bit. But there is little chance that an increasingly critical civil society will buy into such a story (Beschorner 2013a: 111).

As a result, CSV systematically fails to grasp society's expectations and challenges, because social contexts cannot be understood by exclusively relying on categories of utility.

In this regard, Wieland and Heck (2013: 17) pointed out that the term "shared value" is used in the European Commission's (2011: 6) new CSR definition, although it is understood differently from Porter and Kramer:

> While Porter/Kramer predominantly focus on businesses and society as a whole, the European Commission stresses that companies recognise stakeholder interests as they integrate CSR into strategic management (Wieland and Heck 2013: 17; our translation).

Wieland and Heck (2015) elaborated on this observation in an email correspondence with the authors of this article:

> The normative expectations of government and society must be taken seriously by businesses and need to be addressed, if they want to exist on the market on a long-term basis and generate competitive advantages. Stakeholders of companies are no longer external claim-

ants, but rather constructive elements of everyday business whose interests should be included in business decisions. This normative understanding of 'shared value' has to be distinguished from Porter's and Kramer's concept of 'shared value', whose point of reference is the development of market opportunities for a company. The latter can be a result of the normative strategic orientations of a company, but not the limitation of strategy to market development only (our translation).

The problem with the CSV-approach is not only its emphasis on utility, which is also used by strategic stakeholder approaches (cf. e.g. Ulrich 1997: 438ff.; Waxenberger and Spence 2003), but also the business-centered "framing" of the relationship between business and society, which is prominent in the wider academic literature (including business ethics). It is a perspective on "relationships established between the focal organisation and stakeholders" (Jonker and Foster 2002: 190); the planet "business" is in the centre, stakeholders orbit it as satellites.

We demonstrated elsewhere in more detail (cf. Beschorner 2004, 2013b) that a theoretically and empirically appropriate understanding of the relationship between business and society requires a research perspective that examines the constellations and interactions of actors. We think that neither the distinction between a constitutional and an extra-constitutional level (rules of the game and playing the game), nor the analysis of (merely bilateral) stakeholder relationships are sufficient in this regard.

This perspective is accompanied by a shift from a "society-oriented theory of the firm to a business-oriented theory of society" (Beschorner 2004), which draws on sociological neo-institutionalism and the concept of the "organisational field" (cf. Powell and DiMaggio 1991, 1983). On the one hand, a "business-oriented theory of society" extends the planet-satellite-model of the stakeholder approach. On the other, it clarifies the distinction between "the rules of the game" and "playing the game". It no longer assumes that the rules of the game are solely prescribed from the outside, but quite often result from communication and negotiation processes between regulating and regulated organisations, as Edelman and Suchman (1997: 507) demonstrate.

In this perspective, businesses (and other organisations) are seen as active co-creators of the rules of the game and therefore as subjects of regulatory (co-) responsibility (cf. in more detail Beschorner 2004; Beschorner and Schank 2012). Through the lens of organisational fields businesses are located within society and can thereby be addressed as societal and governance actors in the first place.

3.5 … and the Role of Social Sciences

No, Porter and Kramer are not exactly modest. CSV – and by no means CSR – had led to "substantial changes in behaviour of corporations around the world", they claim (Porter and Kramer 2014: 149). CSV had understood the world, as it really is:

it aligns social progress with corporate self-interest in a concrete and highly tangible way, including with those 'old strategy models' that capture the reality of competition and prevailing corporate practice (ibid.: 150).

Not to mention its empirical validity, this telling remark on the (presumed) practice raises the question concerning the role and responsibility of scholars in the discourse with practitioners. We can acknowledge that by using the formulation of "creating value" instead of "responsibility" or even "ethics" Porter and Kramer not only do good (self-) marketing, but possibly also set the right tone in order to be heard by "practitioners". At the same time and given their influence in management, such statements reinforce those economic practices which they had previously identified as risks to the legitimacy of capitalism. Porter and Kramer thus give their scholarly blessing to a system they consider besieged due to its mode of operation so far.

Like Dyllick (2014) we could accept this as part of the "ambiguity" that is probably shared by all scholars in business ethics. On the one hand, they do discuss the limitations of concepts like CSV within academic contexts (such as conferences and publications) and thus in the interaction with peers. On the other hand, they emphasise the "business case", reputational gains, competitive advantages etc. when teaching students and particularly practitioners in order to better relate to this audience. Yet even if this was true for most of executive education and even general university teaching, it raises the question why the current state of the art in the business ethics debate should not be taught. Do seasoned professionals and managers lack the ability to tackle topics and questions that challenge their cherished views? Should business ethics scholars take the path of least resistance and ignore fundamental questions of responsibility in favour of easily digestible contents and feel-good seminars?

We do not deny that especially executive education needs substantiation of theoretical positions and scholarly concepts in order to be useful to practitioners. However, there is a big difference whether we talk about practical instruments and adequate processes by which responsibility can be implemented or whether we sell an intellectual snake oil and thereby deny business people's moral responsibilities and reflective capabilities.

Dealing with issues and solutions in business ethics is challenging, both for scholars and practitioners. However, we need to face these challenges with suitable concepts. CSV is not one of them.

References

Beschorner, Thomas. 2004. Unternehmensethische Untersuchungen aus gesellschaftlicher Perspektive. Von der gesellschaftsorientierten Unternehmenslehre zur unternehmensorientierten Gesellschaftslehre. *Zeitschrift für Wirtschafts- und Unternehmensethik* 5(3): 255–276.

———. 2013a. Creating shared value: The one-trick pony approach – a comment on Michael Porter and Mark Kramer. *Business Ethics Journal Review* 1(17): 106–112.

———. 2013b. Kulturalistische Wirtschaftsethik: Grundzüge einer Theorie der Anwendung. *Zeitschrift für Wirtschafts- und Unternehmensethik* 14(3): 346–372.

Beschorner, Thomas, and Thomas Hajduk. 2012. Vom ehrbaren Kaufmann zur Unternehmensverantwortung. *Forum Wirtschaftsethik Online* 2: 2–7.

Beschorner, Thomas, and Christoph Schank. 2012. CSR – zur Bürgerrolle und Verantwortung von Unternehmen. In *Corporate social responsibility: verantwortungsvolle unternehmensführung in Theorie und Praxis*, ed. A. Schneider, and R. Schmidpeter, 155–164. Berlin: Springer.

Beschorner, Thomas, Thomas Hajduk, and Samuil Simeonov (ed). 2013. *Corporate responsibility in Europe. Government involvement in sector-specific initiatives*. Gütersloh: Verlag Bertelsmann Stiftung.

Crane, Andrew, Guido Palazzo, Laura J. Spence, and Dirk Matten. 2014. Contesting the value of the shared value concept. *California Management Review* 56(2): 130–153.

Curbach, Janina. 2009. *Die Corporate-social-responsibility-bewegung*. Wiesbaden: VS Verlag für Sozialwissenschaften.

Donaldson, Thomas. 2014. Shared values that are lost in translation. *Financial Times*, April 23.

Dyllick, Thomas. 2014. The opposing perspectives on creating shared value. *Financial Times*, April 24.

Edelman, L.B., and M.C. Suchman. 1997. The legal environments of organizations. *Annual Review of Sociology* 23(1): 479–515.

European Commission. 2011. A renewed EU strategy 2011–14 for Corporate Social Responsibility. Access to European Union law. http://eur-lex.europa.eu/legal-content/EN/TXT/PDF/?uri=CELEX:52011DC0681&from=EN. Accessed 29 Oct 2015.

Friedman, Milton. 1970. A Friedman doctrine – The social responsibility of business is to increase its profits. *The New York Times Magazine*, September 13.

Gelbman, Ulrike, and Rupert J. Baumgartner. 2012. Strategische implementierung von CSR in KMU. In *Corporate Social Responsibility*, ed. A. Schneider, and R. Schmidpeter, 285–298. Berlin: Springer.

Hajduk, Thomas. 2014. *Stichwort: Ehrbarer Kaufmann*. Stichwortverzeichnis: *CSR NEWS* http://csr-news.net/main/2014/03/23/ehrbarer-kaufmann. Accessed 29 Sep 2015.

Hajduk, Tomas. 2015. Bei Friedman nichts Neues. Anmerkungen zu einem falsch verstandenen Klassiker der CSR-Diskussion. In *Markt und Verantwortung. Wirtschaftsethische und moralökonomische Perspektiven*, ed. D. Aufderheide, and M. Dabrowski, 89–98. Berlin: Duncker & Humblot.

Hajduk, Thomas, and Christoph Schank. 2016. The model of the honourable merchant: Bridging compliance and integrity? In *Handbook of virtue ethics in business and management*, ed. A.J.G. Sison. Berlin and Heidelberg: Springer (in press).

Hartman, L.P., and P.H. Werhane. 2013. Shared value as an incomplete mental model. *Business Ethics Journal Review* 1(6): 36–43.

Jonker, Jan, and David Foster. 2002. Stakeholder excellence? Framing the evolution and complexity of a stakeholder perspective of the firm. *Corporate Social Responsibility and Environmental Management* 9(4): 187–195.

Lorentschitsch, Bettina, and Thomas Walker. 2012. Vom integrierten zum integrativen CSR-Managementansatz. In *Corporate social responsibility*, ed. A. Schneider, and R. Schmidpeter, 299–316. Berlin: Springer.

Matten, Dirk, and Andrew Crane. 2005. Corporate citizenship: Toward an extended theoretical conceptualization. *Academy of Management Review* 30(1): 166–179.

Palazzo, Guido, and Andreas G. Scherer. 2007. Toward a political conception of corporate responsibility: Business and society seen from a Habermasian perspective. *Academy of Management Review* 32(4): 1096–1120.

Porter, M.E., and M.R. Kramer. 2011. Creating shared value. How to Re-invent capitalism – and unleash a wave of innovation and growth. *Harvard Business Review* 89(1): 62–77.

———. 2014. A Response to Andrew Crane's et al.'s article. *California Management Review* 56(2): 149–151.

Post, James E., Lee E. Preston, and Sybille Sachs. 2012. *Redefining the corporation. Stakeholder management and organizational wealth*. Stanford: Stanford University Press.

Powell, Walter W., and Paul DiMaggio (ed). 1991/1983. *The new institutionalism in organizational analysis*. Chicago/London: The University of Chicago Press.

Preston, Lee E. 1975. Corporation and society: The search for a paradigm. *Journal of Economic Literature* 13(2): 434–453.

Schmiedeknecht, Maud H., and Josef Wieland. 2012. ISO 26000, 7 Grundsätze, 6 Kernthemen. In *Corporate social responsibility*, ed. A. Schneider, and R. Schmidpeter, 259–270. Berlin: Springer.

Scholz, Markus. 2014. *Stichworte: Creating shared value, shared value*. Stichwortverzeichnis: *CSR NEWS* http://csr-news.net/main/2014/03/23/creating-shared-value-2. Accessed 29 Sep 2015.

Scholz, Markus, and Gaston de los Reyes. 2015. Creating shared value – Grenzen und Vorschläge für eine Weiterentwicklung / Creating shared value – limits and suggestions for further development. *Zeitschrift für Wirtschafts-und Unternehmensethik* 16(2): 192-202.

The Economist. 2011. Oh, Mr Porter. *The Economist*, March 10.

Ulrich, Peter. 1997. *Integrative Wirtschaftsethik. Grundlagen einer lebensdienlichen Ökonomie*. Haupt Verlag: Bern/Stuttgart/Wien.

Waxenberger, Bernhard, and Laura J. Spence. 2003. Reinterpretation of a Metaphor: from stakes to claims. *Strategic Change* 12(5): 239–249.

Wieland, Josef. 1999. *Die Ethik der governance*. Marburg: Metropolis.

Wieland, Josef, and Andreas E.H. Heck. 2013. *Shared value durch stakeholder governance*. Marburg: Metropolis.

———. 2015. Creating Shared Value: E-Mail correspondence with Thomas Beschorner and Thomas Hajduk from 7 Jan 2015.

Wolf, Klaus D., and Sandra Schwindenhammer. 2011. Vom business case zum public case? Der Beitrag privater Selbstregulierung zu Global Governance. *Zeitschrift für Wirtschafts- und Unternehmensethik* 12(1): 10–28.

Zadek, Simon. 2001. *The civil corporation: The new economy of corporate citizenship*. London: Routledge.

Chapter 4
Corporate Social Responsibility (CSR). Cui bono?

Aloys Leo Prinz

Abstract Corporate Social Responsibility (CSR) is a concept that has become widely accepted as an ethical claim for firms. It reflects a more recent distribution conflict over the economic rents created by large firms. In this respect, these firms resemble political institutions more than economic entities. To take up this observation theoretically, rent-seeking theory is employed in this paper to analyze CSR more thoroughly. First, CSR may be a form of productive rent-seeking or rent-creation if it provides goods and services with those ethical standards that are coincidental with customers' preferences. Second, CSR could be unproductive rent-seeking if existing rents were simply redistributed. Third, CSR could be rent-shrinking if redistributing rents diluted control incentives within firms with the effect to reduce firm output or profitability. However, the CSR-induced rent competition between owners/shareholders, managers and stakeholders may also alter the rent allocation of firms to the advantage of owners/shareholders via stakeholder preferences. Prudent forms of CSR, therefore, can enhance welfare.

4.1 Introduction

Corporate Social Responsibility (CSR) is apparently accepted by citizens, politicians and even larger firms (corporations) as a criterion to evaluate a firm's performance beyond profits. Nonetheless, it is not so clear whether the just mentioned groups understand CSR in the same way. Within firms, CSR might be considered as a marketing concept to gain reputation with the so-called stakeholders of the firm. In contrast, politicians seem to believe that firms should (and would, perhaps even voluntarily) take over tasks for the general public which otherwise would be assigned to public policy. Citizens, sometimes represented by respective lobby

---

This part of the title is inspired by Stigler (1971)

A.L. Prinz (✉)
Universität Münster, Münster, North-Rhine Westfalia, Germany
e-mail: Aloys.Prinz@wiwi.uni-muenster.de

J. Wieland (ed.), *Creating Shared Value – Concepts, Experience, Criticism*, Ethical Economy 52, DOI 10.1007/978-3-319-48802-8_4

organizations, expect that firms provide something valuable for them as e.g. job opportunities, financial support and sponsorship for culture, sports, health care etc. As a consequence, CSR is not a clearly defined notion with the same meaning for firms, shareholders, stakeholders, politicians and others. Not surprisingly, general definitions of CSR are quite imprecise:

> "While there is no universal definition of corporate social responsibility, it generally refers to transparent business practices that are based on ethical values, compliance with legal requirements, and respect for people, communities, and the environment". (Catalyst Consortium 2002: 2)

> CSR is "(…) a concept whereby companies integrate social and environmental concerns in their business operations and in their interaction with their stakeholders on a voluntary basis". (European Commission 2001: 6)

From the viewpoint of political economy, such imprecise definitions make sense: they allow a broad spectrum of claims to firms' economic profits from persons and groups that are neither shareholders of the firm nor managers. In this paper, CSR is understood as a *system of moral justifications for claims on firms' rents*[1] *from persons and groups which are not directly involved in the firm.* Since there is no legally justified claim, the justification must be based on some moral aspects that may (or may not) be accepted by the general public. From this perspective, it becomes immediately clear that such claims put the burden of justification for making profits back on firms. However, some firms reacted to this in a manner which was not anticipated by CSR protagonists: they employed CSR themselves as a marketing tool. In a sense, to impose the pressure of moral justification for their economic activities and profits on firms was answered by these firms by giving their actions a moral justification in order to gain a competitive advantage over competitors. Nevertheless, this is not the end of the story. The rest of the paper explains how this new form of interaction between firms and their environment – called CSR – may create, destroy or redistribute rents. In other words, the topic of the paper is rent-seeking via CSR.

The structure of the paper is as follows: In section two the concept of rent-seeking is applied to distinguish between productive and unproductive rent-seeking via CSR. Rent-appropriation conflicts concerning CSR are analyzed in section three. The application of CSR to conflicts between shareholders and management as well as shareholders and stakeholders is discussed in section four. Section five concludes with a brief discussion of the findings.

[1] An economic rent is a payment or benefit for a factor of production (labor services, capital) over and above the amount which is necessary to employ this factor in the firm; cf. The Economist (n.d): "rent".

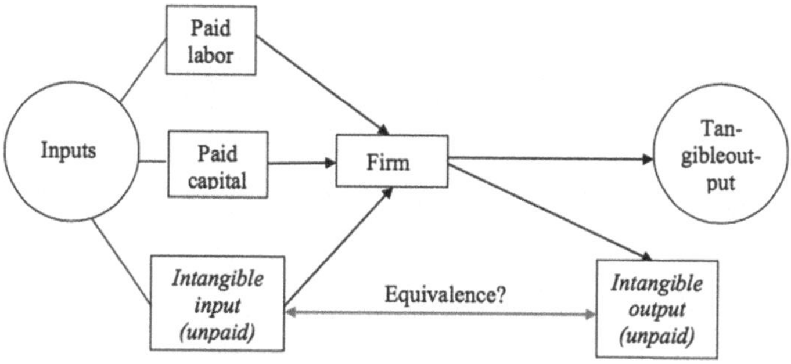

Fig. 4.1 Intangible inputs and intangible outputs of a firm's environment (Source: Own illustration)

4.2 Rent-Seeking via CSR

To explain CSR economically, it may be argued that firms' chances to earn a profit depend on social conditions they are using without paying for them. Put more precisely, there may be intangible input factors that society, communities and so on provide without being paid by firms (cf. Fig. 4.1). Such inputs can be trust, the existence of a market economy, honesty of customers etc. (cf. White 2006, for a definition and examples of intangible inputs). As a consequence, stakeholders from the firm's environment may have a moral claim on part of the rent created by the firm. However, this would be a one-sided argument. The reason is that the firm may also provide unpaid intangible benefits for its environment. Such benefits can be job opportunities, the supply of education within the firm, an infrastructure created by the firm which can also be used by other people e.g., special hospitals etc. As a consequence, it is unclear whether intangible inputs are equivalent to intangible outputs. Nonetheless, it could be conjectured that there is a kind of equivalence since otherwise the firm would relocate or the local public would try to displace the firm.

In this paper, the existence of CSR is explained by *rent-seeking*. We have to distinguish between rent-seeking of the firm (and its owners/shareholders and management) and rent-seeking of persons and groups outside of the firm (stakeholders). First of all, *productive* (competitive) rent-seeking (PRS) (or rent-creation, cf. Buchanan 1980), is to be distinguished from *unproductive* (or redistributive, cf. Dari-Mattiacci et al. 2004) rent-seeking (URS): In the case of PRS, resources are used to generate surpluses and profits from supplying useful goods and services to consumers, whereas in the second case resources are used for the appropriation of already existing rents (cf. Dari-Mattiaci et al. 2007). PRS and URS are depicted in Fig. 4.2.

PRS with respect to CSR might occur when firms satisfy the *moral dimension of demand* for their products (cf., for example Priddat 1998, 2000; Stehr 2007). For instance, if firms provide fair labour standards in their manufacturing locations abroad, this might increase the demand for products of this particular firm in

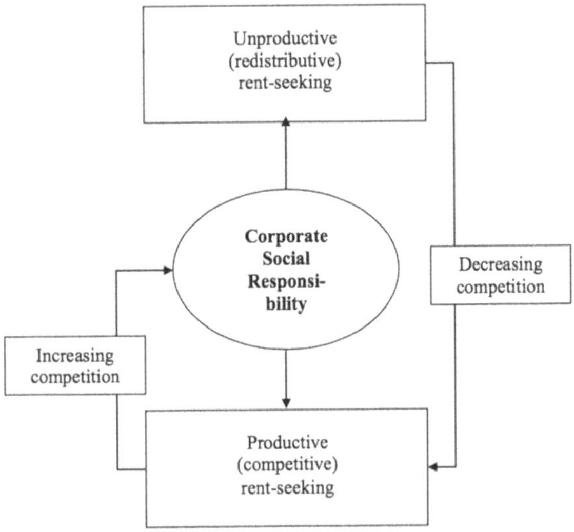

Fig. 4.2 CSR as productive and unproductive rent-seeking (Source: Own illustration)

comparison to a competitor. Insofar this policy may increase firm profits, although applying fair labour standards may also increase production costs but on a lower level. Since at least some consumers are willing to pay a higher price for products manufactured under fair conditions, this can create a rent for the particular firm. The precondition for this rent is, however, that the firm communicates its fair labour policy via marketing. In other words, being recognized by customers as a morally decent firm may pay off economically. This would be part of the *firm's total value* which is to be maximized from an economic point of view (in the words of Jensen 2002, this is called the "enlightened stakeholder theory"; cf. Jensen 2002). In effect, productive rent-seeking increases competition among firms.

But this is not the whole story, unfortunately. CSR may also be used in an unproductive form even by firms themselves. Sometimes it can be easier to lobby for policies that restrict competition (e.g. from abroad) by using CSR. It seems quite easy to allege (and very difficult to prove) that foreign firms do have unmerited cost advantages via social dumping, wage dumping, environmental dumping, and so on. If successful, resources for lobbying are employed to appropriate a rent by restricting competition to protect the own position in the market, with higher prices and profits. Of course, this kind of rent-seeking cannot be considered as rent-creation, provided that the allegations are incorrect. The result will not be different if the allegations mentioned above come from stakeholders of the firm instead of the firm itself. Suppose that a labour union claims wage dumping by foreign firms, although foreign firms have a competitive advantage and do not pay unreasonably low wages. The real reason of the labour union's claim is under these circumstances to protect high wages in the domestic firm or sector of the economy. As a consequence, the claim would be considered as URS on the part of the union. Moreover, stakeholders may involve themselves in URS even if they pretend to protect other persons. Of course, the main intention of employing CSR arguments in these cases is to decrease competition in order to protect an existing rent from the current market position.

URS in combination with CSR may not only be a problem for stakeholders and firms, but also for the management within firms. Managers might overinvest in CSR to appropriate a private rent aiming at being recognized as "good global citizens" (cf. Barnea/Rubin 2005: 1). This overinvestment in CSR is also classified as URS since no values are added that are to the benefit of customers or the society as a whole.

All in all, CSR may be PRS or URS, depending on the fact whether new values for customers and society are created. As a consequence, CSR cannot be evaluated as generally good or bad. Even if URS prevails, the question is whether CSR is really damaging. As argued here, CSR might only be a socially accepted form of justification for claims on rents of firms that would probably be differently justified otherwise, but not abandoned. In the following, *rent-appropriation* is the focal point of analysis. Creation of rents via CSR is not considered further because it does not pose problems, even for economists.

4.3 Rent-Appropriation Conflicts and CSR

4.3.1 Rent-Appropriation

In this paper, an *economic rent* is defined as a reward over and above that level which could be realized with perfect competition. As is well known (cf., for instance, The Economist: "competition"), e.g., the economic profit (and, hence, the economic rent) of a firm under these circumstances is zero. The operating profit on the balance sheet is the market price for equity (plus the market salary for the labour input of the owner in case of an owner-managed firm). In contrast, with imperfect competition – for instance, with a monopoly – an economic rent can be gained. Since markets under perfect competition provide only that level of compensation for the factors of production that is necessary to bring about the required volume and quality of these factors and remunerate the quantity and quality of the firm's output according to customers' demand, there are no rents for distribution (perfect competition assumed). For further analysis, imperfect competition and, hence, the existence of economic rents is supposed.

In general, economic rents can be distributed to firm owners or shareholders, respectively workers, managers, stakeholders, politicians or the general public. The traditional conflict of rent-distribution, however, was between firm owners or shareholders on the one hand and workers on the other hand. This conflict may be dubbed *Marxian Conflict* and it dominated the nineteenth and the first half of the twentieth century. The modern conflict – coming up with firms owned by a large number of shareholders instead of a person or family – was between firm owners, shareholders and managers (given that the share of workers was decided by institutionalized

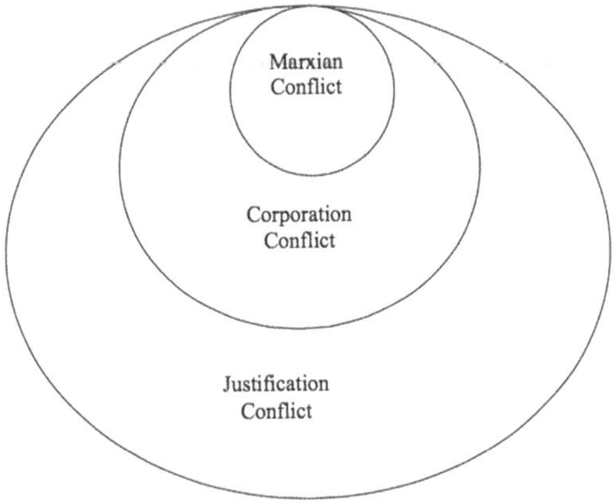

Fig. 4.3 Evolution of rent-distribution conflicts (Source: Own illustration)

negotiations between management and labour unions); this modern kind of conflict may be called the *Corporation Conflict*. The post-modern conflict is between owners/shareholders, managers and stakeholders whereby stakeholders justify their claims mainly by moral reasoning. This puts managers and owners/shareholders under justification pressure; this new kind of fighting for rents is therefore called here *Justification Conflict*. Figure 4.3 depicts the conflicts as circles whereby the first two conflicts are subsets of the *Justification Conflict*. Last but not least, the *Justification Conflict* may be taken as a sign that the perceived nature of (large) firms has changed from "the firm as a subeconomy" (cf. Bengt Holmstrom 1999) to "the firm as a political system" (cf. Steinmann 1985; Rasche et al. 2008; Healy 2014). Hence, the conflict regarding the distribution of firm rents has been enlarged and intensified.

The new quality of the *Justification Conflict* brings CSR into play because it has at least the rhetoric and moral power to change the rent-distribution which obviously could not be changed dramatically by public policy so far. In a sense, CSR can be interpreted either as a substitute for or as a complement to public policy. As a *substitute* it would take over tasks which formerly had been on the political agenda, but could not be realized; as a *complement* it would take over responsibility for tasks which are not (yet) on the political agenda. However, it seems noteworthy to add that stakeholders do not necessarily represent the interest of the general public, but rather special interests of some groups in society.

4.3.2 Political Economy of CSR Goals and Conflicts

First of all, it is crucial to recognize that not all goals of owners/shareholders, management and stakeholders are incompatible with each other. Generally speaking, goals can be classified as *complementary* or *conflict-laden*. Moreover, there may also be a hierarchy of goals which might be legally defined or by the power of the

Table 4.1 Relations between CSR goals according to the type of rent-seeking

Type of CSR rent-seeking	Potential results
Productive CSR	All can win, but conflict about rent-distribution
Unproductive CSR	Some can win, others will loose
Hierarchy of rent claims	Who is entitled to collect the rent in the first instance?

Source: Own illustration

respective group. When goals are complementary, all can win (a so-called win-win situation). With conflicting goals, obviously not all can win (a win-lose situation). A *hierarchy of goals* implies a prioritization for winning. Concerning the types of CSR with respect to rent-seeking distinguished here, the potential goal-related win-lose results are shown in Table 4.1.

According to Table 4.1, with productive CSR all groups can win insofar as the rent to be distributed increases. The size of the rent is consequently a non-conflicting goal in productive CSR. However, the rent-distribution is a win-lose situation because the win of one group is necessarily the loss of another. The difference between productive and unproductive CSR results from the fact that the size of the rent in unproductive rent-seeking does not increase for all groups in society. Therefore, unproductive rent-seeking always implies a win-lose situation between societal groups.

The claims to the rents of a firm are at least partially legally defined, i.e., there is a certain hierarchy of rent claims. Nevertheless, the hierarchy of rent claims is incomplete insofar as the legally defined claims become relevant after the firm's profit is known. In this respect, CSR claims are crucial before the firm's profit is calculated, e.g., CSR causes in some way or other an increase of the firm's cost. From this viewpoint, the hierarchy of rent claims is not only legally defined, but additionally decided by power (cf. Rajan and Zingales 1998, for a theoretical analysis of specific investments and the reason for power in firms). The legal order of claims becomes only relevant *after* CSR claims are (more or less) realized. More precisely, the CSR distribution conflict consists of conflicting goals between shareholders, managers and stakeholders. Managers attempt to maximize *high-risk short-term profits* whereas shareholders strive for *low-risk long-term profits* (cf. Perotti and von Thadden 2006). Stakeholders seem to aim at *social profits* whose exact meaning depends on the particular stakeholder group. The competition among these groups to appropriate firm rents may result in two different effects: a *rent-shrinking effect* and a *rent-redistribution effect*. These effects are demonstrated by using a so-called Peltzman-diagram in Fig. 4.4 and a price-setting diagram in Fig. 4.5.

As assumed at the beginning of the paper, only such firms are considered here that earn an economic rent, i.e., they make a profit above the market price for equity. Without CSR, it is supposed that the firm would maximize profit in a monopolistic way only, as shown by the price p_m in Figs. 4.4 and 4.5. Let this price be the short-term as well as the long-term profit maximizing price (assumed there is no conflict among shareholders and management). CSR may have a *rent-shrinking* as well as a

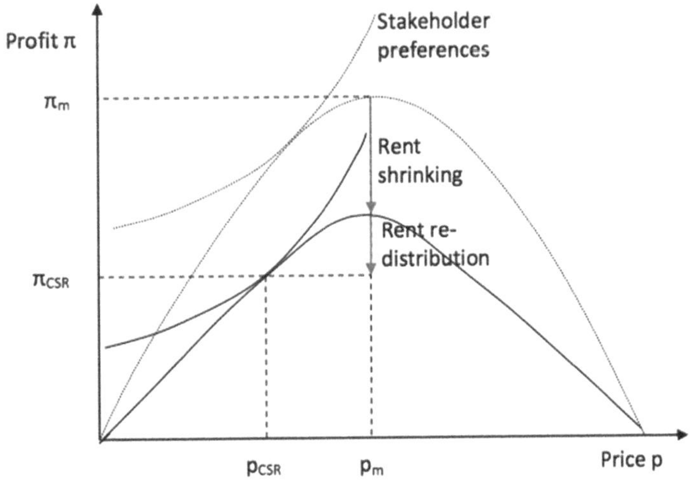

Fig. 4.4 Peltzman-diagram of political economy effects of CSR (Source: Own illustration by adapting Figure II. Peltzman (1976: 224))

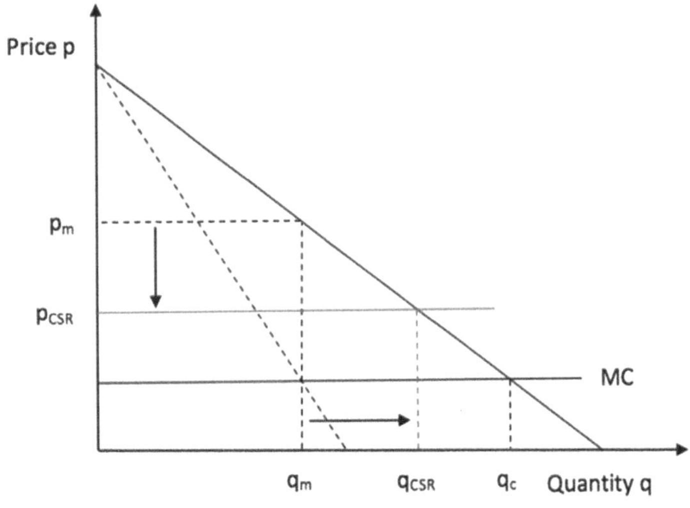

Fig. 4.5 Price and quantity under monopoly pricing and CSR-pricing (Source: Own illustration)

rent-redistributing effect. The *rent-shrinking effect* results from diluting the incentives of both shareholders and management to care about the firm's profit: shareholders may reduce their spending on controlling the management and the management may reduce its cost-containment efforts because a part of the benefits from these costly activities goes to stakeholders. Another version of the story could read as follows: Due to stakeholder activities the firm has to reduce the price of the good from p_m to p_{CSR} which means that the economic rent will also shrink (depicted in Figs. 4.4 and 4.5). Because stakeholders have a preference for social benefits (in this case, a lower price), the stakeholders' indifference curve is tangent to the profit function at p_{CSR} with a profit of π_{CSR}. Due to both the rent shrinking and the rent redistribution effect, shareholders and management lose part of their rents. While the *rent-redistribution effect* may be considered welfare-neutral because it is a pure distribution effect, it might come at a cost via the *rent-shrinking effect*. The cost might be the deterioration of cost control etc. just mentioned. However, it is not self-evident that allocative efficiency is always negatively affected by CSR. To see this, a further look at the *Justification Conflict* is indicated which is analyzed in the following paragraph in more detail.

4.3.3 Owners/Shareholders vs. Management vs. Stakeholders

To fully understand the CSR *rent-distribution conflict* (*Justification Conflict*), it is necessary to go back to the earlier conflict between owners/shareholders and management (*Corporation Conflict*). Due to the evolution of ever bigger firms and of corresponding capital markets, the owner controlled firm was replaced by firms owned by a large number of shareholders which had to employ a management to run the firm (cf. Berle and Means 1932). As is very well known, this evolution was accompanied by severe information and incentive problems (cf. Demsetz and Lehn 1985). Since shareholders have relatively high information costs with little gains from information search, the firm's management gets a large scope concerning firm decisions (cf. van der Burg and Prinz 2006). Beside capital markets, profit sharing with the management and stock options of the firm are tools to give the management incentives to lead the firm according to shareholder goals (cf. Bebchuk and Fried 2003; Bulow and Shoven 2005). But this kind of indirect control over the firm is not perfect, because it implies a lower profit for shareholders in comparison to owner control (*rent-shrinking effect*).

In Fig. 4.6 (which may be interpreted as a generalization of Fig. 4.4 to three groups), the *rent-distribution conflict* is shown. Profit is represented by the Iso-profit curve S = M if owners/shareholders manage the firm themselves. This is the highest level of the Iso-profit curve because the gains from productive rent-seeking (creation of values and profits) are completely internalized. Moreover, it does not involve problems of control regarding information and incentive. However, this might only be true for rather small firms with few owners or shareholders. The *rent-distribution conflict* between owners/shareholders in larger firms implies a lower level of profit, indicated by the Iso-profit curve $S \neq M$. The reason for that is the *rent-shrinking effect* introduced above, which goes back to allocation inefficiencies triggered by information differentials between managers and owners/shareholders. In other words, the management realizes an information rent. This is indicated in Fig. 4.6 by the dashed arrow-lines directing to a position between shareholders and managers.

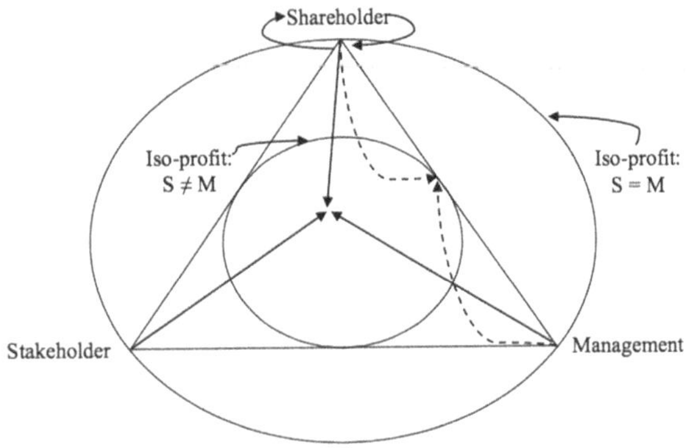

Fig. 4.6 Shareholder, management and stakeholder in the *rent-distribution conflict* (Source: Own illustration)

The occurrence of stakeholders may alter the owners/shareholders-management conflict by strengthening the long-term view of owners/shareholders in their struggle with a semi-autonomous management. Stakeholders are also depicted in Fig. 4.6. According to this figure, the Iso-profit curve is not changed by stakeholders. However, whether or not this is true depends crucially on the question whether the *rent-shrinking effect* of CSR due to incentive dilution by third-party rent-sharing is smaller or larger than the *rent-shrinking effect* of partial management autonomy. In Fig. 4.6 it is supposed that both *rent-shrinking effects* are about equal size. If this is actually the case, second-best rents are distributed among three instead of two parties. This is indicated by three line-arrows directing to the center of the Iso-profit curves. A particularly interesting question is whether the inclusion of stakeholders into rent-sharing arrangements might intensify or mitigate the owners/shareholders-management conflict. As argued above, the management of big firms has some scope to spend resources on that kind of CSR that benefits managers most. The intrusion of firm-external stakeholders could then be in the interest of shareholders because they may gain from stakeholder activism since they probably share at least some interests with stakeholders (and not with managers). Part of the rent which goes to stakeholders might also benefit shareholders. As a consequence, shareholders might benefit at the cost of managers even if the total rent does not change. An institutional instrument to enforce such a redistribution of rents between management and big shareholders on the one side and the large number of small shareholders on the other side could be intensified shareholder activism (cf. van der Burg and Prinz 2006). Hence, empowerment of small shareholders, in combination with active stakeholders, might trigger a redistribution of firm rents towards small shareholders at the cost of large shareholders and the management. However, not all stakeholders are treated equal in this respect. The reason is that the preferences of some stakeholders might be more similar to those of large shareholders and the management whereas the preferences of other stakeholders might be similar to those of small shareholders.

To sum up, it is not clear how exactly the new *Justification Conflict* will alter the rent-distribution between owners/shareholders and the management within a firm. Nonetheless, it seems possible that small shareholders might even benefit from

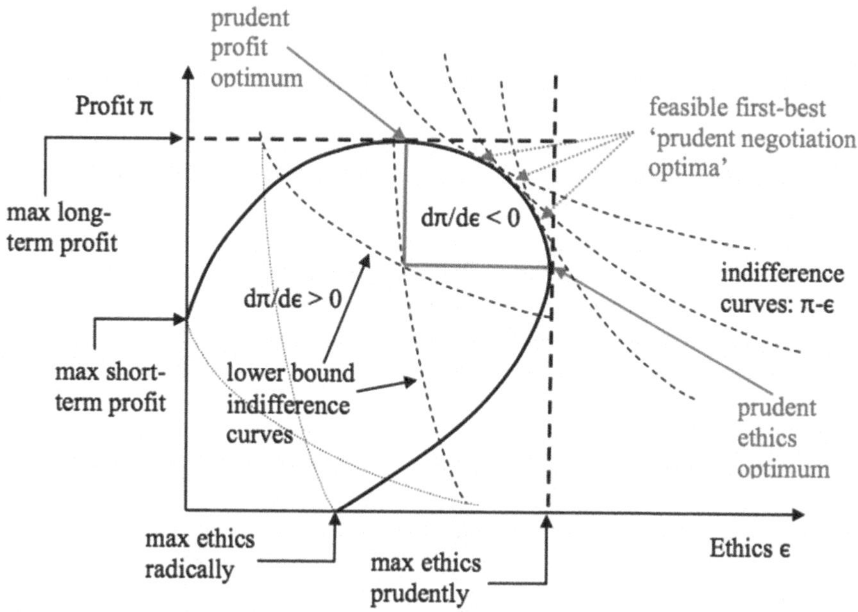

Fig. 4.7 The Profits-Ethics-Possibility Frontier (PEPF) (Source: Own illustration)

stakeholder activism if (a) the preferences of stakeholders are more similar to those of shareholders than to those of the management and if (b) the part of the rent which is appropriated by stakeholders comes from the management.

4.4 Prudent Equilibria

The story so far is one of mixed results. Although it cannot be said that CSR has negative effects only, it would be overly optimistic to tell that it has mainly beneficial effects. After all, it seems that the main effects of CSR come from redistributing firm rents. From an economic point of view, both long-term profit maximization and the maximization of social benefits may be sustainable objectives for society as a whole. This might not be said of the management's attempt to maximize short-term profits. Taking this into account, Fig. 4.7 depicts the trade-off between shareholders' (long-term) profit objectives and stakeholders' social or ethical aims.

In Fig. 4.7, it is supposed that the *Profits-Ethics Possibility Frontier* – which contains all efficient combinations outcomes of 'profits' (π) and 'ethics' (ϵ), e.g., social benefits – has parts with positive slope ($d\pi /d\epsilon > 0$) and a part with negative slope ($d\pi /d\epsilon < 0$). This can be interpreted as follows: Starting with short-term profit maximization on the profit axis, both (long-term) profits and the social benefits can be increased by a change of the time-perspective of the firm. This may also be true if one started at the point on the ethics-axis of radical ethical maximization;

introducing profit goals may make it possible to enhance the material result of production; this would make it possible to distribute more benefits ethically.

For the general construction and meaning of such (utility-possibility) frontiers see Chipman (2010), who also cites the origins of such diagrams. For the version of the possibility-curve applied here see Recktenwald (1987: 25) and Olsen (1997: Fig. 4.3) with an application to a distribution analysis in health economics.

However, at $d\pi / d\epsilon = 0$ the point of long-term profit maximization is reached, at a certain level of ethical standards. At $d\pi / d\epsilon = -\infty$, the point of maximum ethical standards is realized, at a certain level for long-term profits. The first point mentioned is called the 'prudent profit optimum', the latter 'prudent ethics optimum'. Obviously, both optima lie on different points of the PEPF. All attainable first-best points are on the line between the prudent profit optimum and the prudent ethics optimum.

As depicted in Fig. 4.7, there are *two different ways* to see economic and social values. Starting from a dominance of economic values, the trajectory of possibilities starts at short-term profit maximization and ends at the prudent profit optimum. Starting from a dominance of social values, the trajectory of possibilities starts at the radical ethics point and ends at the prudent ethics optimum. Obviously, there is a gap between these trajectories of possibilities. In practice, both trajectories can be taken and firms on both trajectories may survive in economic competition. That there are two different trajectories emphasizes that there is nevertheless a distribution conflict. The trajectories show *efficient* possibilities for both kind of firms, avoiding inefficient points *inside* the trajectories, i.e., inside the PEPF. This holds even true for the region of conflict on the part of PEPF with negative slope, the region between the prudent optima.

In this framework, CSR and the recently proposed concept of *Creating Shared Value* (CSV) (Porter and Kramer 2011) can be located. CSV emphasized the coexistence of economic and social values by stressing the opportunity for business to make more profit by incorporating some social values in their strategy. In this respect, the CSV optimum would be identical with the prudent profit optimum in Fig. 4.7. This is the highest point attainable from an economic point of view. Beyond this point, a further increase in the provision of social value by firms would reduce (long-term) profitability. On the other side of the spectrum, the CSR optimum can be identified with the prudent ethics optimum of this paper, as shown in Fig. 4.7. At this point, a further increase of economic value would reduce social values. Consequently, the area of harmonic increases of economic and social values ends at the respective prudent optima. The trajectory of possibilities has, then, a negative slope between the prudent optima. However, there are also *prudent negotiation equilibria* on that line segment of PEPF which has a negative slope. These optima are called 'prudent' as it is not feasible to find other points with higher levels of welfare. Nevertheless, these optima encompass the *Justification Conflict* of rent-distribution. Because this segment of PEPF has a negative slope, the gain in 'ethics' is paid by lower long-term 'profits', and vice-versa. The risk of negotiations is, however, that the points on this line segment are missed and a combination of profits and ethical standards is established which lies inside PEPF. Obviously, it is not so easy to match the points on the line since the line itself might not be transparent for shareholders, stakeholders and the management. Therefore a trial-and-error process of looking for the best attainable solution is likely.

4.5 Conclusions

CSR has shown that there is a new kind of conflict in (large) firms, which is called the *Justification Conflict*. This new kind of conflict about the distribution of economic rents created by firms may be interpreted as a signal that nowadays these firms resemble rather political institutions than economic entities. The size of these firms, measured in monetary units of their output, is often larger than the GDP of not-so-well developed countries. Moreover, in addition to their output of goods and services, these firms may also produce 'public bads' (cf. Prinz and van der Burg 2011) for which they are not fully accounted. If public policy is not able to internalize these public bads effectively and efficiently, stakeholders may take over responsibility and try to enforce ethical standards (social benefits) on these firms.

However, this picture may be over-optimistic concerning the role of stakeholders. The main argument is that even shareholders have an interest on the internalization of public bads because they also suffer from them. As a consequence, shareholders as well as stakeholders may have some common preferences. In this paper, it is supposed that shareholders are interested in long-term profit maximization which incorporates at least some negative effects of production bads. Firms will have some incentives from their customers to produce their products according to ethical standards and they may gain market shares by committing themselves to these standards.

From a less-optimistic perspective, stakeholders are rent seekers in an unproductive rent-seeking competition. If this is the case, CSR might dilute property rights of the firm's shareholders with the consequence of rent-shrinking. In addition to that, CSR changes the distribution of the firm's rent (*rent-redistribution effect*). However, stakeholders may alter the *Corporate Conflict* between shareholders and management. In the best case, stakeholders may gain that part of the rent which would be appropriated otherwise from the management. In the worst case, CSR is employed by the management to enhance its own reputation at the cost of the firm.

Prudent CSR consists of a combination of long-term profit maximization (also called firm value maximization) and the application of prudent ethical standards in firms. To claim more than that may hardly be justifiable by ethics. CSR might be a viable instrument in the first instance to mitigate the societal disadvantages of short-term profit maximization. Taking this seriously, prudent forms of CSR may be welfare enhancing, e.g., prudent CSR might be beneficial for society as a whole.

References

Barnea, Amir, and Amir Rubin. 2005. *Corporate social responsibility as a conflict between shareholders. McCombs School of Business*. Burnaby: University of Texas at Austin, Austin, and Simon Fraser University http://apps.olin.wustl.edu/jfi/pdf/csr.conflict.pdf. Accessed 23 Aug 2016.

Bebchuk, Lucian A., and Jesse M. Fried. 2003. Executive compensation as an agency problem. *Journal of Economic Perspectives* 17(3): 71–92.

Berle, Adolf A., and Gardiner Means. 1932. *The modern corporation and private property*. New York: MacMillan.

Buchanan, James M. 1980. Rent seeking and profit seeking. In *Towards a theory of the rent-seeking society*, ed. James M. Buchanan, Robert D. Tollison, and Gordon Tullock, 3–15. College Station: Texas A&M University Press.

Bulow, Jeremy, and John B. Shoven. 2005. Accounting for stock options. *Journal of Economic Perspectives* 19(4): 115–134.

CATALYST Consortium. 2002. What is Corporate Social Responsibility? http://pdf.usaid.gov/pdf_docs/Pnada498.pdf. Accessed 23 Aug 2016.

Chipman, John S. 2010. The utility-possibility frontier. In *Famous figures and diagrams in economics*, ed. M. Blaug, and P. Lloyd, 252–261. Cheltenham/Northampton: Edward Elgar Publishing.

Commission of the European Communities. 2001. Greenpaper: Promoting a European framework for corporate social responsibility. Brussels, 18 July 2001. COM(2001) 366 final.

Dari-Mattiacci, Guiseppe, Eric Langlais, Bruno Lovat, and Francesco Parisi. 2007. Crowding-out in productive and redistributive rent-seeking. *Public Choice* 133: 199–229.

Demsetz, Harold, and Kenneth Lehn. 1985. The structure of corporate ownership: causes and consequences. *Journal of Political Economy* 93: 1155–1177.

Healy, Robert. 2014. *Corporate political behavior: Why corporations do what they do in politics*. New York: Routledge Chapman Hall.

Holmstrom, Bengt. 1999. The firm as a subeconomy. *Journal of Law, Economics, and Organization* 15(1): 74–102.

Jensen, Michael C. 2002. Value maximization, stakeholder theory, and the corporate objective function. *Business Ethics Quarterly* 12: 235–256.

Olsen, Jan A. 1997. Theories of justice and their implications for priority setting in health care. *Journal of Health Economics* 16: 625–639.

Peltzman, Sam. 1976. Toward a More General theory of regulation. *Journal of Law and Economics* 19(2): 211–240.

Perotti, E.C., and von E.-L. Thadden. 2006. The political economy of corporate control and labor rents. *Journal of Political Economy* 114(1): 145–174.

Porter, M.E., and M.R. Kramer. 2011. Creating shared value. How to re-invent capitalism – and Unleash a wave of innovation and growth. *Harvard Business Review* 89(1): 62–77.

Priddat, Birger P. 1998. *Moralischer Konsum. 13 Lektionen über die Käuflichkeit*. Stuttgart/Leipzig: S. Hirzel Verlag.

———. 2000. moral hybrids: Skizze zu einer Theorie moralischen Konsums. *Zeitschrift für Wirtschafts- und Unternehmensethik* 1(2): 128–151.

Prinz, Aloys, and Tsjalle van der Burg. 2011. Public bads and private firms: efficiency and sustainability with different allocations of voting rights. *European Journal of Law and Economics* 36: 423–445. doi:10.1007/s10657-011-9266-3.

Rajan, Raghuram G., and Luigi Zingales. 1998. Power in a theory of the firm. *Quarterly Journal of Economics* 113(2): 387–432.

Rasche, Andreas, Dorothea Baur, Mariëtte van Huijstee, Stephen Ladek, Jayanthi Naidu, Cecilia Perla, Esther Schouten, Michael Valente, and Mingrui Zhang. 2008. Corporations as political actors: A report on the first swiss master class in corporate social responsibility. *Journal of Business Ethics* 80(2): 151–173.

Recktenwald, Horst C. 1987. *Über Geben und Nehmen im Kollektiv. Sicht und Einsicht des Ökonomen*. Akademie der Wissenschaften und der Literatur, Mainz. Abhandlungen der Geistes- und Sozialwissenschaftlichen Klasse, Jahrgang 1987, Nr. 9, Stuttgart: Franz Steiner Verlag Wiesbaden.

Stehr, Nico. 2007. *Die Moralisierung der Märkte. Eine Gesellschaftstheorie*. Suhrkamp: Frankfurt a.M.

Steinmann, Horst. 1985. The enterprise as a political system. In *Corporate governance and directors' liabilities*, ed. K.J. Hopt, and G. Teubner, 401–428. Berlin/New York: Walter de Gruyter.

Stigler, George. 1971. The theory of economic regulation. *The Bell Journal of Economics and Management Science* 2(1): 3–21.

The Economist (n.d). Rent and Rent-Seeking. Economics A–Z terms. http://www.economist.com/economics-a-to-z/r#node-21529784. Accessed 07 Aug 2016.

Van der Burg, Tsjalle, and Aloys Prinz. 2006. Empowering small shareholders: A comparison of three instruments. *Corporate Governance: An International Review* 14: 406–417.

White, Allen L. 2006. Business Brief: Intangibles and CSR. Business for Social Responsibility. https://www.bsr.org/reports/BSR_AW_Intangibles-CSR.pdf. Accessed 23 Aug 2016.

Chapter 5
Just When You Thought It Couldn't Get Worse, You Hear: "The Business of Business Is Business"-Some Reflections on a Self-Fulfilling Prophecy and Alternative Perspectives on the Purpose of Companies

Michael Fürst

Abstract Business seems to have lost its sense of purpose and the relationship between business and society appears to be broken. Relevant parts of society question whether business is creating value for the many or just for a few. At the same time there is an expectation that business contributes to solutions to huge challenges such as poverty or climate change. In such an environment, the concept of Shared Value is catching a lot of attention from academics and business practitioners because it appears to offer an appealing narrative about how business can develop innovative solutions to societal challenges that are creating business and societal value simultaneously. According to the authors, this requires a re-definition of the role and the purpose of business in society, a definition that would be fundamentally different compared with the most prominent economic and business theories that in turn claim that business has to maximize profits or respectively has to create value for the shareholders first and foremost. This situation analysis raises some important questions that this article tries to explore: How could it happen in the first place that business is under such scrutiny, given that companies are creating considerable value for societies? And for what reason have economists been at least ambivalent if not even agnostic concerning moral values, ethics and social responsibilities of companies in modern societies for so many years? And what alternative concepts – in regards to the role and responsibilities of business as possible tools to address societal challenges – were offered in former times and can be seen as foundations for the Shared Value concept? The article makes a rather explorative attempt to offer some perspectives to these questions and specifically to how companies could

When not otherwise indicated, statements made in this article represent the personal opinion and perspective of the author and not of the affiliated organization.

Reference for this quote is the famous article from Milton Friedman about the social responsibility of business that we will reflect on within a subsequent paragraph of in this article.

M. Fürst (✉)
Novartis International AG, CH 4002 Basel, Switzerland
e-mail: michael.fuerst1@gmail.com

J. Wieland (ed.), *Creating Shared Value – Concepts, Experience, Criticism*, Ethical Economy 52, DOI 10.1007/978-3-319-48802-8_5

respond to these expectations. We propose that companies should operate with a strategic portfolio approach, i.e. using a portfolio of interventions – of which Shared Value is one – with the aim to optimize the positive impact on society and minimize the negative footprint. Lastly, the article discusses some of the concerns that were raised against the Shared Value concept, either because these are an inherent element of it or because of how it is positioned within the academic debate on the corporate responsibilities of companies.

5.1 Introduction

Business seems to have lost its sense of purpose. The relationship between business and society appears to be broken. There is an easy way to find out whether there is some truth in this assumption though this might not become a pleasurable experience: Just flip through the daily headlines in newspapers or try to engage in a discussion about the benefits business is bringing to society respectively – at a more theoretical level – about the role of business in society. It will not take long time to find negative views or comments about companies and business leaders in the media. What is more, during discussions, the person arguing in favor of business being a positive force in society will be rather quickly a lonely soul or will not be even able to finish the thought because being overwhelmed by a verbal swirl of mistrust towards business, spurred by human rights violations in sweatshops, environmental pollution, corruption and bribery, greed and excessive salaries and bonuses, legal but morally at least doubtful tax practices, exploitation of countries, the mantra of almost unlimited profit seeking joined up with dangerous incentives and lax regulation leading to financial meltdowns – all this resulting in benefits for the few at the expense for the most.[1] This sounds like an executive summary of the list of sins from Dante's Inferno, emerging from unbalanced desires, emotions, greed etc. and we consider these issues, it is not too far away from reality to say that people generally do not see business as a force for good but rather as the opposite or even as a psychopathic affair that belongs on the couch of a psychologist.[2]

Let us be clear: This is for sure an exaggerated and provocative view – however the generally negative perception is backed by recent findings from the Edelman Trust Barometer that shows that the informed public perceives technology, business growth and greed money as the biggest drivers for change in business – whereas improving people's lives or making the world a better place is perceived as less relevant driver of change in business.[3]

[1] For some of these arguments see Stiglitz (2010) "Freefall" or (2012) "The price of inequality".

[2] For such an analysis see the movie "The Corporation" or the website http://thecorporation.com (accessed 30.03.2016).

[3] Edelman Trust Barometer 2015 "Trust and Innovation" http://www.edelman.com/insights/intellectual-property/2015-edelman-trust-barometer/ (accessed 30.03.2016).

This raises some important questions: How could it happen that business – as one of the most powerful institutions in modern society – that mostly operates within democratically legitimized legal frameworks, works with employees who for sure have a disposition and preference for ethical conduct, that develops and offers products or services which were or are crucially important for societal advancements – is under such scrutiny? And for what reason have economists been at least ambivalent if not even agnostic concerning moral values, ethics and social responsibilities of companies in modern societies for so many years? And what alternative concepts – in regards to the role and responsibilities of business as possible tools to address societal challenges – were offered in former times or are heavily debated currently?

Undoubtedly, it cannot be the ambition of this article to develop a full exegesis of the extensive economic literature or the meanwhile growing research about corporate responsibility. However, we make indeed a rather explorative attempt to offer some perspectives and insights in regards to which concepts or frameworks would be appropriate and helpful in articulating how the purpose and role of business in modern societies could be understood and which strategies and frameworks could be adequate propositions in regards to how companies can become powerful actors that aim to create positive societal impact and economic value.

As a starting point, we shed light on Milton Friedman as one of the most influential advocates of a narrow view in regards to whether companies should assume social responsibilities. We proceed then with an analysis concerning why his famous dictum of "the social responsibility of business is to increase its profits" (Friedman 1970) missed out many important factors that companies need to consider.

In a next step, to contrast Friedman's perspective, we reflect on Peter Drucker's view on the topic of social responsibility and the purpose of business – a voice worthwhile to consider since he is one of the most influential management thinkers of the recent decades though sometimes underestimated in his thinking in regards to the societal role of business

This inspection of Friedman's and Drucker's thinking then helps us in a further step to reference some roots of the Shared Value concept from Michael Porter and Mark Kramer (2011) that is heavily debated in academic circles and got considerably positive attention and traction in practitioner circles. We then try to dissect some of the roots of the Shared Value concept that is an important phenomenon since Porter and Kramer claim that their concept can overcome the historical and current shortcomings of business and its relation to society as outlined above. From our point of view, their intent derives in its origins from a narrow conception of business when they write that it can relegitimize business, redefine the purpose of the corporation, reshape capitalism and to supersede corporate social responsibility, the latter aim being a rather misguided one since it is in our view built on a theoretically and practically ill-informed understanding of corporate responsibility.

Besides this particular shortcoming in regards to their understanding of CR and some others that we will analyze and highlight in this article, there are good reasons why the Shared Value concept got such traction and actually moves the field of CR in a positive direction indeed. Eventually we will flag some of the areas in the

Shared Value concept and the wider CR debate that need further exploration and offer some approaches as to how the debate around strategic CR could further unfold.

Lastly, it is important to mention that this article does not have the ambition to be an in depth theoretical analysis – and might therefore be an outlier in this publication. It is rather written from a practitioner's perspective that however should have some relevance in academic debates about a real world topic such as business and society although it is of course up to the reader to judge whether she or he finds the particular arguments pointed out in this article valuable.

5.2 The Manifesto of Libertarian Economics[4]

Friedman is one of the most cited pundits of specific social responsibilities of companies that he considered to be barely justifiable from a theoretical perspective and difficult to manage in practice, since social responsibilities do negatively impact effective resource allocation and economic performance. He though accepted ethical boundaries of business transactions when he argued that

> (...) there is one and only one social responsibility of business – to use its resources and engage in activities designed to increase its profits so long as it stays within the rules of the game, which is to say, engages in open and free competition without deception or fraud. (Friedman 1962, 1970)

This limiting argument of staying within the rules of the game is close to Adam Smith for whom societal benefits arise from economic activities that are conducted within moral and legal boundaries. Friedman, however, was of the definite opinion that corporate executives are no good judges of what social interests are and therefore must not try to involve themselves in such issues. Friedman's basic assumptions in regards to who has which responsibilities are that ethical responsibilities can only be borne by individuals and not by corporations. As a result, expectations for corporate responsibility can only be directed to the executives of a company as individual actors but not to a company as a collective actor. However, these executives are agents of the owners and have an accountability towards the principal to conduct business in accordance with the principal's desires which is to make as much money as possible while conforming to the basic rules of society but surely not to invest money into social causes. From a libertarian point of view, profit maximization and moral disinterest are justified as they reflect the basic rights and liberties that every individual has. Misperceived responsibilities conflict with basic principles of free markets and finally lead to inferior results. Whereas liberal economic competition has beneficial consequences as it represents the driving force behind the invisible hand that is based on the single-minded pursuit of profit maximization that automatically transforms corporate self-interest into social welfare.

---

[4] For many of the arguments in this chapter cf. Donaldson (1982).

Furthermore Friedman was of the opinion that holding an employed business executive accountable for taking on social responsibilities means that they act in a way that is not in the interest of the principal and would spend someone else's money for a general (sic!) social interest. This would de facto impose a tax by spending the principle's money and – even worse – the executive would also decide on how to spend the tax. In this sense corporate responsibility is a quasi political mechanism for resource allocation, although markets should be and are the appropriate mechanism to determine efficient resource allocation. It is obvious that Friedman did very much disagree with the idea that a company is or should be a quasi political actor. In his view it is about quite the opposite, i.e. companies should rather focus on economic activities and nothing else.

When reflecting about Friedman's position, it appears that his arguments are reasonable in so far that it is a right to be guaranteed to make voluntary agreements, i.e. that executives can sign a voluntary agreement to conduct business in the interest of the principal and that the pursuit of profits is legitimate except if the profit seeking activity conflicts with the social contract. The social contract can jeopardize those voluntary agreements whose consequences would commit managers to act contrary to the terms of the social contract because rights can be in conflict, i.e. some right can outweigh another right such as voluntary contracts and to act against a right is legitimate if justified by an overriding public interest. Therefore Friedman's claim that the social responsibility of business is to increase its profits is either an error or incomplete. It is an error if it is meant to imply that the "force" of a fiduciary duty prevents a manager from using the social contract as a yardstick for responsible managerial activity since the right to make voluntary agreements has exceptions if conflicting with other rights and moral considerations. It is incomplete if it is meant to imply that the existence of a voluntary agreement generates a prima facie obligation for the manager to pursue profit. This is because other responsibilities might be overriding as based on a moral obligation generated through the social contract.

Corporate responsibilities are not a violation of property rights as the concept of property refers to the social contract itself.[5] The right to property must at minimum be compatible with other rights in a sense that property rights must also carry a liability for the negative consequences of property use, i.e. activities based on property must not damage the property of others, corporations are obliged not to create unreasonable danger of life (i.e. right to life of individuals) and not to infringe on rights of future generations[6]. All these obligations derive from the right to property rights itself.

Free competition, understood in the sense of the standard economic theory as a concept for maximizing benefits for society, is highly doubtful and at least built on incomplete assumptions: Transformation of self-interest into public good through free markets requires perfect information which is in reality a very unrealistic scenario. Perfect rationality, as assumed in neoclassical economic theory, and perfect knowledge are even contradictory because acquiring information means costs that

---

[5] Cf. Hobbes (1982) for the constitution of rights to property through a social contract.

[6] For the limits of property rights in the state of nature cf. Locke (1980).

could be spent profitably elsewhere by a rational market participant. Additionally, the assumption that free competition maximizes social welfare is questionable which can be demonstrated by the facts that common goods are typically systematically undervalued and underpaid, or that contracts can create negative impacts which are not borne by the producers but rather pushed to the community and hence become external costs.

Furthermore, there seems to be a confusion over "purpose" and "motive": The question in regards to social responsibility refers primarily to the purpose of a business which relates to the question of "What for", and not to the motive which is concerned with the psychological forces that move us to act such as the wish to maximize profits (Drucker 1973, 2001a, b, c).

Therefore, it seems that Friedman is wrong since the purpose of business is to provide goods and services that satisfy the customer; whereas making a profit is a motive and a limitation as shown by Drucker. Furthermore corporations are moral agents that can indeed assume moral responsibilities as was shown by the works of Wieland (2001), Goodpaster (1982) and French (1979).

To sum it up, property rights are not absolute and related activities must not damage the rights of others. The well known assumption that free markets will maximize social benefits such as lowering income inequality is rather theoretical and fails the reality test as recently shown in a study from the IMF (cf. Dabla-Norris et al. 2015). Piketty has also demonstrated in his analysis that inequality in developed countries has risen since 1980 and that "… the distribution of wealth has always been deeply political, and it cannot be reduced to purely economic mechanisms." Piketty 2015: 69 Furthermore, Adam Smith, one of the most important historical reference points in terms of economic theory, pointed out that the pursuit of self-interest has to be limited by sympathy or the interest in the fortunes of others. However, with all the well justified criticism towards Friedman's approach, it also has to be recognized that he was not advocating for a vulgar capitalism but rather insisting that economic actors have to adhere to basic norms, including defending a right based approach from a libertarian perspective. Business and markets are powerful institutions for efficient resource allocation; hence the – not so rare – unstrategic and erratic investments into social causes are neither ethically justifiable, nor socially beneficial nor economically efficient.

Nevertheless, as shown, this critical point is not an argument against the engagement of business in society that Friedman propelled so strongly in economic theory and by which he influenced business practitioners to a huge extent. This then contributed to a situation in which business got more and more disconnected from society and unfortunately lost its sense of purpose and sometimes legitimacy – for the reason mentioned above – in the view of many.

Porter and Kramer's Shared Value concept takes root in Friedman's theory in so far that it argues that corporate self-interest within the rules of the game would lead to superior results for business and society. The authors also share some reservations in regards to corporate responsibility if the respective activities and investments are not done with a strategic view and therefore fail to optimize the positive societal impact, hence they argue for Shared Value as a superior concept as it has an explicit strategic dimension. However, this line of argument seems to be misguided or at least build on a conception of corporate responsibilities that either serves as a straw man to differentiate and promote the own concept as being completely distinct or it draws on an old-fashioned understanding of what corporate responsibility really is and ought to be as it equals corporate responsibility with philanthropy (cf. Crane et al. 2014). We would rather recommend to work with a definition of corporate responsibility that is able to include different types of interventions that aim to positively influence societal, neglected problems – of which a Shared Value type of intervention is one category –, that are all well aligned with the core capabilities and the most material topics of a company, that serve tactical and strategic business needs and that simultaneously drive positive societal impact. We will leave a further drill down on this argument to a later section of this article in which we will proceed to examine the critical points that can be made on the concept of Shared Value.

5.3 Corporate Responsibility Is a Management Task[7]

Whereas Friedman laid out his perspective in terms of accepting social responsibilities of companies mostly from an *economic* and a *libertarian* point of view, Drucker is maybe one of the early and also most relevant sources that should be considered when thinking about social responsibilities of companies from a *managerial* point of view. For Drucker it was without a shadow of doubt obvious that companies have to account for social responsibilities. He differentiated between two different categories:

Firstly, companies need to assume responsibilities for the negative impacts on societies and communities they create throughout their value chain. This relates to the old dictum of "primum non nocere" and is concerned about minimizing the negative impact on society through business activities. Secondly, companies have responsibilities for a society in regards to the problems that exist in a given society itself, a position that automatically leads to the question what companies can do for society in order to solve these problems. This second domain is clearly related to the purpose of business that is about serving the customer with goods and services and not about maximizing profits. Both responsibilities exist because companies live "[...] of necessity in society and community." (Drucker 1993: 326) And therefore they have to consider the interests rooted in society and in communities when taking business decisions.

(a) *Management's responsibility for impacts caused*

With his argument that companies are responsible for minimizing their negative impact in society, Drucker obviously refers back to a for him very basic ethical principle that one has to take responsibility for the impact one causes – independent of whether the impact was intended or unintended (Drucker 1993: 327). For Drucker,

[7] For the following see Drucker (1993).

negative impacts that are not minimized or avoided – even when they are minor – are or will most likely become serious threats to the business since communities or society as a whole understand these as an offense and attack on its integrity which will then result in punitive actions such as stronger regulatory frameworks or reputational harm. In this sense, negative impacts turn into friction and become non-productive costs that have to be avoided from a managerial perspective. Ignoring both perspectives on the problem "[…] is to put ego, desire for power, and vanity ahead of the good of the institution and of the community. And this is irresponsible." (Drucker 1993: 329).

The analysis in regards to how to mitigate negative impacts has according to Drucker always to be weighted up in the light of the basic idea that (a) only impacts related to the true purpose of the company are acceptable and (b) the fewer impacts the better. As an example, a pharmaceutical company that develops, manufactures and markets a needed cancer treatment will also have a negative footprint for e.g. the environment with this mentioned activity. As long as there is a consensus in society that these products are either manufactured for an ethical reason (which is most likely the case for an oncology drug) or are at least legitimately produced, the negative impact on environment seems to be assessed as being inferior and in Drucker's terms they are acceptable if related to the company's real purpose. However, the company has an obligation to avoid as many negative impacts as possible, e.g. related to CO_2 emissions, water, waste etc. Now, in principle it should not be news that these trade-offs are an obvious element of almost any business transaction and that the negative impact should be managed beyond legal obligations. For some managers and also for some academics, however, that share Friedman's view on social responsibilities of companies, it sounds rather uncomfortably new – uncomfortably because managers now have to get used to engage in public discourse about these trade-offs in order to achieve a societal agreement about legitimate and illegitimate activities as well as about their responsibility to mitigate and minimize trade-offs. This follows logically from Drucker's proposal that

> "[...] even the most private business enterprise is an organ of society and serves as a social function [...]" and "[...] that the very nature of the modern business enterprise imposes responsibilities on the manager." (Drucker 1954: 375)

Whenever an activity or a transaction that is not needed to deliver the product or the service can be eliminated, these should be eliminated, even if this causes difficulties. The best case is, of course, to analyze the activity or transaction that causes a negative impact with an opportunity minded view and generate a new business opportunity from minimizing or eliminating that very negative impact. In case that the activity cannot be eliminated – which might frequently be the case because it is business critical and required to fulfill the company's purpose – then the impact of this activity has to be minimized. Unfortunately, the inconvenient truth is that in many cases eliminating or reducing impact comes along with an increase in costs as these were hitherto externalized to the society. To accept this increase in costs is an acid test for the sincerity of the ethical ambition However as costs are a very crucial elements in regards to the sustainability of a company's business model, additional costs cannot be absorbed infinitely. Therefore, management has, due to an enlightened self-interest, the responsibility to think ahead and has to work with governments on a regulatory framework that can contribute to a solution at a sustainable cost basis and with the greatest possible benefit to the public. Interestingly, in our view, companies were rather reluctant to engage in a transparent policy dialogue in the described sense, since the neoliberal mantra – that one can also find in Friedman's line of arguments – was that regulation should be avoided and as weak as possible. This approach can lead to a situation of adverse effects, i.e. the absence of regulations implies that the least ethical actors cashes in, whereas the ethically motivated actors have to internalize the previously externalized costs, which results in an economically disadvantageous situation. Not accepting this task and shunning away from engaging with the numerous stakeholders in a policy dialogue, has proven to be willful blindness, as the ever increasing regulatory environment in the compliance and corruption area very vividly demonstrates[8]. Having said this, involvement in policy dialogue in a self enlightened manner requires a particular set of skills and capabilities that allow to understand, evaluate and weigh arguments from different stakeholders that follow their function-specific logic that is different from the narrow economic logic. This means that companies as polylingual systems need to be able to understand and process different "language games" that are relevant in a polylingual stakeholder setting and that typically go beyond the market logic of profit and loss.[9]

When identifying impacts on society, Drucker was not primarily referring to a normative criterion that would allow to judge whether the activity is ethically right, but rather to the question whether the activity that causes the impact is integral to the purpose of the business and if not it should be stopped. This perspective is not without complications as it is agnostic about the fact that a purpose of a company – even if legally allowed – is not per se socially favorable and beneficial or ethically acceptable. It makes therefore sense to enrich this argument with the perspective of Josef Wieland who has demonstrated with his work (2014) that any economic cooperation requires social cooperation. This can be for example expressed via the acceptance of responsibility for a particular societal issue, since this is the only possibility to mobilize the required resources and to generate societal legitimacy. According to Wieland, a firm is therefore a social cooperative project of multiple stakeholders that exploit their resources under the conditions of economic competition. It is a contractually constituted form that enables organized cooperation (Wieland 2009: 282). Although this does not result in a normative determination regarding the purpose of the company, it implies a linkage to the normative social legitimacy of corporate objectives and business activities. This embraces the desirability and necessity of corporate contributions to social welfare beyond the legal requirements. The social character of an enterprise and its nature is thus defined as endogenous – for economic reasons –, because otherwise transactions and cooperations cannot be managed successfully (cf. Fürst 2014).

[8] Cf. e.g. Wieland et al. (2014) trends and topics around Compliance.

[9] For this argument, cf. in more detail the work of Josef Wieland (2001, 2014).

This is a clear difference to the standard economic theory – as for instance proposed by Friedman – that defines institutional settings in the business environment as an exogenous behavioral restriction and theoretically excludes the role of the company as a responsible collective actor in society. Wieland's train of thought also represents a required additional perspective to the ethically agnostic argument from Drucker that we briefly outlined above.

(b) *Social problem as a corporate responsibility and business opportunity*

In the previous chapter we mainly discussed the responsibility of companies to avoid negative impact. However, corporate responsibilities of companies can also be seen through a lens of opportunities. For Drucker, societal problems are a crucial source of business opportunities and it is the main function of business to satisfy the need that arises from or is connected with such a societal problem (Drucker 1993: 327). This means that business has the task to convert challenges and societal problems into innovation. In the context of major societal problems such as access to healthcare or water, climate change or food security – to name just a few – it would be a mistake to assume that innovation that builds the business opportunity and contributes to solutions to these challenges is mainly related to technology. To a considerable extent it is distinct business model innovation that has the potential to lead to a unique positioning in a market, to generate market share or drive profits and simultaneously contributes to solving the societal problems. These opportunities shape up when companies take responsibility in areas where e.g. market failure, weak or dysfunctional political governance or gaps in the public infrastructure exist and where huge societal needs occur but if no sufficient purchasing power exists that is required to make the traditional business models work. That is, in other words, precisely in those areas where companies have not seen a strong sense of obligation or area of involvement as they did not and could not see relevant commercial opportunities in these socio-economic segments of the global income pyramid. C. K. Prahalad pointed out very lucidly that people in low income segments of the global income pyramid have a certain level of purchasing power which is indicating opportunities for companies, if they understand to develop catalytic business models that meet the needs of the poor and provide them with goods and services and finally with social opportunities (cf. Prahalad 2004; Prahalad and Hammond 2002; Hammond et al. 2007). On the other hand, companies can also try to endogenously identify these challenges as opportunities without being pushed by societal expectations but rather while proactively analyzing the business environment and societal problems. Companies could redefine these as potential business opportunities by analyzing them through sustainability lenses. This is surely a different approach than the one many companies used in the past, which was to try to either negate the problem or to lobby against policy action by regulatory authorities.

In principle it is in the enlightened self-interest of companies to accept this increased level of responsibility and to focus on business minded solutions to societal challenges, but – and this needs to be pointed out very clearly – only if they define their specific spheres of responsibilities as precisely as possible; a process which needs to consider the individual core competencies and resources of each organization. This is important to understand as the change in the tectonics of the governance of modern societies (Wieland 2014) definitively does not mean that business can be held accountable for providing solutions to any societal problem or for being the only solution provider. Other stakeholders such as governments, NGOs etc., must accept their specific responsibility in shared dilemmas based on their resources, skills and expertise and must contribute to solutions by means of cooperation and collaborative models. If we accept these developments as facts, it should not be an overly guarded secret anymore that business and entrepreneurship are increasingly seen in terms of social responsibility and that this insight must trigger a more strategic approach regarding how to manage this topic in order to be perceived as a legitimate business and to successfully compete in a changing society. When we condense this theoretically we can state that the organizational ability to cooperate becomes an increasingly important factor and the success in such a cooperation driven economy will be dependent on the effective integration of factors such as morality, ethics or culture into the governance of an organization (cf. Wieland 2014; Fürst 2005).

We can summarize that a greater involvement of business in solving societal challenges that are outside of – though connected with – the scope of the traditional business strategies, is on the one hand expected by society and is on the other hand a chance for new business opportunities, growth, and profit. From this perspective the task of business is to reframe and understand societal challenges as opportunities and to solve these challenges with business means. In this role business is about satisfying

> [...] a social need and at the same time serve their institution, by making resolution of a social problem into a business opportunity. (Drucker 1993: 337)

Drucker has highlighted this already early in his work. However, he did not work in depth on this topic that would have allowed him to develop a conceptual model for this. In recent years, Clayton Christensen – maybe the most prominent author and researcher on innovation – tried to conceptualize a model on the topic of solving societal challenges through business activities. He applied his theory of disruptive innovation to the issue of solving societal challenges with business means and to social change. Clayton Christensen et al. coined this as catalytic innovation (Christensen et al. 2006). Disruptive innovations challenge existing products or services by

> "[...] offering simpler, good enough alternatives to an underserved group of customers [...]". "Catalytic innovation can surpass the status quo by providing good enough solutions to inadequately addressed social problems." (Christensen et al. 2006: 2)[10]

The difference to the underlying core concept of disruptive innovation is that disruptive innovations can unintentionally cause social change whereas catalytic innovation focus on social change or social benefit as the primary objective. This

[10] We will not discuss the concept of disruptive innovation in detail but refer to Christensen (2011) for further reference and detailed reading.

idea of simplifying goods or services to meet the needs and the purchasing power of a specific – maybe poor – customer segment to have positive social impact is also articulated in the base of the pyramid-concept of Prahalad (2004).

For the majority of businesses it is a difficult task to come up with catalytic innovation and according to Christensen, companies with strong business models are almost incapable to disrupt themselves as they mostly assume that catalytic innovations "[...] could sabotage their current offerings." (Christensen et al. 2006: 3) Existing businesses have a natural tendency to persevere their existing business model and they do this powerfully by bringing their resources, partnerships and processes into play. This leads often to an opportunity for entrants that come from outside into the market to generate or gain market share. Christensen et al. (2006) point to the fact that catalytic innovation is very often not in focus and ignored by existing players as the – sometimes perceived – difference of profitability between the established business model and the one to be built on catalytic innovation seems to be too huge and makes this innovation space unattractive for further investments. The authors highlight an important point that is a relevant reason why companies can be hesitant of being engaged in catalytic or social innovation as they have a tendency to allocate resources into opportunities that have a profitability that either the capital markets would expect from their investments or that were defined by internal targets in the scorecards of management. Successful companies are mostly able to analyze und understand their existing markets quite accurately and to operate in those very efficiently. However, this is categorically different for new market segments that could be created through catalytic innovations as these are not their established playground. As Christensen writes, it requires upfront investments in terms of building up market intelligence, the capabilities and the organizational structure to discover the markets (Christensen 2011: 165ff.) and to develop and operate catalytic business models. Furthermore, investment in business models with a lower margin expectation because of e.g. high upfront investments and because of lower selling prices relative to the operative costs can be margin dilutive to the overall profitability of the business. In the starting phase of a catalytic business model, when sales and income are relatively small compared to the sales and income of the established business model, the margin dilution is relatively small. However, this might change at that moment when the catalytic business scales-up and grows more rapidly compared to the established business model. This can lead to a situation in which business growth of the catalytic business model is recognized as a hindrance and risk to achieve the overall profit margin goals.

Another issue that impedes established businesses to develop and run new catalytic business models is the concern that it could lead to cannibalization of existing sales. This fear is justified if the catalytic business was in direct competition with existing sales generated from an existing customer base. However, if the catalytic innovation underlying the business model taps into new customer segments that were not reached by the existing products and services since these were too expensive or did not match the needs of this new customer group, then cannibalization will not emerge but new business opportunities will be created Although this sounds logical and simple, this is a rather complex endeavor in reality as it requires a thorough understanding of (a) the determinants of the societal challenge that should be addressed by the catalytic innovation, (b) the needs of the new customer group, (c) a segmentation from distinct customer groups as precise as possible to avoid cannibalization and (d) a proper internal alignment of targets incl. profitability targets and incentives in order to enable an organization to run two distinct business models with distinctly intended profit margins.

5.4 Some Remarks About the Concept of Shared Value and About Some Recent Critics

If we reflect – in the context of the Shared Value concept – on the arguments in the previous chapters about the ethical responsibility of a company to mitigate harm and minimize negative impact, it is obvious that Porter and Kramer do not focus on this important dimension in their work. This does not mean that they ignore this ethical responsibility of business activities but they assume that this would be within the focus of classical corporate responsibility and compliance activities that they regard as prerequisites for responsible business and companies. If the concept is not properly understood or analyzed, it might appear as if Porter and Kramer were glancing over the fact that trade-offs and negative impacts exist. However, we would rather argue that they focus on a particular topic that they would like to address and comment on which is about solving societal issues with creative business solutions and we consider such a particular, deliberatively chosen focus as perfectly legitimate.

The question brought up in the article from Crane et al. (2014) where the prerequisite of obeying the law and behaving ethically fits in the Shared Value concept is quite easy to answer. It fits as a prerequisite of the concept – period. Porter and Kramer do not assume that managers can or shall claim that they have all "ethical dilemmas licked" but they assert that there are better ways to address some – not all – societal problems than applying a minimizing or a philanthropic approach only. As a consequence of this particular focus and this hypothesis, they propose a concept that makes an attempt to elaborate how this can be done in practical terms and with a strategic perspective. We believe that some might misunderstand the concept of Shared Value, maybe because Porter and Kramer are wrongly belittling the achievements of corporate responsibility in theory and practice, because they do not give sufficient credit to the early sources of similar thinking in the academic literature or since they artificially distinguish Shared Value from corporate responsibility instead of seeing Shared Value as an element of a corporate responsibility portfolio that entails a number of distinct interventions of which Shared Value is one as philanthropy is one, or zero profit models etc., – a thought that we will explain within a following chapter.

Crane et al. claim that Porter and Kramer "[...] are hiding all the tough challenges" (Crane et al. 2014: 152) instead of trying to get behind the real meaning of what Porter and Kramer say when they point out that

> The purpose of the corporation must be redefined as creating shared value, not just profit per se. (Porter and Kramer 2011: 4)

In our understanding this concept of *sharing and going beyond pure profit seeking* has an ethical notation and embraces the notion that tough choices and trade-offs exist and have to be managed in the interest of the involved stakeholders that should get a share, instead of allocating all the profits exclusively to the shareholders. It is irritating if some insinuate that the Shared Value concept is ignorant about the tough choices managers are confronted with as if it is not reality that tough choices come up every day when developing or managing a Shared Value business model. This idea sounds rather naive and far away from the reality one can experience when actively involved in such Shared Value business models. Porter and Kramer do not claim – at least we were not able to identify where – that their concept is without or cannot also generate some negative impact, but they do also not stop with just managing these negative impacts. They want to go beyond and encourage companies to apply another lens to societal problems and they articulate an ambition to come-up with a business minded solution that creates Shared Value and has the potential to achieve scale and can be replicated. This seems to be a worthwhile effort to us and not a cherry on the cake approach. And even when we recognize the sometimes bold "marketing language" in the article it appears to be an interesting attempt to innovate for superior solutions that benefit vulnerable stakeholders communities. We all should know that innovation is a risky business and might not lead to the intended positive outcomes and impacts. However it is worthwhile to test if it can be legitimately assumed that the results would be superior from a perspective of Creating Shared Value and of mitigating harm.

If we consider the Shared Value concept as a strategic approach to foster competiveness, then the concept of Shared Value is an extension of Porter's competitive strategy model (Porter 1998) which is rooted in industrial economics and argues that companies will only grow and survive if they are able to gain or maintain a position that is less vulnerable than by the key competitors and if they are able to manage a unique supply chain that will allow a company to deliver on its unique positioning. This approach is recognizable in the Shared Value concept in which companies can achieve this superior competitive position by either developing products for unserved needs, or through local investments and cluster development or through improvements in the supply chain. This competitive argument is inherently accompanied by the objective of solving societal challenges with business means in order to regain legitimacy for business.

Overall, for us, it is astonishing to see with which verve the Shared Value framework is criticized by some and which kind of arguments are to some extend used against the concept. Just pointing to some Shared Value examples from companies to underpin one's own argument that Shared Value is a cherry on the cake approach and a hoax without being able to underpin this allegation with any piece of evidence, is neither scientifically solid nor a well founded argument against the concept. Instead of being too comfortable with one's own perspective, we believe that it would be helpful if some particularly critical reviewers of the Shared Value concept would at least try to understand the real difficulties and dilemmas in regards to the development of sustainable business models to real world challenges and would come up with constructive proposals for implementable, sustainable solutions instead of brushing over those real problem. This would be hugely beneficial for the advancement of the field and more productive than just belittling Shared Value models or uncritically repeating one-sided arguments on difficult issues that are far more complex than just being of reputational nature. We do not judge in this article which opinion someone should have about these issues but we would expect that the line of arguments is presented in a more nuanced and less one-sided manner compared to what we can read in the article from Crane et al.

If the Shared Value concept is criticized – and we think it should it be criticized – we propose to focus on its serious weakness that the concept is currently suffering from. This is the affirmative nature of the concept and the lack of proper measurement and evaluation of outcomes and impact of the models that they qualify as being examples for Shared Value models. This is not an inherent problem but an obvious one at the current state of the debate. It seems that many examples that Porter and Kramer refer to, provide information and data on activities, input and output. However, the real proof of the concept lies in the outcomes and the impact of both sides of the Shared Value equation. We are very cognizant of the fact that this is more easily written than done, since measurement and evaluation for Shared Value models at the level of outcomes and impact are theoretically ambitious and practically complex endeavors. There are mainly two reasons why this needs to be done. First of all, it is in the interest of the concept itself in order to provide empirically relevant data that has the potential to prove that the concept is actually generating Shared Value. This would be immensely helpful to either counter some of the arguments that were brought forward against the concept or to prove these. Either way, it should be done. Secondly, data on outcomes and impact of Shared Value programs is genuine management information that is crucially needed to derive metrics that can be used to manage Shared Value models, to mitigate negative impact and to optimize the positive benefit. The lack of a coherent measurement and evaluation approach is not a criticism against the concept itself but if not addressed properly, the concept will not be able to prove its proclaimed positive and superior value in theoretical and in practical terms.

5.5 Corporate Responsibility as a Strategic Portfolio Approach[11]

Historically corporate responsibility had an overproportional focus on philanthropy that can create social impact if conceptualized with a strategic view but has genuine problems in terms of scalability and replicability. Based on these limitations, the

[11] See Fürst (2014).

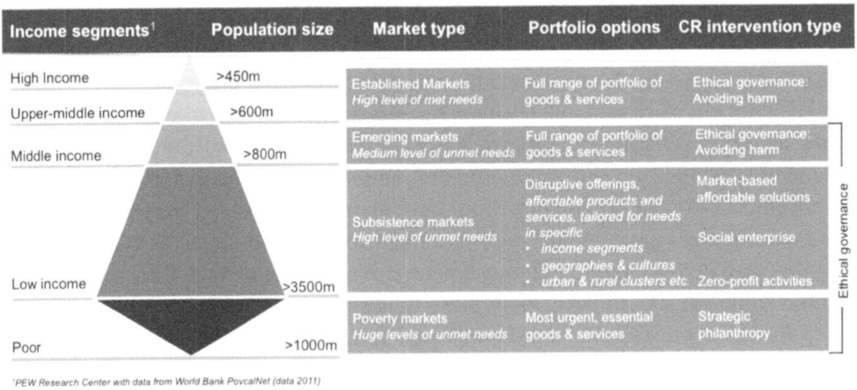

Fig. 5.1 Differentiating CR intervention types according to income levels, needs and market types. Own illustration with data from PEW (see additional data 11 references in illustration).

genuine entrepreneurial activity, understood as a mechanism to create new, sustainable business models through the transformation of societal challenges into innovative and sustainable services, needs to be emphasized and specifically addressed in a strategic approach to CR. Therefore, as this is increasingly understood, the trendlines point in the direction of having more focus on activities that are aligning social and commercial ambition and can result in large-scale responsibility engagement. This without ignoring the basic ethical responsibility of "do no harm" and philanthropic or zero profit initiatives if such kind of interventions contribute to solving societal challenges. Strategic CR should therefore aim to operate with a portfolio of tailored activities, comprising philanthropic initiatives, zero profit, Shared Value or lower margin business models that are all closely linked to a company's strategy and core competencies and are operated via a strong ethical governance. Figure 5.1 explores this rationale and typology by showing that specific CR intervention types should be differentiated along the different income segments of the global income pyramid.

Typically, business models of multinational companies are tailored to serve the needs of consumers at the top of the pyramid. Companies can work here with the full spectrum of products and services they have in their portfolio, typi cally with a focus on highly innovative offerings. CR is here mostly focused on ensuring – through integrity management – that business is done in line with ethical standards (cf. Fürst and Schotter 2013) and that negative external effects are avoided or minimized.

The next level of the global income pyramid comprises two different income segments that represent emerging markets with a medium level of income and unmet needs at the upper end and subsistence markets with a high level of unmet needs at the lower end.

In the segment of emerging markets with middle to low income customers, companies can approach the existing needs from a CR perspective with market-based solutions that typically should operate with lower prices and therefore offer the possibility to new consumer segments to satisfy their needs with relevant goods and services. The portfolio would here offer solutions such as "low-end disruption" that do not offer the full functionality or "new-market disruptions" that focus underserved needs of potential customers.[12] Furthermore these models could systematically intervene at the systems level to drive productivity increases or strengthen local cluster development (Porter and Kramer 2011). We could coin these interventions as Shared Value models that allow a rather quick scale up since they generate an appropriate level of profitability or business value. Companies need to very carefully differentiate the specific income segments within this income bracket and understand different factors influencing buying decisions. These factors can be the purchasing power of a customer, the prices of products and services (very often the price for basic goods is higher in these market segments than in established markets), the rural versus urban distribution of population, informal solutions that are provided, cultural determinants, educational and awareness levels, infrastructure gaps, supply chain constraints etc., as only the consideration of these factors will allow to develop a holistic and successful intervention. Typically such social business models are built as volume models, i.e. they operate according to the principle of economies of scale, in order to keep the margin levels of the unit low and therefore the product affordable. This is of course problematic during the starting phase of such kinds of models as it needs a certain level of upfront investment in order to quickly achieve scale and pass break-even.

In the next level of the middle of the pyramid – the subsistence market – where significant unmet needs exist and where many people are working in an informal economy, the CR intervention types should be focused on zero-profit models that offer a more limited but still existing potential for scale and can definitively improve the frame conditions for (social) business in the long run[13].

At the bottom of the income pyramid where people live in total poverty, CR should operate with philanthropic models that have a strong strategic rationale for the company and therefore unfold an appropriate level of impact.

The dictum to avoid unnecessary, negative external effects does apply throughout the whole pyramid. And similar to the activities in mainstream business all the activities in the middle or the base of the pyramid have to be conducted in accordance with strong ethical standards that a company has committed to as part of its organizational self-governance (cf. Fürst and Schotter 2013). Corporate responsibility would then refer to the legitimate generation of shared benefit by focusing on trying to solve these societal challenges where a company has competencies and the needed resources. The linkage back to the legitimacy criterion ensures firstly that only those activities are considered that are socially acceptable and desirable and secondly that they are carried out in accordance with ethical principles. Connecting CR with the strategic value drivers and core competencies aims to narrow down the range of activities as only this integration will generate sustainable solutions that are replicable and scalable. If this integration is not done successfully many CR initia-

[12] For the distinction cf. Christensen et al. (2006, 2011).

[13] As an instructive article in regards to segmenting different income levels in the lower range of the global income pyramid we recommend Rangan et al. (2011).

tives – however interesting they may be, and independent from a strong moral motivation – are often considered by decision-takers to be primarily cost-generating, not value-adding and therefore to be up for disposition if another economic crisis arises or priorities need to be changed.

The Shared Value concept from Porter and Kramer is in this understanding a distinct, business minded intervention for societal advancement besides other intervention types that have a legitimate reason to exist and to be deployed, dependent on the strategic goals and capabilities of a company and the companys' view on the world in regards to which models are most appropriate means to an end.[14] Shared Value is not a unprecedented superior model that overrides all other interventions but rather a piece in the overall puzzle of minimizing negative impact and creating opportunities from societal challenges.

5.6 Making Sense of Societal Challenges[15]

In the following section we describe one reason why societal challenges have not been widely perceived and understood in the way Drucker described them as an opportunity so far. This misperception results in a situation that the many companies still operate their corporate responsibility programs on the basis of philanthropic activities and not with a holistic corporate responsibility strategy that has a focus on scalable and replicable business minded models, let us call those Shared Value, social enterprise, inclusive business etc. and also entails other intervention types that are used and deployed by a company in case needed.

We explore this question by analyzing how the individual and collective mental process of identifying and reframing societal challenges to opportunities does occur that is how such cognitive processes work at the level of an individual but even more importantly of a collective actor. For most of the cases we assume that large companies do not have such a set of cognitive and cultural preferences at their disposal that would facilitate an early identification of social challenges as a business opportunity. This is of fundamental importance since we know that the perception and identification of opportunities and risks is always based on cultural patterns, values or identity semantics of social entities[16]. Perception processes are based on existing values and on cultural patterns that describe social entities and define their identity. Such a constructed perceptual process is indispensably and closely linked to the self-description and self-observation of social system (Fürst 2005: 140)[17]. A process of "sense-making" happens in organizations which can be described as a method to search, analyze and interpret critical changes and to subsequently enables individu-

[14] Cf. for a similar argument Werhane and Hartmann (2013).

[15] Cf. Fürst (2014).

[16] Cf. the work of Weick to the topic of "sensemaking in organizations", Weick (1995), Weick and Roberts (1993), Weick and Sutcliffe (2003).

[17] Referencing Japp (1996), Douglas and Wildavsky (1982).

als to take "rational" decisions within the given cultural and institutional frame (Weick 1995). "Sense-making" in the context described here is the construction of an organization's identity and institutionalized self-description and entails processes that can enable an organization to perceive societal challenges as a business opportunity and to develop relevant business strategies to address these challenges. The beliefs and the values of a distinct social unit are defined and described in this organizational culture. Jesper Sørensen formulated this as follows, with reference to Karl Weick (1985) and Edgar Schein (1992):

> Organizational cultures can codify the organization's understanding of itself and its environment, and thereby clarify the organization's belief and goals for members. (Sørensen 2002: 80)

Distinct institutions represent cultural determinants from the perspectives of systems theory and institutional economics. These determinants shape specific behavioral dispositions and constitute an environment for individuals that provide them with a certain degree of reliability and safety as they understand what is expected and how they should decide form an ethical, legal or economic point of view. The establishment of distinct institutional settings (values, morals, interpretation patterns, policies, etc.) leads to the emergence of a kind of "collective mind" (cf. Weick for this term) that represents perception, interpretation, and behavior patterns of individual and collective actors and thus determines the perception and the selection of distinct opportunities.

Belief systems work like glasses, i.e. they allow on the one hand distinct perceptions of issues and sharpen the view one these but on the other hand they literally fade-out issues and realities that are outside of scope (Schramm 2004). In the context described here, the relevant belief systems work like sustainability glasses, i.e. an organization is enabled to perceive societal challenges as existing and relevant and to subsequently develop appropriate strategies and social business models to manage these challenges successfully and sustainably.

In conjunction with theoretical considerations of the New Institutional Economics and Organizational Economics, we can say that each company owns an organization-specific "shared mental model" (Denzau and North 1994) that represents and determines patterns of perception and behavior.[18] Institutionalization means in this context that a consensus on behavioral expectations exists in each organizational entity. For the negotiated topic in this article this means that both the perception of societal problems as a positive economic opportunity and the related behavior is subject to a specific set of expectations (Japp 1996: 121) of a distinct culture. Establishing perception routines as a crystallization process of cultural patterns is a central process in the context of enabling corporate social entrepreneurship. A company as a collective actor maintains and conveys perception patterns by its own cultural preferences and institutional settings and the task is to establish organiza-

[18] Cf. Schlicht (2008) with reference to Issac et al. (1991) "[...] firms and other institutions provide institutional frames which activate certain types of behavior rather than others."

tional governance and learning, so that societal challenges can be seen through such sustainability glasses and be interpreted as a business opportunity.

This line of argument is based on the assumption that the world is understood only through a construction process and that this in turn is differentiated and determined through different cultural types. Corporate social entrepreneurship can only succeed if value systems exist in the organization that shape specific perceptual patterns and if such a social entrepreneurial venture is within the "zone of acceptance" Barnard (1938/1964) of a collective actor. This informal institutional setting is to be strengthened by establishing a distinct formal governance structures that encourage and incentivize the desired behavior, i.e. in this case social entrepreneurship. The informal and formal institutional layers work reciprocal and reinforce the intended pattern of perception in a recursive process. It is known from the risk research conducted in cultural sociology that the perception bias of an organization is processed by using the distinction of accepting and rejecting information. Pieces of information which fit into the frame of values or the cultural setting are perceived as acceptable whereas information that is not compatible with the specific organizational bias and is outside the "zone of acceptance" is typically rejected. The permanent repetition of accepting or rejection information culturally solidifies perceptual episodes into perception patterns of a collective actor (cf. Japp 1996).

To summarize we can say that institutional settings, values and cultural patterns shape the positive or negative perception of information. This means that specific governance structures of an organization should enable its members to perceive a societal problem as an economic opportunity and to deal with it through Shared Value models or corporate social entrepreneurship. Such governance structures are e.g. performance management schemes or career development programs that actively incentivize social entrepreneurship or leadership development programs that provide managers with the skills to develop and manage corporate social enterprises (cf. Stolz et al. 2012). It is about the design of the context and about "[...] choosing preferences by constructing institutions." (Wildavsky 1987). This kind targeted management should enable companies to reframe societal challenges as opportunities by using different mental models that we tried to sketch out in this article.

5.7 Conclusion

We started this article with the question how it is possible that business as one of the most powerful institutions in modern society that mostly operates within democratically legitimized legal frameworks, has employees that for sure have a disposition and preference for ethical conduct, that develops and offers products or services that were or are crucially important for societal advancements is under such scrutiny. In order to approach an answer we analyzed some of the ideas of one of the most influential economist of the last decades in regards to why economic theory and business have at least been ambivalent if not agnostic about moral values, ethics and social responsibilities of companies in modern societies for so many years or for too long time. A particular narrow view on the purpose and responsibility of companies that has hugely influenced academics and practioners was spotted as one of the reasons for the current distress we see in the relationship between business and society. Then, we were trying to amalgate some of the core thoughts of one of the most influential management thinkers, Drucker, who had distinct views on corporate responsibility and the purpose of a company which in his view is not to maximize profits but to provide goods and services that are needed by consumers, resulting in a hugely successful enterprise also in terms of profits. Based on this historical context we explored what alternative concepts in regards to the role and responsibilities of business as well possible means to address societal challenges are currently offered and debated. The Shared Value concept from Porter and Kramer is in our view such a proposal that offers interesting perspectives in regards to how companies can reframe societal challenges as opportunities and create lasting positive impact for business and society. We also tried to highlight that some of the arguments against the Shared Value concept might not be well founded, but we also pointed to some weaknesses such as the affirmative nature of the model because of the lack of proper measurement and evaluation that proves their claim besides anecdotes or weak data points. Furthermore, since we do not recognize Shared Value as a strategy that would replace corporate responsibility, we proposed to understand a corporate responsibility strategy as a portfolio approach that entails many different options tailored for the needs of particular consumers or responding to societal challenges that are material for companies and their stakeholders. Shared value is then one distinct intervention type for a particular use case, as philanthropy or zero-profit models are other distinct intervention types hat all have to be used by a company – most likely simultaneously – in order to be aligned with its purpose, to minimize the negative impact and to create as much benefits for business and society as much as possible.

References

Christensen, C.M. 2011. *The Innovator's Dilemma*. New York: Harper.

Christensen, Clayton M., Heiner Baumann, Rudy Ruggles, and Thomas M. Sadtler. 2006. Disruptive innovation for social change. *Harvard Business Review* 84(12): 94–101.

Crane, Andrew, Guido Palazzo, Laura J. Spence, and Dirk Matten. 2014. Contesting the value of 'creating shared value'. *California Management Review* 56(2): 130–149.

Dabla-Norris, Era, Kalpana Kochhar, Frantisek Ricka, Nujin Suphaphipat, and Evridiki Tsounta. 2015. *Causes and consequences of income inequality: A global perspective*. International Monetary Fund. https://www.imf.org/external/pubs/cat/longres.aspx?sk=42986.0. Accessed 09 Sept 2016.

Denzau, A.T., and D.C. North. 1994. Shared mental models: Ideologies and institutions. *Kyklos* 47: 3–31.

Donaldson, Thomas. 1982. *Corporations and morality*. New Jersey: Prentice Hall.

Douglas, Mary, and Aaron B. Wildavsky. 1982. *Risk and culture. An essay on the selection of technological and environmental dangers*. Berkeley: University of California Press.

Drucker, Peter. 1954. *The practice of management*. New York: Harper.
Drucker, P. 1973. Management: Tasks, responsibilities and practices. New York: Harper Paperbacks.
———. 1993. *Management: Tasks, responsibilities and practices*. New York: Harper Paperbacks.
———. 2001a. Social impacts and social problems. In *The essential Drucker*, ed. Peter Drucker. New York: Harper Collins.
———. 2001b. The purpose and objectives of a business. In *The essential Drucker*, ed. Peter Drucker. New York: Harper Collins.
———. 2001c. The entrepreneurial business. In *The essential Drucker*, ed. Peter Drucker. New York: Harper Collins.
Edelman Trust Barometer. 2015. *Trust in innovation*. http://www.edelman.com/insights/intellectual-property/2015-edelman-trust-barometer/. Accessed 30 Mar 2016.
Fürst, Michael. 2005. *Risiko-governance. Die Wahrnehmung und Steuerung moralökonomischer Risiken*. Marburg: Metropolis.
———. 2014. *Opening the door to opportunities: How to design CR strategies that optimize impact for business and society*. Berlin: Springer.
Fürst, Michael, and Andreas Schotter. 2013. Strategic integrity management as a dynamic capability. In *Strategic management in the 21st century*, ed. Timothy J. Wilkinson. St. Barbara: Praeger Publishers, Forthcoming.
French, P.A. 1979. The corporation as a moral person. *American Philosophical Quarterly* 16(3): 207–215.
Friedman, Milton. 1962. *Capitalism and freedom*. Chicago: University of Chicago Press.
———. 1970. A Friedman doctrine – The social responsibility of business is to increase its profits. *The New York Times Magazine* September 13: 122–126.
Goodpaster, K.E. 1982. Review: Corporations and morality. *Business and Professional Ethics Journal* 1(3): 101–105.
Hammond, A.L., W.J. Kramer, R.S. Katz, J.T. Tran, and C. Walker. 2007. *The next 4 billion. Market size and business strategy at the base of the pyramid*. Washington: World Resources Institute and International Finance Corporation.
Hobbes, Thomas. 1982. *Leviathan*. Harmondsworth: Penguin Classics.
Isaac, R. M., Mathieu, D., & Zajac, Z. 1991. Institutional framing and perceptions of fairness. Constitutional Political Economy, 2, 329–370.
Japp, K.P. 1996. *Soziologische Risikotheorie. Funktionale Differenzierung, Politisierung und Reflexion*. Weinheim/München: Juventa-Verlag.
Locke, John. 1980. *The second treaties of government*. Cambridge: Hackett Classics.
Piketty, Th. 2015. Putting Distribution Back at the Center of Economics: Reflections on Capital in the Twenty-First Century. In Journal of Economic Perspectives. Volume 29, Number 1, Winter 201, Pages 67–88.
Porter, M.E. 1998. *Competitive strategy: Techniques for analyzing industries and competitors*. New York: Free Press.
Porter, M.E., and M.R. Kramer. 2011. Creating shared value. *Harvard Business Review* 89(1/2): 62–77.
Prahalad, C.K. 2004. *Fortune at the bottom of the pyramid: Eradicating poverty through profits*. Upper Saddle River: Wharton School Publishing.
Prahalad, C.K., and Allen Hammond. 2002. Serving the world's poor, profitably. *Harvard Business Review* 80(9): 48–58.
Rangan, V. Kasturi, Michael Chu, and Djorjiji Petkoski. 2011. Segmenting the base of the pyramid. *Harvard Business Review* 89(6): 113–117.
Schein, E. 1992. *Organizational culture and leadership*, 2nd edn. San Francisco: Jossey-Bass.
Schlicht, E. 2008. Consistency in organizations. *Journal of Institutional and Theoretical Economics JITE* 164(4): S. 612–S. 623.
Schramm, M. 2004. Strukturelle Kopplung und moralökonomisches Kontingenzmanagement. Aus: Wieland, J. (Hrsg.): Governanceethik im Diskurs. Marburg, S. 63–98.

Sørensen, J.B. 2002. The strength of corporate culture and the reliability of firm performance. *Administrative Science Quarterly* 47(1): 70–91.

Stiglitz, J.E. 2010. *Freefall. Amercia, free markets, and the sinking of the world economy*. New York: Norton.

———. 2012. *The price of inequality. How today's divided society endangers our future*. New York: Norton.

Stolz, I., M. Fürst, and D. Mundle. 2012. Managing strategic corporate citizenship at Novartis. In *Corporate Volunteering. Unternehmen im Spannungsfeld zwischen Effizienz und Ethik*, ed. Th. Wehner, and G.-C. Gentile. Berlin: Springer Gabler.

Werhane, P.H., and L.P. Hartmann. 2013. Proposition: Shared value as an incomplete mental model. *Business Ethics Journal Review* 1(6): 36–43.

Weick, K.E. 1985. The significance of corporate culture. In *Organizational cultures*, ed. Peter J. Frost et al., 381–389. Beverly Hills: Sage.

———. 1995. *Sensemaking in organizations*. Thousand Oaks: Sage.

Weick, K.E., and C. Roberts. 1993. Collective mind in organizations: Heedful interrelating on flight decks. *Administrative Science Quarterly*: 357–381.

Weick, K.E., and K.M. Sutcliffe. 2003. *Das Unerwartete managen. Wie Unternehmen aus Extremsituationen lernen*. Stuttgart: Klett-Cotta.

Wieland, J. 2001. *Die moralische Verantwortung kollektiver Akteure*. Heidelberg: Springer.

Wieland, J. 2009. Die Firma als Kooperationsprojekt der Gesellschaft. In J. Wieland (Ed.), CSR als Netzwerkgovernance. Theoretische Herausforderungen und praktische Antworten. Marburg: Metropolis.

———. 2014. *Governance Ethics: Global value creation, economic organization and normativity*. Berlin: Springer.

Wieland, J., R. Steinmeyer, and St. Grüninger (Hrsg.). 2014. Handbuch Compliance Management. Berlin: ESV.

Wildavsky, A. (1987): Choosing preferences by constructing institution: A cultural theory of preference formation. In *American political Science Review*. 81. Jg.: S. 3–21, Washington: American Political Science Association.

Part II
Creating Shared Value: Philosophy and Critique

Chapter 6
How the (Business) World Really Works. Business Metaphysics & "Creating Shared Value"

Michael Schramm

Abstract We are all in favor of some concept of "Creating Shared Value". The question is, accordingly, not *whether* one advocates a "Creating Shared Value", but *which* concept of "Creating Shared Value" is plausible and productive. This paper examines the question as to whether Michael E. Porter's and Marc R. Kramer's *specific* concept of "Creating Shared Value" is convincing or not, through the lens of a research program called "Business Metaphysics", referring predominantly to the "Process Metaphysics" of Alfred North Whitehead and the "Transaction Economics" of John R. Commons. As a result, the paper shows that Porter and Kramer commit the "Fallacy of Misplaced Concreteness", namely of mistaking the abstract (the ideal world of an overall "win-win") for the concrete (the contingent and "messy" world of real business).

From time to time, a new conceptual spectre haunts the world of business. In recent decades, we witnessed for example: "Shareholder Value", "Stakeholder Management", "Corporate Social Responsibility", "Sustainability", and lately the spectre of "Creating Shared Value" (Porter/Kramer Harv Bus Rev 89:62–77, (2011); Porter Harv Bus Rev (2011), Porter Creating shared value (Ideas for Change) (2012); Porter/Kramer Calif Manage Rev 56(2): 149–151 (2014)), which aims at replacing all the other (conceptual) spectres. We are told about "The Big Idea" and "How to Fix Capitalism and unleash a new wave of growth" (Titel page of *Harvard Business Review* Vol. 89 No.1-2 (2011) or "How to reinvent capitalism" (Porter/Kramer Harv Bus Rev 89:62–77, (2011): 63). The way how this "Big Idea" is presented, it almost takes after a religious promise of a "promised land" of a magical capitalism. The question arises as to whether the concept of "Creating Shared Value" can do justice to this ambitious claim. My answer is that it cannot. I will provide the reasons for this answer in the light of a research program which I call "Business Metaphysics".

M. Schramm (✉)
Universität Hohenheim, Stuttgart, Germany
e-mail: Michael.Schramm@uni-hohenheim.de

J. Wieland (ed.), *Creating Shared Value – Concepts, Experience, Criticism*, Ethical Economy 52, DOI 10.1007/978-3-319-48802-8_6

6.1 "Creating Shared Value" (CSV) – Idea & "Presumption"

Modern capitalism is an economic system which presumably has – as far as we can see – no radical conceptional alternative.[1] That does not mean, however, that modern capitalism works without problems – remember e.g. the latest financial crisis or the increasing ecological challenges. Well, Porter and Kramer claim to have found the solution for all these problems the capitalistic system is faced with:

> "The solution lies in the principle of shared value, which involves creating economic value in a way that also creates value for society by addressing its needs and challenges." (Porter and Kramer 2011: 64)

Their slogan – "Creating Shared Value" – aims at a double-sided value creation, namely the simultaneous creation of value for both companies ("economic value") and society:

> "The concept of shared value tries to focus on a tremendous opportunity to create economic value through creating social benefit." (Porter and Kramer 2011)

"Companies can create economic value by creating societal value." (Porter and Kramer 2011: 67)

6.1.1 *The Idea – Gratifying, But Not Developed Systematically*

I welcome the fact that Porter and Kramer are linking the value creation of companies to the needs of society. This has, of course, been a driving concern for a Business Ethicist like me for decades. Every Business Ethicist is in favour of some concept of "Creating Shared Value". But Porter and Kramer do not develop a systematic concept of this link between business and society. It is, rather, merely a pragmatic means to rescue the capitalist system, which is currently under fire.

Hypothesis I: The idea of "Creating Shared Value", namely to emphasize the relation between companies and society, is gratifying! But: Porter and Kramer are supporting this idea for pragmatic reasons only[2]. They do not develop this idea systematically (firms as societal projects).

Porter and Kramer begin with a (moral) appeal to the actors of global capitalism. Companies *"should try"* (Porter and Kramer 2011: 75) to combine economic value and societal value:

> "Every firm *should* look at decisions and opportunities through the lens of shared value." (Porter and Kramer 2011: 65)

---

[1] See, on this, the illustration on the growth of economics in the last 3000 years in Clark (2007: 2)

[2] They came up with this idea in order to get out of the current situation in which "the capitalist system is under siege", so that "businesses can earn the respect of society again." (Porter and Kramer 2011: 64;77)

They should do this for a pragmatic reason only: namely to fix the prevailing negative image of capitalism as well as to rescue the capitalist model, which is – I agree, despite all the problems – "an unparalleled vehicle for meeting human needs, improving efficiency, creating jobs, and building wealth." (Porter and Kramer 2011: 64)

Now, this is the initial shortcoming of the "Creating Shared Value" concept: The link between companies and society is seen as a merely pragmatic one. But in my opinion, we have to systematically emphasize the fact that companies *are* agents of *societal* value creation. The very existence of companies is legitimized only by their contribution to the common good. Corporate profits are solely the incentive for companies to perform this societal task in an efficient way.[3]

6.1.2 The "Presumption" – A Sleight of Hand

The core of all the strenuous efforts of Business Ethics was, is, and will always be the tough and ongoing challenge of bringing economy and ethics into a closer alignment (Paine 2000: 325f). Remarkably enough, Porter and Kramer are presenting an elegant avoidance of this "messy" business. They simply *"presume"* or *"assume"* the compliance of business with moral standards. They are treating this challenge as a *"prerequisite"* to their concept of "Creating Shared Value":

> "Creating shared value *presumes* compliance with the law and ethical standards, as well as mitigating any harm caused by the business, but goes far beyond that." (Porter and Kramer 2011: 75) "[C]ompliance with laws and ethical standards and reducing harm from corporate activities are *assumed*." (Porter and Kramer 2011: 76) "We actually say that legal compliance and a narrow sense of social responsibility are *prerequisites* to creating shared value, but the concept of shared value takes company behavior much further." (Porter and Kramer 2011: 150)

But this "presumed" harmony between economy and ethics is not a given – not at all. It is a hard and ongoing task, and simply to "presume" such compliance is little more than the refusal to face the real problems.

> "The so-called 'prerequisites' are where Porter and Kramer are hiding all the tough challenges. It is a […] trick of assuming away all the messy stuff that is difficult to deal with. But it is exactly in these 'prerequisite' legal and ethical obligations that the complex 'trade-offs' between economic and social value need to be faced. These are the ones that keep managers awake at night." (Crane et al. 2014b: 152)

It is precisely the absence of a (complete) harmony between economy and ethics that is the key challenge for Business Ethics and for companies. It is simply not

[3] Conceptually lucid for example Homann (2015: 47): „Unternehmen sind Agenten gesellschaftlicher Wertschöpfung, nicht privater. Die Legitimation unternehmerischen Handelns kann nur in ihrem Beitrag zum Gemeinwohl bestehen. Die Aussicht auf private Gewinne ist lediglich der Anreiz, diese gesellschaftliche Aufgabe effizient zu erfüllen."

adequate to "presume" a "clean" reality while the real-world business is actually "messy". The integrity of creating value is a *challenge*, and in fact a *tough* one.

Hypothesis II: The conceptual strategy of Porter and Kramer to declare that "compliance with laws and ethical standards" is understood as a prerequisite to the concept of "Creating Shared Value" and can therefore be seen as a given, is nothing more than a sleight of hand.

It is a sleight of hand we are very familiar with. No lesser than Milton Friedman presented this "prerequisites" trick decades ago, namely in his New York Times article with the famous title "The Social Responsibility of Business Is to Increase Its Profits". As this title already indicates, Friedman tried to show, that there is only one responsibility for a company: "to make as much money as possible". He writes:

> "In a free-enterprise, private-property system, a corporate executive is an employee of the owners of the business. He has direct responsibility to his employers. That responsibility is to conduct the business in accordance with their desires, which generally will be *to make as much money as possible*" (Friedman 1970/2007: 173)

But the last sentence does not end here. Despite his assertion that there is "one and only one social responsibility of business"[4], Friedman continues the quotation above by naming a second kind of responsibility:

> "[...]to make as much money as possible while *conforming to the basic rules of the society*, both those embodied in law and those *embodied in ethical custom*."[5]

So, in the second half of the sentence, Friedman smuggles in this concept of "ethical custom" – without making clear what he means, precisely, by "ethical custom". But the entire field of Business Ethics consists of this question, and we are faced with that very question because actual business transactions are not just economic operations, but *multi*dimensional processes, including the moral dimension.

The *"prerequisites"* of Porter and Kramer is more or less a repetition of Friedman's *"while conforming"*. But there is a difference between Friedman and Porter and Kramer. According to Michael Porter the difference is this:

> "Milton Friedman [...] famously argued that the social responsibility of business was to maximize its profits, and this simple act of profit maximization *was good in absolute itself*. That was enough, that was sufficient. [...] What was good for business was sort of *axiomatically good for society*." (Porter 2011a, b)

[4]See Friedman (1962/1982: 133) "The view has been gaining widespread acceptance that corporate officials and labor leaders have a 'social responsibility' that goes beyond serving the interest of their stockholders or their members. This view shows a fundamental misconception of the character and nature of a free economy. In such an economy, there is one and only one social responsibility of business – to use its resources and engage in activities designed to increase its profits".

[5]Friedman (1970/2007: 173f). Similarly he continues the quotation from the previous footnote: "[...]to increase its profits *so long as it stays within the rules of the game, which is to say, engages in open and free competition, without deception or fraud*." (Friedman 1962/1982: 133).

Within the framework of Porter and Kramer's "Creating Shared Value" profit maximization is *not* "good in itself", it is *not* "axiomatically good for society".[6] "Creating Shared Value" is a *challenge*, it is a *task* to figure out how business can create economic by creating societal value. But Porter and Kramer are simply *concealing* this *task* in their "presumed" "prerequisites". And this trick of hiding the difficult tasks is a sort of presuming away of the "messiness" of real-world business: the polydimensional world of business in which there is no "presumed" harmony between economy and ethics. So, the Porter and Kramer's conceptual strategy consists of two steps: As a first step, their concept "presumes compliance with the law and ethical standards" (Porter and Kramer 2011: 75). And as the second step, they present their concept of "Creating Shared Value" *itself* as "pure unadulterated capitalism", which is then – pretty much like in Friedman's view – nothing but "making money":

> "The basic idea which we call 'Creating Shared Value' is about actually applying the capitalist model to addressing issues in society." "'Creating Shared Value' is *pure unadulterated capitalism*. It's about *making money*. So the idea here is actually to get capitalism working not against the interests of society […] but actually integral to addressing the problems of society […]. Then you have the *magic of capitalism* at work." (Porter 2012)

So, as a result, this "trick" to declare "compliance with the law and ethical standards" as a prerequisite, as a given, is nearly the same "sleight of hand" as in Friedman's *New York Times* article. On their front door are slogans like "Nothing but Profit!" or "the Magic of Capitalism" are written – that is, however, possible only by smuggling in compliance with laws and ethical standards through the back door. This enables them to present a clean "reality" of a capitalistic "magic" while elegantly avoiding the "messy" and challenging stuff of an ethical integrity of everyday business.

6.2 The Perspective: "Business Metaphysics"

The research program which I have headlined with the term "Business Metaphysics" deals with the question "how the business world really works (in general)". One of the reasons for this research question is the well-known accusation that economists – and pretty much the same could be said about ethicists – are dealing only with the fanciful world of their theories which have little to do with the actual world of business:

> "A surprising problem is that many economists do not distinguish between economic model and reality." (Greenspan 1984 cited in Andrews 2005: 13)

My hypothesis is that there are deeper reasons for this problem, namely *metaphysical* reasons. So, the specific "lens" through which I want to view the concept

[6] "There's example after example of where actually it's much more complicated than that" (Porter 2011a, b).

of "Creating Shared Value" from now on is the perspective of "Business Metaphysics" (as I called it) (Schramm 2014a, b, c, 2015a, b, 2016). In order to do that (see Sect. 6.3), I have to briefly clarify the terms "Metaphysics" and "Business Metaphysics".

6.2.1 Metaphysics

Of course there are some philosophers who are in favour of "post-metaphysical thinking" or a "post-metaphysical culture" (cf. Rorty 1995; Habermas 1992, 1994[7]), but they are using the term "metaphysics" in a different way than I do. In contrast to these philosophers I understand the term "metaphysics" in a strictly *epistemological* sense. Precisely in this sense, Alan Greenspan, former Chairman of the Federal Reserve of the United States from 1987 to 2006, used the term *"ideology"* for a mental framework that is meant to solve certain problems in the area of modern economy (or financial markets respectively):

> "Well, remember that what an ideology is. It's a conceptual framework with the way people deal with reality. Everyone has one. [...] To exist, you need an ideology. The question is whether it is accurate or not. And what I'm saying to you is, yes, I've found a flaw [...] in the model that I perceived is the critical functioning structure that defines how the world works, so to speak."[8]

If we replace Greenspan's ambiguous term "ideology" with the term "metaphysics",

- We can firstly say that "metaphysics" focuses on the conceptual frameworks with which we *generally* deal with reality. "Metaphysics" sheds light on the question of how the world works *in general* – whereas the various fields of science deal with the question of how the world works *in detail*.
- Secondly, we are faced with the fact that metaphysics is *inevitable* ("everyone has one").
- And thirdly, we always have to ask if the metaphysical worldview in question is reasonable or *"accurate"*, i.e. if it is really problem-solving or not (Table 6.1).[9]

Now, for further clarification of the concept of "metaphysics" I will draw on the philosophy of science which was presented by Karl R. Popper. He distinguished between three types of theory:

[7] For them, "metaphysics" is a pre-modern and idealistic matrix for one's thinking, a tendentially totalitarian and therefore outdated world view, into which everybody and everything has to fit.

[8] See for example *http://www.pbs.org/newshour/bb/business-july-dec08-crisishearing_10-23/* (accessed 18.02.2016).

[9] Metaphysics is *inevitable*, but there is a serious danger to any "metaphysics" (or "ideology"): "The defect of a metaphysical system is the very fact that it is a neat little system of thought, which thereby over-simplifies its expression of the world." (Whitehead 1926/2007: 79) And Alan Greenspan actually "found a flaw [...] in the model that I perceived is the critical functioning structure that defines how the world works".

Table 6.1 Popper's three types of theory

Types of theory	Examples	Refutability
Logical and mathematical theories	if 2 + 2 = 4 then 2 + 2 = 5 is refuted (q.e.d.)	Logical
Scientific (empirical) theories	"All swans are white!" Refutation: one single black swan	Empirical
Metaphysical (philosophical) theories	"There is a real world out there!" (= metaphysical realism) Refutation: impossible "The constants of nature are constant!" Refutation: not yet possible	None

"*First*, logical and mathematical theories.

Second, empirical and scientific theories.

Third, philosophical or metaphysical theories." (Popper 1963/1985: 197).

It is the empirical falsifiability which distinguishes scientific theories (natural sciences) from metaphysical theories:

"According to this view [...] a system is to be considered as scientific only if it makes assertions which may clash with observations." (Popper 1963/1985: 256)

While the theories of the sciences are therefore empirically falsifiable, it is the characteristic of metaphysical theories that they are not falsifiable empirically:

"[N]on-testable theories [...] may be described as metaphysical." (Popper 1963/1985: 257) "[P]hilosophical theories or metaphysical theories will be *irrefutable by definition*." (Popper 1963/1985: 197)

But that does not mean that they are senseless or useless. Quite contrary to any positivistic rejection of metaphysical statements, Popper considers them as very important:

"But metaphysical hypotheses are important for science in at least two ways. First of all, in order to have a general picture of the world we need metaphysical hypotheses. Secondly, in the actual preparation of our research we are guided by what I have called 'metaphysical research programmes'." (Popper in Popper/Eccles 1977/2003: 442[10])

[10] Popper regarded even Darwinism not as a testable scientific theory, but as a metaphysical research program: "And yet, the theory is invaluable. I do not see how, without it, our knowledge could have grown as it has done since Darwin. In trying to explain experiments with bacteria which become adapted to, say, penicillin, it is quite clear that we are greatly helped by the theory of natural selection. Although it is metaphysical, it sheds much light upon very concrete and very practical researches. It allows us to study adaptation to a new environment (such as a penicillin-infested environment) in a rational way: it suggests the existence of a mechanism of adaptation, and it allows us even to study in detail the mechanism at work." (Popper 1976: 171 f).

6.2.2 Three Types of Metaphysics

Over the last millennia mankind invented several metaphysical conceptions. A rough division distinguishes between three types of metaphysics:

- the classical metaphysics of *"substance"* (roughly 500 BC to 1500 AD; e.g. Aristotle or Thomas Aquinas),
- then with the beginning of modern times a mechanistic metaphysics of *"machine"* (just about 1500 AD to the 20th century; e.g. René Descartes, Isaac Newton, Daniel Dennett, Richard Dawkins),
- and at least since the 20th century various metaphysics of evolutionary "processes".

All these metaphysical concepts had an elementary impact on all areas of knowledge, for example on natural sciences and on economic theory.

After the traditional metaphysics of *"substance"*[11] had widely lost its plausibility, the early modern age invented a new type of metaphysics: the metaphysics of the *"machine"*. The development of this new type of metaphysics originates from physical cosmology. As an early example of this mechanical worldview in a letter, Johannes Kepler wrote in 1605:

> "My aim in this is to show that the celestial machine is to be likened not to a divine organism but rather to a clockwork [...]. Moreover I show how this physical conception is to be presented through calculation and geometry."[12]

In a second step, this model of a "celestial machine" provided the basis for the idea that *all* matter is mechanistic in its nature. René Descartes consequently extended the machine idea into the realm of biology, so that all biological bodies turned into machines. According to his machine theory of life, he wrote in 1637,

---

[11]Aristotle distinguished two types of "substance" or "essence" (Greek: ουσία): the "first substance" or "first nature" (πρώτη ουσία) and the "second substance" or "second nature" (δευτέρα ουσία). Let's illustrate his distictions with the following sentence: "This ear of wheat is ready for harvesting." The word "this" labels the "first substance" (πρώτη ουσία), namely the single, real thing that you can see in front of you: *this* ear of wheat. But this "this" has a certain "essence", in our case it is an ear of wheat. The "essence" or the "nature" of "this" thing actually is wheat – and this "nature" Aristotle called the "second nature" (δευτέρα ουσία) or "the underlying thing" (Latin: "sub-iectum" or "sub-stantia"). This invisible "second substance" (δευτέρα ουσία) determines the particular "form" (μορφή) of our ear of wheat, namely by shaping the undetermined "matter" (ύλη). In addition, it is the underlying "substance" that is breathing life into our ear of wheat. The invisible "substance" (ὑποκείμενον) is the stimulating *soul* of a living thing, of a plant, an animal or a human being – while the visible features of a plant or a human are only externally added "accidents" (Latin: adcadere). For example: this ear of wheat is "ready for harvesting". Aristotle regarded this condition as a visible, but only additional property ("accident"; συμβεβηκός). – Perhaps the most critical problem of this substance metaphysics is that nobody has ever seen such a "substance"; the "second nature" (Greek: δευτέρα ουσία; Latin: "sub-iectum" or "sub-stantia") always remained merely a theoretical postulate. Therefore it's not surprising that with the arrival of the Early Modern Era, the metaphysical assertion of such "substances" (or "souls") became more and more suspect.

[12]Letter to Herwart von Hohenburg (February 10, 1605), cited in: Holton (1973/1988: 56).

"those who know how wide a range of different automata or moving machines [...] will consider this body *[of animals or human beings]* as a machine [...] , having been made by the hand of God".[13]

The triumph of machine metaphysics continued when Sir Isaac Newton published his *"Principia Mathematica"* in 1687, a book which laid the foundation for classical mechanics. As early as in the very first sentence of the preface to his *"Principia"* he referred to all those thinkers who

"considered *mechanics* to be of the greatest importance in the investigation of nature and science"[14].

In Newton's worldview it was still God who was the creator and sustainer of the world machine – a cause of the universe which has to be "very well skilled in mechanics"[15] but during the 19th century God was finally dissolved out of the scientific worldview and only the inanimate world machine was left.

6.2.3 *Economic Slaves of Defunct Metaphysicians*

Later, the early economists began to (re-) construct the economic system according to the pattern of physical mechanics and the underlying machine metaphysics. For example, Léon Walras and William Stanley Jevons thus adopted the metaphysical paradigm of mechanics in economics:

---

[13] Descartes (1637/2006: 46). To be sure, Descartes still used the word "substance" and called the realm of physical entities "corporeal substance" or "res extensa". In his dualistic worldview (metaphysics) there exists another "substance": the non-physical and non-mechanical, but *mental* substance which he calls "res cogitans". (Alongside he believed in a third substance: God.) The dualism of two realms confronted him with the problem of the interaction of corporeal and mental substances because the mind or soul of man seemed like an immaterial ghost in the mechanical machinery of the human body (Sheldrake 2012: 34). Descartes himself "solved" this problem by assuming that the body is interacting with the mind at the pineal gland, which allegedly is the seat of the soul. But apart from man's mind, the whole world of physical things (including the human body) was, according to Descartes, merely a mechanistic machinery.

[14] Newton (1687/1999: 381) Newton assumed that matter consists of "solid, massy, hard, impenetrable, moveable Particles" (Newton 1730: 375 Book III) whose movements he described with his famous three universal laws of motion. However, with Newton's gravitation a non-mechanical force had actually found its way into classical mechanics. Newton left open the question as to whether there is a hidden "mechanical" explanation of gravitation or if gravitation is an "occult" power metaphysically: "I have not as yet been able to deduce from phenomena the reason for these properties of gravity, and I do not feign hypotheses. […] [A]nd hypotheses, whether metaphysical or physical, or based on occult qualities, or mechanical, have no place in experimental philosophy. In this experimental philosophy, propositions are deduced from the phenomena and are made general by induction. The impenetrability, mobility, and impetus of bodies, and the laws of motion and the law of gravity have been found by this method. And it is enough that gravity really exists and acts according to the laws that we have set forth and is sufficient to explain all the motions of the heavenly bodies and of our sea." (Newton 1687/1999: 943).

[15] Newton (2004: 96 Letter "To the Reverend Dr Richard Bentley", December 10, 1692).

„The Theory of Economy thus treated presents a close analogy to the science of Statical Mechanics". (Jevons 1871/1965: vii)

Interestingly, the self-interest of "man" – later "homo economicus" – is understood as the equivalent to Newton's gravitational force:

"Utility only exists when there is on the one side the person wanting and on the other the thing wanted. [...] Just as the gravitating force [...] utility is an attraction" (Jevons 1981: 80)[16].

The self-interest is modelled as a force of *attraction* in a mechanical system in order to make the overall system predictable:

„[T]he theory here given may be described as *the mechanics of utility and self-interest.*" (Jevons 1871/1965: 21)

And so the machine metaphysics actually survived in economic textbooks up to this day. The development of economic theories does not happen independently of current metaphysical ideas – on the contrary. Rephrasing the famous passage from Keynes' "General Theory"[17], one could say:

Hypothesis III: Metaphysical ideas are more powerful than commonly understood. Indeed the world is run by little else. Economists and (some) Business Ethicists, who believe themselves to be quite exempt from any ideological influences, are usually the slaves of some defunct metaphysician.

And here is the problem: "The age of the machine" (Davies/Gribbin 1992: 11) was a success story (especially with regard to the countless innovations of engineering), but the underlying metaphysics of this age, the mechanistic paradigm, has simply turned out to be *wrong*. Evidently, the universe is *not* a machine, but radically *evolutionary* and *processual*:

- A machine does not evolve or grow. But since Charles Darwin's theory of "natural selection" we do know that the biological world *is* evolving and constantly producing something new.[18] And since the findings of Georg Lemaitre, Edward Hubble, Arno Penzias and Robert Wilson the "Big Bang" theory is the orthodox model for the universe and its cosmological evolution. We *are* faced with a growing and evolving universe. This universe does not look like a machine at all. It is

[16] And the price is the equivalent to the centrifugal force.

[17] See Keynes (1936/1953: 306): "The ideas of economists and political philosophers, both when they are right and when they are wrong, are more powerful than is commonly understood. Indeed the world is run by little else. Practical men, who believe themselves to be quite exempt from any intellectual influences are usually the slaves of some defunct economist. [...] It is ideas, not vested interests, which are dangerous for good or evil."

[18] To be sure, Darwin's theory of "natural selection" doesn't imply that there is a kind of goal for the whole universe or for the evolutionary process of life on earth. What Darwin discovered was a mechanism of effects. If you do, however, apply the principle of evolution to the entire cosmos, the result is a universe that doesn't look like a machine at all.

much more like an evolving and growing organism.[19] So, a "Philosophy of Organism", like the cosmology of philosopher Alfred North Whitehead, is a much more adequate metaphysical concept than the old machine thinking.[20]

- No (traditional) machine is able to change its form. But Albert Einstein's "Theory of Relativity" showed "that space and time are not independent and absolute, as Newton had thought, but are enmeshed and relative" (Greene 2004/2005: 9). Newton's unchangeable "absolute space" and "absolute time" are changing all the time, "space and time [...] can warp and curve in response to the presence of matter or energy." (Greene 1999/2006: 6) Science fiction became science.[21]
- A machine is made of solid mechanical components and has a structure which is stable and invariable. But quantum physics showed that, in fact, not only does the old "machine" of the universe evolve, but its smallest "components" are actually quantized *events* (*processes*) of fluent energy. So, again a philosophy of *events*, a "*Process* Philosophy", like Whitehead's is needed.[22]

If on the one hand everybody has a "metaphysics" and if on the other hand we always have to ask whether the metaphysical worldview in question is "accurate" or not[23], then philosopher Charles Sanders Peirce is right:

Hypothesis IV: „Every man of us has a metaphysics, and has to have one; and it will influence his life greatly. Far better, then, that that metaphysics should be criticized and not be allowed to run loose." (Peirce 1960: ch.1,129)

6.2.4 Process Metaphysics & Business Metaphysics

Machine Metaphysics has outlived its usefulness because it is very likely that it is simply wrong. According to modern physics our universe is not a machine:

> „[M]aterialism is dead. [...] [T]here is no machine." (Davies and Gribbin 1992: 13,309)

---

[19] In the words of Sheldrake (2012: 53): "The machine metaphor has long outlived its usefulness [...]. Our growing, evolving universe is much more like an organism, and so is the earth, and so are oak trees, and so are dogs, and so are you."

[20] Whitehead explicitly called his metaphysical concept the "Philosophy of *Organism*" (e.g. Whitehead 1929/1978:xi. 7,18ff.).

[21] "The eighteenth century opened with the quiet confidence that at last nonsense had been got rid of. Today we are at the opposite pole of thought. Heaven knows what seeming nonsense may not tomorrow be demonstrated truth." (Whitehead 1925/1967:114).

[22] Whitehead's major work is called "*Process* and Reality" (Whitehead 1929/1978) and is best known as "*Process* Philosophy" which is a philosophy of *events* (also termed "actual *occasions*").

[23] As quoted above: "[A]n ideology is [...] a conceptual framework with the way people deal with reality. Everyone has one. [...] To exist, you need an ideology. The question is whether it is accurate or not." (Alan Greenspan in 2008; *http://www.pbs.org/newshour/bb/business-july-dec08-crisishearing_10-23/* (accessed 18.02.2016).

Instead, the nature of reality is radically *evolutionary*. So, a new and more adequate metaphysical cosmology is needed. In my view, such a metaphysics actually exists: the cosmology of the mathematician, physicist and philosopher Alfred North Whitehead (as already mentioned).

In this part of the paper, I proceed in two steps: (a) Whitehead's "*Process Metaphysics*" forms the *philosophical* point of departure for (b) the development of the *moral-economic* concept of "*Business Metaphysics*".[24] Within this paper, I can neither give a comprehensive description of Whitehead's cosmological "Process Metaphysics" nor a detailed portrayal of the research program "Business Metaphysics". Therefore, I will concentrate on a few features which are useful for a critique of the concept of Porter and Kramer's "Creating Shared Value". To make my analysis easier to follow, my arguments are structured via the following table:

6.2.4.1 Process Metaphysics

It was chiefly his main work "*Process and Reality*" in which Alfred North Whitehead presented a cosmological metaphysics that he himself mostly called a "Philosophy of Organism" but which has now become better known as "Process Philosophy".

1. "*Creativity*". As Quantum Physics views *energy* as the raw *material* of the universe and elementary particles as concrete embodiments of this energy, so Whitehead's *metaphysics* describes the universal basic *character* of the world with the term "*creativity*"[25] (which was presumably coined by himself!). With this term, Whitehead aims at expressing the fact that we live in a universe of *activity* and precisely not in a universe of dead and passive matter:

   > "'Creativity' is [...] divested of the notion of passive receptivity [...]; it is the pure notion of the activity [...]. It is that ultimate notion of the highest generality at the base of actuality." (Whitehead 1929/1978: 31)

   Due to this creative basic character of reality/ies, things are made fluid and become dynamic in an *evolutionary* way: everything is in flow (cf. Heraklits πάντα ῥεῖ = "everything flows"). New things are "born", grow and decay.

2. "*Events*". With reference to Quantum Physics, Whitehead initially assumes micro-analytically the existence of many realities which are linked in processual relativity, and energetic process-droplets that he calls "*events*", "*actual entities*", or "*actual occasions*":

[24] A similar approach is the process-based theory of organization of Tor Hernes and others. Cf. Hernes 2008; Helin et al. 2014; 2015.

[25] The completely elementary and foundational meaning of the term "creativity" in Whitehead's metaphysics can already be seen by the fact that he calls "creativity" "the ultimate" (Whitehead 1929/1978: 20), the "universal of universals characterizing ultimate matter of fact" (Whitehead 1929/1978: 21), the "ultimate principle" (Whitehead 1929/1978: 21) or "that ultimate notion of the highest generality at the base of actuality" (Whitehead 1929/1978: 31).

> "This epoch is characterized by electronic and protonic actual entities, and by yet more ultimate actual entities which can be dimly discerned in the quanta of energy." (Whitehead 1929/1978: 91)

In terms of *metaphysics*, it is important at this point that the universe is made up of entities which have the character of *process droplets* which are *genetically relative* and exist in a *minute temporal period* (maybe on billionth of a second).

> "'Actual entities' – also termed 'actual occasions' – are the final real things of which the world is made up." (Whitehead 1929/1978: 18)

These "events" or "occasions" are also the basic units of the, thus, micro-analytical conception of Whitehead 's "*Process* Philosophy"[26].

3. "*Societies*". At the *micro* level the universe consists, according to Whitehead, of such *process* droplets ("events", "occasions") while all bigger formations – such as atoms, water drops, ants, stones, trees, people or plants – are more lasting things. These things consist of "actual occasions" which, in a manner of speaking, "*cooperate*" more closely and, in this, achieve a certain *stability of structure*. Whitehead calls these more complex and more lasting things of this world at the *macro*-cosmic level "*societies*":

> "The real actual things that endure are all societies. They are not actual occasions." (Whitehead 1933/1967: 204)

"Societies" are, accordingly, *complex* structures. As (contingently) separate complexes of "events", they depend on a shared characteristic which then defines them as a "society" belonging to each other and which differentiates them from other "societies". Whitehead calls this element of identity, which is common to all elements of a "society", a "*defining characteristic*":

> "A society has an essential character, whereby it is the society that it is." (Whitehead 1933/1967: 204). "The common form is the ‚defining characteristic' of the society." (Whitehead 1929/1978: 34) "The self-identity of a society is founded upon the self-identity of its defining characteristic, and upon the mutual immanence of its occasions." (Whitehead 1933/1967: 204)

Whitehead's "societies" are, in any case, "organic" forms which (have to) reproduce their "defining characteristic" every day in an evolutionary "life"-process.

I do not want to expand on the system of "societies" at this point but I do want to point out, in advance, that *organizations* – such as *business enterprises* – can be imagined, metaphysically, as "societies". (The German word for stock corporation – "Aktien*gesellschaft*" = "*society* of shareholders", is telling.)

4. "*Organisms*". In Whitehead's cosmology all things – the "actual occasions" at the micro level, the "societies" on the meso level and finally the universe on the macro level – are seen as dynamic "organisms":

---

[26] "*How* an actual entity *becomes* constitutes *what* that actual entity *is* [...]. Its 'being' is constituted by its 'becoming'. This is the 'principle of process.' " (Whitehead 1929/1978: 23).

Fig. 6.1 Ludwig Wittengenstein's "thread" and "fibres"

> "Science is [...] becoming the study of organisms. Biology is the study of the larger organisms; whereas physics is the study of the smaller organisms." (Whitehead 1925/1967: 103)

The "final real things of which the world is made up" are not "particles", not dead billiard balls, but "waves". Nothing in nature is like a static machine. Even the whole universe is "growing". And all things within the universe are growing, changing their form, ageing, dying … So, consequently, Whitehead explicitly called his metaphysical concept the "Philosophy of Organism" (Whitehead 1929/1978: xi 7,18ff.). Actuality is an "organic" fabric or network of myriads of events. The philosopher Ludwig Wittgenstein suggested – in a completely different context – a metaphor that expresses this organic "spinning" of the truth quite well:

> " ... as in spinning a thread we twist fibre on fibre. And the strength of the thread resides not in the fact that someone fibre runs through its whole length, but in the overlapping of many fibres." (Wittgenstein 1953/2009: 36, §67)

So, just like the "thread" develops from the "spinning" and the "overlapping of many fibres" in an evolutionary way, the thread of a human life is also spun from a vast number of individual events. The thread of life has to *reproduce* itself day by day. The continuing, ongoing spinning process represents, in this, the distinctive *identity* of this person from their conception to their death, in which, however, nothing remains the same "sub-stantially" but where this human being – this human "society" of "actual occasions" – continually changes over the course of his life, gains experiences, starts turning grey, and at some point this human "society" dissolves. All things in the universe have the same "organic" character – from the atom to the business enterprise, and also a galaxy (Fig. 6.1).

5. *Creating "Value"*. Whitehead's "Process Metaphysics" *is* actually a (cosmological) philosophy of "Creating Shared Value". But, in contrast to Porter and Kramer there is no pretence here that this value creation is an easy thing.

The term "value" takes a central place in Whitehead's philosophy. In contrast to a world of machine metaphysics, where there is pragmatic functioning only but no "value" (economic value; societal value and so on) not to mention moral "values", the world of the "Metaphysics of Organism" is inherently a world of value(s).

Whitehead develops this from everyday experience. For normal human beings it is not a matter of indifference about what will happen to them in the future. Rather, they experience "the value of an individual for itself" (Whitehead 1926/2007: 59), they experience themselves, accordingly, as "self-value" (Whitehead 1926/2007: 101). This experience is taken to a cosmological level by Whitehead. "Value" does thus not just signify, in his system, any objects in an ideal world of value(s), but is a feature of our finite *actuality* itself (and all the different "events" on earth or in the whole universe):

> "The emergence of some actual value depends on limitation […]. Thus an event is a matter of fact which by reason of its limitation is a value for itself" (Whitehead 1925/1967: 194). "Value is inherent in actuality itself. To be an actual entity is to have a self-interest. This self-interest is a feeling of self-valuation […].This self-interest […] is the *ultimate enjoyment of being actual*." (Whitehead 1926/2007: 100) In short: "The actuality is the value". (Whitehead 1925/1967: 105)

The process of the universe is a vast production place of creating actual value.

But the production of value is – in modern terms – a "*network* production". The individual "entity" or "society" creates itself, and creates with that, its own "self-value". This creation process does not occur from the scratch, but always in relation to other "entities" or "societies" only:

> "Each actual entity is *an arrangement of the whole universe*, actual and ideal, whereby there is constituted that *self-value* which is the entity itself."[27]

Metaphysically fundamental is, here, the relatedness of everything (Whitehead's "principle of relativity"[28]). The origination of individual values is interconnected with all other things.

At this point it is crucial to not look at the universe through rose-tinted spectacles. Our universe of value production is shaped by countless *conflicts*. For example, Whitehead stressed that life, by definition, and inevitably, happens at the expense of

---

[27] Whitehead 1926/2007: 101 (emphasis nine). In his last ever talk – a talk with the title "Immortality" in 1941 – Whitehead again extensively addresses the subject of "values". He does, however, undertake a shift in meaning that it is vital to pay attention to. While, in his earlier writing, he has always used the term "value" in the sense of an "*actualised* value", in this talk he now uses the term "value" in the sense of "*possibilities* of value" (Whitehead 1941/1948: 64) When he talks about a "the World of Value" (Whitehead 1941/1948: 62) he does *not* mean the "world" of *actualised value*, but the "world" of the possibilities of value! Whitehead differentiates, in "Immortality", between two "worlds" which combine to form the total of the world: On the one hand there is of course our real world (the cosmos of galaxies, solar systems including our earth and everything that happens on it). Whitehead talks about the "world of activity", the "world of origination", the "creative world", the "world of action", the "world of fact" or the "world of change". And on the other hand the universe contains the "world" of *possibilities* of value. For this, Whitehead uses the phrases "the world of mere possibility" and then nearly consistently, precisely "the world of [*possible*] value". "Thus the two sides of the Universe are the World of Origination and the World of [*possible*] Value." (Whitehead 1941/1948: 63) The two worlds are a package deal: "'The Two Worlds […] require each other, and together constitute the concrete Universe. Either World considered by itself is an abstraction." (Whitehead 1941/1948: 63).

[28] "It belongs to the nature of a 'being' that it is a potential for every 'becoming.' This is the ‚principle of relativity.'" (Whitehead 1929/1978: 22).

other life: "[L]ife is robbery." (Whitehead 1929/1978: 105) The creation of an individual value means the destruction of other values, even if a positive net balance of value is created. To put it in the terms of Porter and Kramer: The world is a place of creation of "shared value" as well as creation of value at the cost of other values.

Whitehead advocates "the concept of the world as a realm of adjusted *values, mutually intensifying* or *mutually destructive*." (Whitehead 1929/2007: 59)

Let us take, for example, us humans and how we create economic value. To feed ourselves and to create economic values (products etc.), we have to destroy other values: we consume plants and animals as food and also use them up within the context of our economic production. Whitehead says:

"[L]ife is robbery. It is at this point that with life morals become acute. The robber requires justification." (Whitehead 1929/1978: 105)

The production or the creating of value cannot happen without conflict in this finite world. It is impossible to live without "getting one's hands dirty". Our universe as a factual given is recognizably not in a state of cosmic peace. Only the myth of paradise "dreams" of a cosmic peace, of the Garden of Eden (cf. Gen 2). Nowadays, we all, however, live "East of Eden". And this is precisely where the conflicts start. In the "world of origination" there is no creation of new value without the eliminating use of existing values:

"[T]here is a struggle for existence. It is folly to look at the universe through rose-tinted spectacles. We must admit the struggle. The question is, who is to be eliminated." (Whitehead 1925/1967: 205)

It is of course often possible to achieve "win-win" situations for some of the actors or creatures concerned, and thus to create universal "shared value" as well as to increase the value intensity in total. But it is by no means rare for *the way in which value* is brought forth to be "messy", and therefore to pose a difficult ethical problem.

6.2.4.2 "Business Metaphysics"

"Metaphysics" is concerned with the question of how the world works *in general* whereas the natural sciences are dealing with the question of how the world works *in detail*. When we transfer this approach to human society and especially to economy, it is possible to say the following. "*Business* Metaphysics" is concerned with the question of "how the *business* world works *in general*" whereas economics is dealing with the question of "how the business world works *in detail*".

By way of introduction, I would like to illustrate the field of the research program "Business Metaphysics" with an example. Let us focus on the well-known debate on the possibility of a "Corporate Social Responsibility" in the context of the "Theory of the Firm". For all his life Milton Friedman for example took the view that only "people" as individuals can have moral responsibility, in contrast to companies, as a company is nothing but an "artificial legal structure"[29]. Lynn Sharp Paine noted, on this (with an ironic undertone):

[29] „Only people can have responsibilities." (Friedman 1970). With companies, according to him, this is not possible due to their nature: „Can a building have moral opinions? Can a building have social responsibility? If a building can't have social responsibility, what does it mean to say that a

> "According to this line of reasoning, advocates of corporate social responsibility are guilty of a grave mistake of metaphysics." (Paine 2003: 87)

And it actually is a question of "Business *Metaphysics*".[30] In this case it is about the "*essence*" resp. the "*nature* of the firm". And regarding this question, the classics of the "Theory of the Firm" also used the argument of Friedman. By the way of example, we are told the following by Michael C. Jensen and William H. Meckling:

> "[O]rganizations are simply *legal fictions*" (Jensen and Meckling 1976: 310). To be sure, there *is* "individual behavior in organizations, including behavior of managers" (Jensen/Meckling 1976: 308), but: "*The firm is not an individual*. It is a legal fiction" (Jensen and Meckling 1976: 311).

Due to this "nature" or "essence of the firm", the organizational "legal fiction" only serves instrumentally as a locus to bring the conflicting interests of the concerned individuals into (the neo-classical) balance:

> "The firm [...] is a legal fiction which serves as a focus for a complex process in which the conflicting objectives of individuals [...] are brought into equilibrium within a framework of contractual relations." (Jensen and Meckling 1976: 311)

> "[A] corporation which hitherto had only a *legal existence* in the state of its incorporation, because it was an *invisible legal entity existing only in contemplation of law*, now became an economic *going concern existing in its transactions*". (Commons 1934/2009: 53)[31]

It is easy to see that this question about organizations as "corporative actors" is precisely about the problem that I just categorized as "a question of metaphysics": the question about the "*nature*" or the "essence of the firm" (Jensen and Meckling 1976: 310). When Commons explains, that a corporation, after the transition that has been diagnosed by him, was *no* longer only an invisible legal entity, which is ontologically present only in the *abstract* way of existing of a legal game rule ("existing only in contemplation of law"), but is now also seen in its *concrete* way of existing as a company, which reproduces itself in its *actual* transactions ("an economic going concern existing in its transactions"), then this is a very fundamental *setting of a course* for the question of how the *business* world works *in general*. The above described problem with Jensen and Meckling on the one side and Commons on the other side ways has the character of a *metaphysical* problem. It is a question of "*Business Metaphysics*".

In the same way that I already used Alfred North Whitehead as an example to affix the idea of an appropriate "Metaphysics", it is also possible, in my opinion, to

---

corporation can? A corporation is simply a artificial legal structure. But the people, who are engaged in it – whether the stockholders, whether the executives in it, whether the employees – they all have moral responsibilities." (Friedman 2003).

[30] Paine has, *admittedly*, made this remark with an ironic undertone and, directly following this, belittled the problem by claiming that it had dissolved in so far as, nowadays, factually all sides demanded CSR, so that the argument was settled "pragmatically" already, but, in my opinion, she underestimates the (indeed) *metaphysical* problem.

[31] The historical background with Commons is a reform of the way companies were valued in the eyes of the (tax) law in 1893 in Indiana, which is, however, not particularly relevant for our context.

Table 6.2 Process metaphysics and business metaphysics

	Process metaphysics	Business metaphysics
No. 1	**"Creativity"**	**"Activity"**
No. 2	**"Events"**, "actual occasions"	**"Transactions"** ("correlates law, economics and ethics")
No. 3	**"Societies"** (with "defining characteristics")	**"Going concerns"** (with "working rules")
No. 4	"Events", "societies" and the whole universe as **"organisms"** ("Philosophy of Organism")	"Transactions", "going concerns" and the whole economy as **organisms**
No. 5	"Origination" of **"value"** ("the world as a realm of [...] values, mutually intensifying or mutually destructive")	**Integrity** of creating **value** as a tough challenge

use John R. Commons as an example for an appropriate "*Business* Metaphysics". Overall, I propose the thesis in this part of the paper, that a "Business *Metaphysics*" in the tradition of Whitehead and Commons presents, *analytically*, an "accurate conceptual framework" which *conceptionally* has a high problem solving potential. Therefore it is *pragmatically* useful for the development of expedient and multidimensional tools for *solving* problems – for example concerning the ethics of management. Referring to Table 6.2 (see above), I would like to sketch the following characteristics:

1. "*Activity*". At the core of Common's conception is the question about "the ultimate unit of *activity*" (Commons 1934/2009: 58). As, with Whitehead, the universal fundamental character of the *world* is described by the term "*creativity*", so Commons calls – metaphorically speaking – the fundamental "stuff" of which the business world is made up "*activity*". What *really* happens in business are forms of this (business) *activity*.
2. "*Transactions*". Just like Whitehead metaphysically sees "actual occasions" ("events", "actual entities") as concrete occurrences of "creativity", so the "*transactions*" function, with Commons, as micro-analytical concrete occurrences of "activity":

   > "Thus the *ultimate unit of activity* [...] is a *Transaction*. A transaction [...] is the smallest unit of institutional economics." (Commons 1934/2009: 58)

   In this, he makes explicit references to the metaphysics of Whitehead:

   > "These [...] transactions are to economics what Whitehead's [...] ‚event[s]' are to physics." (Commons 1934/2009: 58)[32]

[32] That Commons takes a *metaphysical* strategic decision with using this micro-analytical foundation of his economic of institutes can be seen in the numerous parallels he draws in his economics to physics, chemistry, biology and astronomy: "This falls in with an analogy to the recent correlation of the separate sciences of physics, chemistry, and astronomy, by the discovery *of a unit of*

Commons' "transactions" function, accordingly, like Whitehead's "actual occasions". Because of this, it is possible to also describe Commons' position by paraphrasing a Whitehead quote: '*Transactions*' are the final real things of which the *world of economy* is made up.[33] What is metaphysically meaningful in this is that, in the world of economics, it is only these transactions that are *real*. Economic actors exist *economically in* their transactions only , regardless of whether they are individual (manager, consumers) or corporate economic actors (companies). In the same way, economic "laws" or "game rules" only *concretely* exists in corresponding transactions which give life to these "laws". This is because these "laws" or "game rules" remain *abstract* precisely until they reproduce in *concrete transactions*, "become incarnate", *become concrete.*

A further point in reference to Commons' "transactions" is of fundamental importance. "Economic transactions" are, with Commons, no purely economic occurrences. He rather discerns in the *concrete reality* of one individual transaction (at least) *three dimensions*:

"Thus the ultimate unit of activity which *correlates law, economics and ethics* [...] is a transaction." (Commons 1932/1996: 454)

It was exactly this correlation of different dimensions that was the problem from which the classic essay of 1932 departed as its title indicates: "*The Problem of Correlating Law, Economics, and Ethics*". The inherently abstract world of the code of the economic system (± pay, or "to pay or not to pay") exclusively shows the economic dimension only, and thus has a *mono*-dimensional character. This abstract *mono-dimensionality* is precisely *not* applicable for *concrete transactions*, however. To illustrate this line of argument by, let us take the simple example of purchasing something at the supermarket till. A straightforward analysis of such a payment process[34] already shows, at a minimum, the following dimensions:

- Key word "Economics": The concrete transaction of this payment at the supermarket till is an economic process (in the narrower sense of the word) as its medium is money, and the concrete action of payment actualises the code of the economic system ((± pay, or "to pay or not to pay")[35].
- Key word "Law": The concrete transaction of this payment at the supermarket till also has a legal dimension. This is because there is a legal duty to pay at the

activity common to all of them. Roughly speaking, the former units in physics had been molecules, the units in chemistry had been atoms, the units in astronomy had been planets and stars. And the 'energies' which made these units go were heat, electricity, chemical affinity, gravity. But *nowadays* the *unit common to all of them is a unit of activity*, the interaction of corpuscular wavelengths" (Commons 1934/2009: 55). Because we live precisely in *one* and *only* in one real universe, Commons is able to word his basis for a *metaphysical* conceptualization, "how the *economic* world works (in general)", in analogy to Whitehead's cosmological concept of metaphysics, "how *the* world works (in general)".

33 See Whitehead (1929/1978: 18).

34 The "metaphysical complexity" of such a simple event is described by Searle (1995/1996: 3f)

35 „Zahlen oder Nichtzahlen – das ist [...] die Seinsfrage der Wirtschaft." (Luhmann 1990: 104)

super market till if you wish to take home a yoghurt. If someone refused to believe this

- they would soon be told by the owner of the super market and informed of the unhappy perspective of having the police called in case of non-payment
- Key word "Ethics": Lastly
- our banal supermarket situation also has an ethical dimension. This is because
- if I were about to try to conceal the yoghurt from the grocery clerk in a bid to escape notice
- another customer watching this would take moral umbrage to this indecent act

The concrete "transactions" are precisely "events"in which (at least) three mono-dimensional dimensionswhich are abstract themselvescome together and become concrete ("actual") only then

3. "*Going Concerns*". As Whitehead differentiates between "events" ("actual occasions") on the one hand and "societies" (as "cooperations" or "cooperations" of "events") on the other, so John R. Commons' concept of has on the one hand the "transaction" and on the other hand what he calls a "going concern". Here as well, he explicitly follows Whitehead:

> "These going concerns and transactions are to economics what Whitehead's 'organic mechanism' [*later called: "society" or "organism"; M.S.]* and 'event' are to physics." (Commons 1934/2009: 96) "[T]ransactions [...] are functionally interdependent, and their interdependence constitutes the whole which, following American usage, we name a going concern. [...] This going concern is itself a larger unit, and is analogous to that which in biology is an 'organism,' or in physics a 'mechanism.' But its components are not living cells, nor electrons, nor atoms – they are transactions." (Commons 1932/1996: 454)

Metaphysically decisive is here the theory's strategy to construct "going concern" in a way that only its actual (real) transaction has concrete existence:

"[W]e must perceive that the true unit of economic theory is not an individual but a going concern composed of individuals in their many transactions". (Commons 1932/1996: 335) It is "*an economic going concern existing in its transactions*". (Commons 1934/2009: 53)

A further point that is conceptionally important is that the transactions that build up to a "going concern" need a shared characteristic that turns them into transactions of *this* "going concern". And like Whitehead's "societies" are marked by a "defining characteristic", so the "going concern" is, with Commons, *structured* by what he calls "*working rules*":

> "A *going concern* is a *joint expectation* of beneficial bargaining, managerial and rationing transactions, kept together by '*working rules*.' When the expectations cease, then the concern quits going." (Commons 1932/1996: 454)

4. "*Organisms*". Commons sees, like Whitehead, all "things" as "events" or dynamic "organisms":

> "Whitehead has observed that the Eighteenth Century method of science had no notion of the *organic unity* of the whole in a changing relation of the parts to the whole. [...] But the mechanism [*of an 'organic unity' or an 'going concern'*] itself is '*organic*' in that it is a kind of prolonged *interweaving* of changing events [*or 'transactions'*], having, as Whitehead says, a past, a present realization, and a future life in its present events." (Commons 1934/2009: 619)

This "organic" character shapes all sorts of things on earth. In the same way that human beings are born, grow, age and die, so companies – Commons' "going concerns" –, too, can be "born" (emerge), they can grow, they can shrink or "die". Organizations are *not* "simply *legal fictions*" (Jensen and Meckling 1976: 310), they are *not* invisible legal entities existing only in contemplation of law, but "economic *going concern[s] existing in its transactions*" (Commons 1934/2009: 53). Viewed as actualities, organizations are – we remember Wittgenstein's metaphor cited above – "threads" existing in the ongoing "spinning" of "fibres" ("transactions").

5. *Creating "Value*". Just like Whitehead's "Process Metaphysics" had already shown a *cosmological* concept of "Creating Shared Value", it can also be said, now, for "Business Metaphysics": The concept of "Business Metaphysics" *is* a philosophy of "Creating Shared Value", too. In contrast, however, to Porter and Kramer , it does not pretend that just by labeling the concept with the slogan "Creating Shared Value". The all-deciding question of *how exactly* this origination of *shared* value in the context of the numerous *tensions* between economic and social value creation in everyday business can be achieved concretely, has been answered already.[36] Porter and Kramer simply *conceal* this *tough task* in their "presumed" "prerequisites". Such kind of assuming away the "messiness" of real-world business is simply not adequate to reality, namely to the poly-dimensional world of business in which there is no "presumed" harmony between economy and ethics on the level of operative management. As Lynn Sharp Paine has rightly argued:

> "The supposed alliance between ethics and economy is highly contingent. It depends both on how ethical behavior is defined and on the surrounding social and institutional context. [...] It is naïve to think that ethics pays any time and any place." (Paine 2000: 325f)

Undoubtedly, it is always desirable to seek "win-win" opportunities and to create "*shared* value". But there is simply no evidence that there is always a "business case" for "Creating Shared Value". As David Vogel writes on the question as to whether there is a business case for virtue in the following:

> "Unfortunately, a review of the evidence, including academic studies of the relationship between profitability and responsibility [...], finds little support for the claim that more responsible firms are more profitable." (Vogel 2005/2006: 45)

[36] "Porter and Kramer claim to 'move beyond' any such trade-offs, largely by (it would seem) ignoring them. While seeking win-win opportunities is clearly important, this does not provide guidance for the many situations where social and economic outcomes will not be aligned for all stakeholders." (Crane et al. 2014a: 136).

To be sure, this does not mean that there is no business case for virtue at all. Thus, Lynn Sharp Paine continues her just-quoted thoughts on "contingency", the "alliance between ethics and economy", as follows:

> "It is naïve to think that ethics pays any time and any place. It is also naïve to suppose that the two cannot be brought into a closer alignment." (Paine 2000: 325f.)

And David Vogel adds:

> "[T]his does not mean that there is no business case for virtue." (Vogel 2005/2006: 45)
> "CSR [...] makes business sense for some firms in some areas under some circumstances." (Vogel 2005/2006: 3)

The contingency in the relation of creating economic value and creating societal value is precisely the point at which Business Ethics comes into the equation. There simply is no clean "reality" of a capitalistic "magic". Every problem-oriented and useful theory has to face the "messy" and *challenging* stuff of an ethical integrity of everyday business. A "Business Metaphysics" which takes its point of departure from Whitehead's "Process Metaphysics", does *not* look at the universe or the economy through rose-tinted spectacles.

6.3 Business Metaphysics on "Creating Shared Value". Three Observations

With the metaphysical equipment of Sect. 6.2, I would like to continue the critique of the concept of Porter and Kramer with three further observations.

6.3.1 "Creating Shared Value" and the "Fallacy of Misplaced Concreteness"

In my hypothesis II (Sect. 6.1) I argued that the conceptual strategy of Porter and Kramer to declare "compliance with laws and ethical standards" as a "prerequisite" to their concept to be nothing more than a sleight of hand. I continue this by arguing for the thesis that the deeper root of this sleight of hand is in a metaphysical fallacy that Alfred North Whitehead calls the "Fallacy of Misplaced Concreteness":

> "There is an error; [...] it is [...] the [...] error of mistaking the abstract for the concrete. It is an example of what I will call the 'Fallacy of Misplaced Concreteness." (Whitehead 1925/1967: 51)

Whitehead himself addressed this fallacy in the context of the physical mechanics of the Early Modern Era.[37] I myself would like to illustrate the fallacy with a

[37] This is about how "matter" can be imagined. As already quoted above, Newton assumed that matter consists of "solid, massy, hard, impenetrable, moveable Particles" (Newton 1730: 375

further simple example: the traffic rule "stop at a red traffic light!" which is as such still *abstract*. It only gains *concrete reality* when people actually stick to it in their concrete behavior, when they really suspend their action of driving[38]. This is because what happens *concretely* at the *actual* red traffic light is significantly more "colourful" (poly-dimensional) than the "clean" *abstract* world of mechanic, and thus perfect, rule following: Some drivers stop indeed; others do not notice the red traffic light as they are daydreaming; others ignore it intentionally because their individual interest to get from A to B quickly takes precedence in this situation. If, however, you only focus on the *abstract game rules*, i.e. here on the *abstract* model of a traffic regulation system, all these possibilities of the concrete and "messy" reality will remain invisible. As Whitehead recognized:

> "The disadvantage of exclusive attention to a group of abstractions [...] is that [...] you have abstracted from the remainder of things. In so far as the excluded things are important [...], your modes of [*abstract*] thought are not fitted to deal with them." (Whitehead 1925/1967: 59)

Whitehead proposed while facing the "Fallacy of Misplaced Concreteness" the thesis that it is precisely here where the important job of *philosophy* or, respectively, of *metaphysics* begins:

> "You cannot think without abstractions; accordingly, it is of the utmost importance to be vigilant in critically revising your modes of abstraction. It is here that philosophy finds its niche as essential to the healthy progress of society. It is the critic of abstractions." (Whitehead 1925/1967: 59) So, considering "the 'fallacy of misplaced concreteness' [...] [i]t is the office of metaphysics to determine the limits of the applicability of such abstract notions." (Whitehead 1929/1978: 93)

[Book III]). Accordingly, he imagined these "particles" as "billiard balls", which are only affected in terms of their location: As a "billiard ball" a "particle" or an atom can mechanically be pushed around in space – in Newton's words: it's "moveable" – and therefore changes its location, but in itself the "particle" isn't affected by anything else – it's "solid, massy, hard, impenetrable". Whitehead calls this notion the fallacy of "*simple location*" (e.g. Whitehead 1925/1967: 49). By that, he means that it's *simply* the *location* that constitutes a relation to other things, but in itself the "billiard ball" doesn't change its nature. With a physical *mechanics* that is conceptualized like this, physicians – and, by extension, technicians – were able to work very well: "This is the famous mechanistic theory of nature, which has reigned supreme ever since the seventeenth century. It is the orthodox creed of physical science. Furthermore, the creed justified itself by the pragmatic test. It worked. Physicists took no more interest in philosophy." (Whitehead 1925/1967:50) It worked for certain purposes, but it turned out that scientifically it was wrong. There are no immutable "billiard balls", but fluent energetic events. The "mechanistic theory of nature" turned out to be an *abstraction* of the real and *concrete world* which we now know through quantum mechanics. This concept of "particles" and the "mechanistic theory of nature" is therefore "an example of what I will call the 'Fallacy of Misplaced Concreteness.'"

[38] "Habit" is an important term in Whitehead's philosophy. Like Charles Sanders Peirce, who spoke of "the laws or habitudes of nature" (Peirce 1893-1913/1998: 53), and William James, who saw "the laws of nature" as "habits" (James 1909/2008: 79), Whitehead gave his "occasions" metaphysical priority and regarded the natural laws as consequent "habits of nature": "People make the mistake of talking about 'natural laws.' There are no natural laws. There are only temporary habits of nature." (Whitehead in: Price 1954/2001: 363). So, the so-called "laws" of nature are not completely fixed but in fact "widespread habits of nature" (Whitehead 1936/1968: 154).

Bearing in mind, too, the pertinent conceptualization of economics, it is fundamentally important to avoid the "Fallacy of Misplaced Concreteness", that is to understand that *concrete reality* is only granted to *actual moves in the game*, or respectively *transactions*. Those which *really* happen are only concrete *moves in the game*. Without these moves, the rules of the game would remain *abstract*. The abstract *rules* of the game only attain empirical reality in the "habits" of the players (moves in the game). Methodologically controlled *abstractions* are useful and unavoidable in the scenes, but it is important to always consider additionally that they are abstractions and *not concrete* reality itself. It is of course necessary to analyse scientifically the rules of the modern economic system, but these rules are as such *abstract* ones, only the real transactions are *concrete*. And without doubt it is useful to see a corporation through the lens of law in its legal existence, but – again – this is an abstraction because what is concrete is "an economic *going concern existing in its transactions*". (Commons 1934/2009: 53)[39]

If we now look at the concept of "Creating Shared Value" by Porter and Kramer through the lens of the "Fallacy of Misplaced Concreteness", hypothesis V emerges:

Hypothesis V: The strategy of Porter and Kramer to "presume compliance with the law and ethical standards" *wants* to get into the "comfortable" position to present a purely economic (*one*-dimensional) "solution" to all the "messy" problems of the manager's daily business. This *intentional* ignorance towards the concrete and *poly*-dimensional ("messy") actuality of the real economy is exactly the "Fallacy of Misplaced Concreteness".

In contrast to this, Business Ethicists have been pondering, with reference to the term "*Corporate Social Responsibility*", the question about *how exactly* it would be possible to solve all these "messy" problems of the manager's daily business, *how*,

[39] In addition it should be said, however, that there is, besides the "*Fallacy of Misplaced Concreteness*" also the opposite fallacy: the "Fallacy of Disregarded Abstractness". In how far? On the side of the *abstract* (the ideals, the concepts) is, firstly, the *abstract idea* of a market system (invented by Adam Smith or whoever else), on the other side is the concreteness of the *real* events, the *concrete* transactions from the simple act of shopping at the supermarket till up to introducing the *Apple iPhone* to the market in 2007. *Concrete reality* is only gained by the abstract concept of the market system when real people in their economic transactions actually go by these *abstract ideas* and make it their habit to play by its rules. Nevertheless, the invention of the abstract market system is a societal achievement of the first order. This is because humankind's ability to leave the narrow frame of the antique idea of "household management" (οἰκονομία) and to put their trust into an (in itself) *abstract* market mechanism, and so allow themselves to be led in their *actual* moves or transactions by the rules of the game of this (in itself) *abstract* economic system (market competition) at least partially – an economic system that has, as a "discovery procedure" (Friedrich August von Hayek) brought forth an enormous economic growth. This is where the "Fallacy of Disregarded Abstractness" comes into play: here, the concrete reality is not ignored (as with the "Fallacy of Misplaced Concreteness"), but it is not seen, for example, that the enormous, hunger-overcoming processes of growth of Western capitalism are productive effects of the (in itself) *abstract market system*. In parallel to Whitehead's definition of the "Fallacy of Misplaced Concreteness" the "Fallacy of Disregarded Abstractness" can be defined as follows: *There is the error of ignoring the abstract. This error can be called "the fallacy of disregarded abstractness"* (These phrases are my staff member Christoph Wagner's.).

Table 6.3 Type of situations and concepts

Type of situations	Concept
Win-Win Situations ("Shared Value" Situations)	"Creating Shared Value"
"**Dilemma** Situations"	"Corporate Social Responsibility"
"**Contingency** Situations"	"Corporate Social Responsibility"

then, profitability and responsibility could be brought "into a closer alignment" (Paine 2000: 325f.). In simply "*presuming*" or "*assuming*" the compliance of business with moral standards, Porter and Kramer are indeed doing a "kind of cherry-picking" (Crane et al. 2014b: 152): they concentrate only on the desirable "win-win" situations ("shared value" situations) and they disregard the "messy stuff" of all the difficult moral-economic "*dilemma* situations" – situations in which ethics costs – or "*contingency* situations" – situations in which it is contingent if ethics will pay or cost. Hence they leave the imperfect situations to the old-fashioned guys of "Corporate Social Responsibility" – the Business Ethicists, as Porter says, out of "the CSR bucket"[40]. So, it seems that Table 6.3 shows this intended division of labor:

The crucial point is that the *actual* reality of daily business consists of all *three* types of situations, so not only of the enjoyable "*win-win*" or "*shared value* situations", but also of difficult and "messy" "*dilemma*" and "*contingency* situations". To only cherry-pick the "*win-win* situations", is an abstraction of *actual* reality and thus falls in the category of the "Fallacy of Misplaced Concreteness". To avoid the "Fallacy of Misplaced Concreteness", both economists and ethicists will have to learn to live with "messy" realities:

> "As I see it, the economics profession went astray because economists, as a group, mistook beauty, clad in impressive-looking mathematics, for truth. [...] [E]conomists will have to learn to live with messiness." (Krugman 2009)

> "What is important is that practical problems, unlike the idealized thought experiments of the philosophers, are typically ‚messy'. They do not have clear-cut solutions." (Putnam 2004/2005: 28ff.)

6.3.2 "Creating Shared Value" and the Ontology of the Moral Dimension

My main criticism of Porter and Kramer's concept comes out of the fact that they simply presuppose the "compliance with ethical standards", and thus presuppose the moral integrity as a prerequisite for their approach. While doing so, they

[40] Porter (2012), 00:07:37 min. This term in itself shows that Porter and Kramer work with a caricature of "Corporate Social Responsibility" which they only build up as a "straw man" (Beschorner 2013: 109).

externalise the *moral*-economic challenge. This externalisation naturally leads to a *subjectivisation* of moral demands: Porter and Kramer are leaving the moral-economic problems to the individual *subjects*, mainly the managers. This strategy of *subjectivising* morals rests, from the point of view of my "Business Metaphysics" on a metaphysical error regarding the ontological status of the logic of modern ethics, the ethical *logic of impartiality*, which, in my opinion, is *not* "ontologically *subjective*", but "ontologically *objective*".

The differentiation between "ontologically *subjective*" und "ontologically *objective*" is of decisive importance for the argument of this paragraph. I adopt this useful term differentiation from the philosopher John Searle (Searle 1995/1996; 2010/2011). Searle developed a concept called "Social Ontology" – which he considers to be a part of "the metaphysics of [...] social relations." (Searle 1995/1996: 3) In general, ontology deals with the question of what the big categories of existence are, in short: "ontology (what exists)" (Searle 1998/1999: 5). Traditionally, there are three categories: the *physical* (atoms, molecules, stones, bodies, planets, galaxies etc.), the *mental* (minds, thoughts etc.) and the *abstract* (numbers, logic etc.) ones. On the back of this differentiation, Searle adds one more category to these traditional ones: the category of the "*social*".

> "[T]he puzzling character of social ontology is [...] an apparent paradox in our understanding of social reality. We make statements about social facts that are completely objective [...]. And yet, though these are *objective* statements, the facts corresponding to them are all created by human *subjective* attitudes. An initial form of the paradox is to ask, How is it possible that we can have factual *objective* knowledge of a reality that is created by *subjective* opinions?" (Searle 2010/2011: ix)

A typical example of this "Social Ontology" is money: money is something that does not occur naturally, but was created by us humans, i.e. by human *subjects* (out of nothing) – but money is nevertheless an *objective* reality.

> "[A] type of phenomenon is money only if we think it is money [...], only if it is accepted as money." But: "How can there be an objective reality that is what it is only because we think it is what it is?" (Searle 1998/1999: 112f)

Money *objectively* is money because we *subjectively* think it is money. More precisely: Social entities like money are "*ontologically subjective*" ("we *think* it is money"; "it is accepted as money") but "*epistemically objective*" (it "is money").

We do not have to go further into this riddle of "Social Ontology" at this point. Within the framework of this paper only the combination of the terms "*ontologically*" and "*epistemically*" as well as the combination of "*subjective*" and "*objective*" are of interest. In Table 6.4 I apply these combinations of terms to the *economic* and *moral* dimensions of business and examine how these two dimensions are reflected in three different conceptualizations: in Porter and Kramer's concept of "Creating Shared Value", in Josef Wieland's concept of "Governance Ethics" and in my own concept of "Business Metaphysics".

If we apply these distinctions to the view on the *economic* and *moral* dimension of the operative management (daily business) in three distinct concepts of Business Ethics, we acquire the following table (in my view):

Table 6.4 The ontology of economic and moral dimension of business

	"Creating Shared Value"	"Governance Ethics"	"Business Metaphysics"
***Economic* dimension**			
Ontologically...	Subjective	Subjective	Subjective
Epistemically...	Objective	Objective	Objective
***Moral* dimension**			
Ontologically...	Subjective	Subjective	Objective
Epistemically...	Subjective	Objective	Objective

If we look at first at the *economic* dimension of daily business, we can see that there is a consensus between the three conceptualizations. All three conceptualizations explain the *economic* dimension as

- "*Ontologically subjective*": the system of modern capitalism (markets; competition; money; firms etc.) is not a natural ("ontologically objective") thing, but our invention ("we *think* that ... "), and as
- "*Epistemically objective*": there *is* market competition, this *is* indeed money, it's objectively true that this firm *is* a firm and so on.

This consensus however dissolves when we look at the *moral* dimension. Regarding this, the three conceptualizations have different positions.

(a) The problem of the *ontology* of the moral dimension is about the question as to whether this moral dimension is an *invention* of humankind (which would make it "ontologically subjective") or whether the moral dimension is, at least in some ways, something that we do not simply make up, but that we *discover* as something that is objectively given.

(b) In relation to *epistemology* it is about the question as to whether – first option – the moral dimension is an *objective* part of the situation with which managers are confronted in daily business, and thatv they should therefore, if they are competent, be able to *recognize* this moral dimension which can *objectively* be seen (and can be dealt with, too), or whether – second option – a moral dimension of the situation *does not have to be recognized* because it does *not objectively* belong to the given situation and hence the business of executives can limit itself to creating "value" – "economic value and/or "societal value") – without having to take into account moral "values".

1. "*Creating Shared Value*" (Porter and Kramer).

(a) *Ontology*. In relation to the *ontology* of the moral dimension the difficulty is here, that Porter and Kramer are not explicitly dealing with the moral dimension or *moral* values as such (the terms "moral" or "morality" do not appear at all, the term "ethical" only appears twice). Solely the term "*societal* value" (Porter/Kramer 2011:67)[41] is used. Therefore, we can conclude that Porter and Kramer categorize

[41] Porter and Kramer (2011: 67) "Companies can create economic value by creating societal value."

moral values as "ontologically *subjective*", as they are *subjective* values or preferences of the members of *society*.

(b) *Epistemology*. As discussed earlier, the concept "*presumes* compliance with the law and ethical standards" (Porter and Kramer 2011: 75). The whole issue of moral values is outsourced into the preliminary stages of the conceptualization so that, *within* the strategy of "Creating Shared Value", it is only about producing *economic* value and "*societal* value". Genuine *moral* values do not play a role here anymore – and they do not cause a disturbance either. Rather, the whole task of executives can be reconstructed by using the *economic* premise of *self-interest*:

> "Creating shared value [...] is [...] *self-interested* behavior to create economic value by creating societal value." (Porter and Kramer 2011: 77)

So, *within* the concept of "Creating Shared Value" the moral dimension of the *moral*-economic management problem is ignored because the concept simply leaves this problem to the individual *subjects*, that is to the executives. (Crane et al. 2014b: 152) The moral dimension is epistemically categorized as a purely subjective matter ("epistemically *subjective*").

2. "*Governance Ethics*" (Josef Wieland).

(a) *Ontology*. In Wieland's "Governance Ethics" the moral dimension is conceptualized clearly as "ontologically *subjective*". Moral values are not discovered but created or invented by human *subjects*:

> "From the standpoint of Governance Ethics it is the task of philosophy to create normatively justified values and guiding principles for society, to stockpile them and to feed them into social discourses." (Wieland 2014: 99) So: "Values are *statements* about what is desirable and are part of the moral culture of a society [...]. They express what is valued in a society". (Wieland 2014: 162)

Values are a *creation* or an invention of mankind. Moral values are values because people *think* that certain things are ethically desirable. The moral dimension of a management problem is also seen as "ontologically *subjective*". This is different, however, for the epistemic dimension:

(b) *Epistemology*. According to Wieland, a good executive has to have the ability to recognize or to perceive the moral dimension as an *objective* or inherent feature of the genuine management problem:

> "[M]orality [...] should not only be conceived of as [...] generated externally, from outside the economy. It should also be seen as one (and only one) of the elements of decision programmes on resources internal to the economic organization, which, in its allocational effects, must be set in relationship to the other logics, for example the economic or legal logics of the company." (Wieland 2014: 11)

As a result, an effective management requires the capability of (what Wieland calls) "*polylinguality*".

"[P]olylinguality is the essence of leadership excellence." (Wieland 2014: 11)

The moral as well as the economic or legal logics are conceived as "epistemically objective" features of the genuine management problem.

3. "*Business Metaphysics*" (my own research program).

(a) *Epistemology*. The concept of "Business Metaphysics" completely agrees with Wieland's "Governance Ethics" in relation to the "*epistemological objectivity*" but disagrees with regard to the *ontology* of the moral dimension.

(b) *Ontology*. "Business Metaphysics" claims that the logic of *modern* ethics, the ethical logic of impartiality, is *not* "ontologically *subjective*", but "ontologically *objective*". This requires a more lengthy explanation, and a philosophical or metaphysical justification.

To anticipate a potential misunderstanding first, I would like to point out in advance that the following is *not* about some *specific* moral demands, which, say, a "God" has arbitrarily commanded to humankind and to which he now demands obedience (for example to sacrifice Isaac, to stone adulteresses, or to crash planes into the World Trade Center). Such contingent demands would be precisely "ontologically *subjective*", because a *subject* – in this case admittedly a divine subject, but nevertheless a *subject* – is the originator of the arbitrary moral demand. What the following is about, is the logic of modern ethics, that is the *ethical logic of impartiality*. Now, the standard view concerning modern ethics holds that the logic of morality is a human *invention* – "ontologically *subjective*" and *not* an *objective* "part of the fabric of the world" (Mackie 1977/1990: 24). The representatives of the ethical mainstream assume that there is *no objectively* existing ethical logic, and thus *no discovery* of an *objective* moral "truth" either. The philosopher John Leslie Mackie writes concisely:

> "There are no objective values." (Mackie 1977/1990: 15)

Thus, the subtitle of Mackie's book also speaks of "*Inventing Right and Wrong*". Equally concisely, the expert on the theory of justice John Rawls informs us:

> "[T]here are no moral facts." (Rawls 1980: 519)

The physicist and Nobel Prize winner (1979) Steven Weinberg accordingly sees things like this:

> "*There is a moral order*. It is wrong to torture children. And the reason it is wrong to torture children is *because* I say so. And I don't mean much more than that. I mean that not only I say so, John says so, probably most of us say so. But it's *not a moral order out there*. It is something we *impose*." (Weinberg 1999)

The (double) message of Weinberg's is, accordingly: The universe "out there" is *objectively without* meaning or moral logic. The only ones who are able to bring a "moral order" into the world are we ourselves ("because *I* say so"; "most of *us* say so"; the "moral order [...] is something *we* impose").

I would like to defend the thesis now that this position of the authors named above is only half the truth. Granted, Weinberg is completely right when he points out that we – and we alone – are the ones being able to balance the reasons for and against, and that it is also us who then have to formulate moral sentences and who have to agree on moral game rules. But at the same time – and this is the thesis here – there is an *objective logic of the moral discourse*, an *objective logic of impar-*

tiality, because it is *not* up to us to impose any ethical *logic* we want. The logic of modern ethics, the *logic of impartiality is ontologically objective*. To put it more philosophically: I agree with Weinberg's "because I say so" in an *epistemological* sense, but *not* in an *ontological* sense.

Well, what is more I draw here on a – in my view – remarkable book: "*The View from Nowhere*", written by the philosopher Thomas Nagel (Nagel 1986). This book is about a single, but very comprehensive problem, the problem of "*objectivity*".[42] Finally, it is a book on the possibility of scientific *objectivity* and *objective truth* in science and in ethics.

(a) *The "objective" point of view in natural sciences*. To illustrate this point just with a small example, I go back to a problem that was topical at the beginning of the Early Modern Era: whether the sun orbits the earth, or rather the earth orbits the sun. When we watch a sunrise, we get a very clear *subjective* impression: the sun moves while the earth remains completely still. Judging from this *subjective* impression the conclusion is that the sun orbits the earth! When we now try to *transcend* this narrow subjective view and take a broader perspective – for example a point of view at a certain distance to our solar system – then we can establish that our first subjective impression deceived us and that, in truth, the earth orbits the sun. This *broadened* point of view is more "objective" than the first subjective impression.

> Objectivity "requires a detachment from particular perspectives and transcendence of one's time and place." (Nagel 1986: 186f)

(b) *The "objective" point of view in ethics*. The logic of the ever greater objectivity applies, according to Nagel, also to ethics:

The problem of objectivity "is the most fundamental issue about morality". (Nagel 1986: 3)

This point of view, to see the ethical problem as a problem of ever greater objectivity, is not new. It stands for the *modern* view of ethics in general. It would be possible, of course, to refer the reader to Immanuel Kant at this point. But as my paper deals with an economic concept, I would like to quote the classic of early economics: the moral philosopher Adam Smith. This is because it is possible to see Smith's figure of the "impartial spectator" as a conceptional predecessor of Nagel's "View from Nowhere". Smith wrote:

> "We endeavour to examine our own conduct as we *imagine* any other *fair and impartial spectator* would examine it [...] placing ourselves in his situation" (Smith 1759/1790/2009: 133)

When we construe this theory of the "*impartial sympathetic spectator*" or "ideal observer theory" a bit more formally, it can be described as follows:

---

[42] "This book is about a single problem: how to combine the perspective of a particular person inside the world with an objective view of that same world, the person and his viewpoint included. It is a problem that faces every creature with the impulse and the capacity to transcend its particular point of view and to conceive of the world as a whole. Though it is a single problem, it has many aspects." (Nagel 1986: 3).

> "The main idea is that ethical terms should be defined after the pattern of the following example: 'x is better than y' means 'If anyone were, in respect of x and y, fully informed and vividly imaginative, impartial, in a calm frame of mind and otherwise normal, he would prefer x to y'." (Brandt 1959: 173)

The view of this "impartial sympathetic spectator" is an *objective* one. Of course, in Smith's theory this "Spectator" is a *fictitious* figure ("as we *imagine*" this spectator), but his ethical *logic* is *objectively* given. Smith puts this a bit more poetically:

> "[…] the supposed impartial spectator […]. If we place ourselves completely in his situation, if we really view ourselves with his eyes […], his voice will never deceive us. We shall stand in need of no casuistic rules to direct our conduct." (Smith 1759/1790/2009: 268)

If we really *could* "view ourselves with his eyes", if we really *could* hear the voice of this fictitious figure, then his voice would "never deceive us", that is: this voice would speak the *truth* – the *objectively* given *moral truth of impartiality*. We are *not* this person, and we *cannot really* take on his comprehensive point of view, but the *direction* in which our imagination of the ethical logic must lie is *objectively* given.

The view of this "impartial sympathetic spectator" is Thomas Nagel's "*View from Nowhere*" (insofar as this view is an ethical one):

> "What really happens in the pursuit of objectivity is that a certain element of oneself, *the impersonal or objective self*, which can escape from the specific contingencies of one's creaturely point of view, is allowed to predominate." (Nagel 1986: 9)

Nagel's "impersonal or objective self" has the same function in ethics as Smith's "impartial spectator".

> "[E]thics [...] requires a detachment from particular perspectives and transcendence of one's time and place." (Nagel 1986: 186f)

This so-called "transcendence" is Nagel's "View from Nowhere" – "from *nowhere*" because for Nagel as a self-declared atheist there is actually no "God" viewing the universe from "*somewhere* above". And so, the "View from Nowhere" is not a real person, but only the given *logic of ethical objectivity*.[43]

> "Objectivity is the central problem of ethics. Not just in theory, but in life." (Nagel 1986: 138)

> "We begin with a partial and inaccurate view, but by stepping outside of ourselves and constructing and comparing alternatives we can reach […] a higher level of objectivity." (Nagel 1986: 140)

[43] Although the ethical validity of this theory does not, therefore, depend on the actual existence of a *real* ideal observer – or "*ideal feeler*" (Griffin 2001: 316) –, theistic ethics holds, *ontologically*, the "notion of God, which is simply the ideal observer regarded as actual." (ibid.: 314 f) So, in a theistic universe, God is the actual representation of the moral ideals.

According to Nagel this logic of impartiality – the logic of the "View from Nowhere" – is *objectively* real.[44] It is not up to us to impose any ethical logic we want – just like the logic of mathematics:

> "[I]t seems that we're not free to impose any mathematics or any logic we want." This "isn't something we can just make up or decide." (Putnam 1979: 238)

If things are in ethics like they are in mathematics, then, in both cases a non-arbitrary logic is *objectively given* which can be labelled as "*normative realism*":

> "Normative realism is the view [...] that there are reasons for action, that we have to discover them". (Nagel 1986: 139)

The logic of impartiality is precisely *different* to, say, musical creations: Johann Sebastian Bach created "*Die hohe Messe in h-moll*" and The Beatles created "*Penny Lane*" – but they could just as easily have done otherwise. Maybe mankind invented numbers (I doubt it) – but as soon as some numbers had been invented, the *logic* of numbers was *objectively* given. There were no choices left to make.[45] This is the case, too, with the ethics of impartiality. It is therefore not surprising that this ethical logic of impartiality is still presupposed by all major contemporary ethical concepts. For example, the "original position" with its "veil of ignorance" (in John Rawls' "Theory of Justice" or in John Harsanyi's utilitarianism) is actually an equivalent of this "ideal observer" or the "View from Nowhere".[46]

Hypothesis VI: The logic of modern ethics – the logic of the "impartial spectator" (Adam Smith) or the "View from Nowhere" (Thomas Nagel) – is ontologically *objective* ("moral realism"; "normative realism"). In other words: This logic of *modern* ethics has the structure of a hypothetical "*God Simulation*".

Two more remarks on my term "*God Simulation*":

(a) The term "God" is used here independently of the question as to whether such a God does indeed exist, or whether he does not. In our context, this "God" or "impartial spectator" is used as a *fictitious* figure, which signifies only the *methodology* of the logic of impartiality: precisely Nagel's "detachment from particular perspectives and transcendence of one's time and place". (b) All we can do is a "*God Simulation*". Theists (like me), too, have no other option than to decide for *themselves* whether a moral norm can be seen to be fair and impartial or *not*. They, too, do not "own" moral truth with certainty (as they are not "God") and have to posit

---

[44] In response to John Leslie Mackie's "argument from queerness", that "objective values [...] be entities [...] of a very strange sort" (Mackie 1977/1990: 38), Nagel insisted repeatedly "that realism about value is not a metaphysical postulation of extra entities or properties" (Nagel 2012: 105).

[45] This was Karl Popper's view: "[M]en may have invented the natural numbers [...]. But the existence of prime numbers [...] is something we discover." (Popper 1974/2002: 216) So, even if numbers are an invention (according to Popper), the "[l]ogical relations [*e.g. between numbers*] [...] are [...] timeless" (ibid: 216). In contrast to Popper, I do think that we not only discover the logical relations between numbers, but we also *discovered* the natural numbers themselves – not as Platonic ideas (as ultimate actualities), to be sure, but as a realm of *possibilities*.

[46] See Rawls (1971: 185ff.) But, in contrast to Rawls, I don't think that a rational and impartial spectator necessarily leads to utilitarianism.

hypotheses – like everyone else, too – *themselves* on what is morally acceptable and what is *not.*[47] I am thus not asserting objectivity in an epistemic sense. None of us "owns" moral truth with certainty after all, and so I explicitly agree with Weinberg's "because I say so" (cited above) in an *epistemological* sense. But I disagree *ontologically*. This is why "Business Ethics" categorises the ontological status of the moral dimension in Table 6.4 as "*objective*".

6.3.3 "Creating Shared Value" as Supernaturalistic "Theology"

Porter and Kramer are promoting a "magic of capitalism" that is allegedly "Moving B*eyond* Trade-Offs".

> By "Moving Beyond Trade-Offs" (Porter and Kramer 2011: 74) the "concept of shared value resets the boundaries of capitalism" (Porter and Kramer 2011: 77) and promises a 'win-win' world of a "reinvent[*ed*] capitalism" (Porter and Kramer 2011: 73) that "unleash[*es*] a wave of innovation and growth" (Porter and Kramer 2011: 73). In short: With "Creating Shared Value" "you have the magic of capitalism at work." (Porter 2012)

From the point of view of my "Business Metaphysics" this is a "crypto-theological" promise of a salvation "beyond", of a "supernaturalistic" place where the "magical" capitalism of "Creating Shared Value" could be practiced, if not automatically, then at least unburdened by the "messy" problems of real-world business.

> "At its worst, the 'shared value' concept becomes a kind of Happy Land in Business dream, in which [...] clever managers can always effect a 'win-win' outcome for profit and values. The land of sugar and honey, perhaps, but not the land of real-world business."[48]

This biblical phrase (e.g. Ex 3,8: the promised land "flowing with milk and honey"; by the way: not "sugar", but "milk") reminded me of a theological difference concerning the question of how value creation actually works:

Traditional theism (e.g. Thomas Aquinas) described God as "actus purus" or "summum bonum" and therefore claimed that the transcendent God is the eternal actualisation of all possible value(s).

According to the Process Philosophy of Alfred North Whitehead this concept of traditional theism is mistaken about the way how the actualisation (creation) of value actually works:

> "[I]n abstraction from actuality, the eternal activity is divorced from value. For the actuality [*our universe*] is the [*actual*] value." (Whitehead 1925/1967: 105) Apart from the actual world "God" only includes "all *possibilities* of physical value *conceptually*" (Whitehead 1926/2007: 153).

---

[47] This search for what is ethically right connects them to "all people of good will".

[48] One of the anonymous reviewers for Crane et al. (2014a); cit. Crane et al. (2014b: 153).

So, Whitehead's metaphysical hypothesis concerning the question of how the world of value creation (actualization) works in general, holds that value is not created in paradise or heaven, but only here on earth (or somewhere else within the universe). And the crucial point – as shown in 2.4.1 (5) – is that our universe is a finite world where generally we have to expect a lot of trade-offs. So, in creating value there is no simple "Moving Beyond Trade-Offs".

Hypothesis VII: In real-world business there is no simple "Moving Beyond Trade-Offs" of creating value. Porter and Kramer are promoting a kind of crypto-theological promise of a redemptive supernaturalistic "land of milk and honey" "beyond" the messy problems of real-world business.

References

Andrews, Elmund L. 2005. 'Maestro' leaves stellar record and murky legacy. *International Herald Tribune*, August 26, 13–17.

Beschorner, Thomas. 2013. Creating shared value. The one-trick pony approach. *Business Ethics Journal Review* 1(17): 106–112.

Brandt, Richard. 1959. *Ethical theory. The problems of normative and critical ethics*. Englewood Cliffs: Prentice Hall.

Clark, Gregory. 2007. *A farewell to alms. A brief economic history of the world*. Princeton/Oxford: Princeton University Press.

Commons, John R. 1932/1996. The problem of correlating law, economics, and ethics. In *Wisconsin Law Review* 8: 3–26 (1932). qtd. in: Commons, John R. 1996. *Selected essays*, ed. Malcolm Rutherford and Warren J. Samuels, 453–473. London: Routledge.

———. 1934/2009. *Institutional economics. Its place in political economy*. Vol. 1, 3rd Printing 2009. New Brunswick/London: Transaction Publishers.

Crane, Andrew, Guido Palazzo, Laura J. Spence, and Dirk Matten. 2014a. Contesting the value of "creating shared value". *California Management Review* 56(2): 130–149.

———. 2014b. Reply (to Porter & Kramer). *California Management Review* 56(2): 151–153.

Davies, Paul, and John Gribbin. 1992. *The matter myth. Dramatic discoveries that challenge our understanding of physical reality*. New York/London/Toronto/Sydney: Simon & Schuster.

Descartes, René. 1637/2006. *A discourse on the method of correctly conducting one's reason and seeking truth in the sciences*, translated with an Introduction and Notes by Ian Maclean (Oxford World's Classics). Oxford/New York: Oxford University Press. Original titel: Discours de la méthode.

Friedman, Milton. 1962/1982. *Capitalism and freedom*, Reprint. Chicago/London: The University of Chicago Press.

———. 1970. A friedman doctrine – The social responsibility of business is to increase its profits. *The New York Times Magazine*, September 13, 32–33 & 122–126.

———. 2003. Statement, in the documentary film *The Corporation*, directed by Mark Achbar & Jennifer Abbott, Canada, 0:41:34 – 0:42:01.

———. 2007. The social responsibility of business is to increase its profits. In *Corporate ethics and corporate governance*, ed. Walter Ch. Zimmerli, Klaus Richter, and Markus Holzinger, 173–178. Berlin: Springer.

Greene, Brian. 1999. *The elegant universe. Superstrings, hidden dimensions, and the quest for the ultimate theory*. London: Vintage/Random House.

Green, Brian. 2004. *The fabric of the cosmos. Space, time, and the texture of reality*. New York: Vintage/Random House.
Griffin, David R. 2001. *Reenchantment without supernaturalism. A process philosophy of religion (Cornell studies in the philosophy of religion)*. Ithaca/London: Cornell University Press.
Habermas, Jürgen. 1992. *Post-metaphysical thinking. Between metaphysics and the critique of reason*. Cambridge, MA: Polity Press.
Helin, Jenny, Tor Hernes, Daniel Hjorth, and Robin Holt. 2014. *The oxford handbook of process philosophy and organization studies*. Oxford: Oxford University Press.
Hernes, Tor. 2008. *Understanding organization as process. Theory for a tangled world*. London/New York: Routledge.
Holton, Gerald James. 1973. *Thematic origins of scientific yhought. Kepler to Einstein*, 56. Cambridge, MA/London: Harvard University Press.
Homann, Karl. 2015. Wir sind mit unseren intuitiven Moralvorstellungen noch nicht in der Moderne angekommen (Interview). *Perspektiven der Wirtschaftspolitik* 16(1): 44–54.
James, William. 1909. Final impressions of a psychical researcher. In *Memories and studies*, ed. William James, 72–85. Rockeville, MD: Arc Manor.
Jensen, M.C., and W.H. Meckling. 1976. Theory of the firm: Managerial behaviour, agency costs and ownership structure. *Journal of Financial Economics* 3: 305–360.
Jevons, William Stanley. 1871/1965. *The theory of political economy*, 5th ed., reprinted 1965. New York: Sentry Press.
———. 1981. *Papers and correspondence of William Stanley Jevons*, ed. by R. D. C. Black, Volume VII: Papers on political economy. London: Macmillan.
Keynes, John Maynard. 1936. *The general theory of employment, interest and money*. New York: Harcourt Bracc Jovanovich.
Krugman, Paul. 2009. How did economists get it so wrong?. *The New York Times Magazine*. http://www.nytimes.com/2009/09/06/magazine/06Economic-t.html?_r=1&pagewante=&pagewanted=print. Accessed 18 Feb 2016.
Luhmann, Niklas. 1990. *Ökologische Kommunikation. Kann die moderne Gesellschaft sich auf ökologische Gefährdungen einstellen?* Opladen: Westdeutscher Verlag.
Mackie, John Leslie. 1977. *Ethics. Inventing right and wrong*. London/New York: Penguin.
Nagel, Thomas. 1986. *The view from nowhere*. New York/Oxford: Oxford University Press.
———. 2012. *Mind & cosmos. Why the materialist neo-Darwinian conception of nature is almost certainly false*. Oxford: Oxford University Press.
Newton, Isaac. 1687/1999. *The Principia. Mathematical principles of natural philosophy. A new translation (by I. Bernard Cohen and Anne Whitman, assisted by Julia Budenz)*. Berkeley/Los Angeles/London: University of California Press.
———. 1730. *Opticks or, A treatise of the reflexions, refractions, inflexions and colours of light (first english ed. 1704, latin Translation 1706)*, The fourth edition, corrected. London: William Innys.
———. 2004. *Philosophical writings*, ed. Andrew Janiak *(Cambridge texts in the history of philosophy)*. Cambridge/New York/Melbourne: Cambridge University Press.
Paine, Lynn Sharp. 2000. Does ethics pay? *Business Ethics Quarterly* 10: 319–330.
———. 2003. *Value shift: Why companies must merge social and financial im-peratives to achieve superior performance*. New York/Chicago/San Francisco/et al.: McGraw-Hill.
Peirce, Charles Sanders. 1893–1913/1998. *The essential peirce*. Selected Philosophical Writings, Volume 2 (1893–1913), ed. The Peirce Edition Project, Bloomington/Indianapolis: Indiana University Press.
———. 1960. *Collected papers*. Volumes I – VI (ed. by Charles Hartshorne/Paul Weiss), Cambridge, MA: Harvard University Press.
Popper, Karl R. 1963. *Conjectures and refutations. The growth of scientific knowledge*, 4 edn. London/Henley: Routledge and Kegan Paul.
———. 1974. *Unended quest. An intellectual autobiography*. London/New York: Routledge.
———. 1976. *Unended quest. An intellectual autobiography*. La Salle: Open Court.

Popper, Karl R., and John C. Eccles. 1977/2003. *The self and its brain. An argument for interactionism*. New York: Routledge.
Porter, Michael E. 2011. Rethinking capitalism. *Harvard business review*. http://www.youtube.com/watch?v=LrsjLA2NGTU. Accessed 18 Feb 2016.
———. 2012. Creating shared value (Ideas for change). World Economic Forum. https://www.youtube.com/watch?v=xuG-1wYHOjY. Accessed 18 Feb 2016.
Porter, Michael E., and Mark R. Kramer. 2011. Creating shared value. How to invent capitalism – and unleash a wave of innovation and growth. *Harvard Business Review* 89: 62–77.
———. 2014. A response to Andrew Crane et al.'s article. *California Management Review* 56(2): 149–151.
Price, Lucien. 1954. *Dialogues of Alfred North Whitehead*. Boston: Nonpasreil Book.
Putnam, Hilary. 1979. The philosophy of science. Dialogue with Hilary Putnam. In *Men of ideas. Face to face with fifteen of the world's foremost philosophers*, ed. Bryan Magee, 224–239. New York: The Viking Press.
———. 2005. *Ethics without ontology*. Cambridge/London: Harvard University Press.
Rawls, John. 1971. *A theory of justice*. Cambridge/London: The Belknap Press of Harvard University.
———. 1980. Kantian constructivism in moral theory. *Journal of Philosophy* 77: 515–572.
Rorty, Richard. 1995. Toward a post-metaphysical culture. *The Harvard Review of Philosophy Spring*: 58–66.
Schramm, Michael. 2014a. Business metaphysics. *Forum Wirtschaftsethik* 22: 51–58. http://www.dnwe.de/forum-wirtschaftsethik-online-1-2014.html. Accessed 18 Feb 2016.
———. 2014b. Das Abstrakte und das Konkrete. TTIP aus der Sicht einer Business Metaphysics. *AMOSinternational. Gesellschaft gerecht gestalten. Internationale Zeitschrift für christliche Sozialethik* 8(4): 12–18.
———. 2014c. The social nature of existence. Eine evolutionäre Metaphysik der Solidarität. *Jahrbuch für Recht und Ethik/Annual Review of Law and Ethics* 22: 383–413.
———. 2015a. Die Ethik der Transaktion. Warum eine Business Metaphysics im operativen Management nützlich ist. In *Vom Praktisch-Werden der Ethik in interdisziplinärer Sicht. Ansätze und Beispiele der Institutionalisierung, Konkretisierung und Implementierung der Ethik*, ed. Matthias Maring, 173–191. Karlsruhe: KIT Scientific Publishing.
———. 2015b. Die menschliche Natur "schubsen". Moralökonomisches Anreizmanagement in der behavioral business ethics. In *Wirtschaftsethische Perspektiven*, ed. Reinhard Neck, 228(X): 95-128. Berlin: Duncker & Humblot.
———. 2016. Business metaphysics. Konturen eines Forschungsprogramms. In *Wirtschaftsethische Perspektiven*, ed. Reinhard Neck, 228(XI): 95–128. Berlin: Duncker & Humblot (in print).
Searle, John R. 1996. *The construction of social reality*. London: The Penguin Press.
———. 1999. *Mind, language and society*. New York: Basic Books.
———. 2011. *Making the social world. The structure of human civilization*. Oxford/New York: Oxford University Press.
Sheldrake, Rupert. 2012. *The science delusion. Freeing the spirit of enquiry*. London: Hodder & Stoughton/Coronet.
Smith, Adam. 1759/1790/2009. *The theory of moral sentiments (edited with Notes by Ryan Patrick Hanley; Introduction by Amartya Sen)*. London/New York: Penguin Books.
Vogel, David. 2006. *The market for virtue. The potential and limits of corporate social responsibility*. Washington, D.C.: Brookings Institution Press.
Weinberg, Steven. 1999. *Cosmic q uestions. Steven Weinberg and John Polkinghorne - an Exchange*. www.counterbalance.org/cqinterv/swjp-frame.html. Accessed 18 Feb 2016.
Whitehead, Alfred N. 1925. *Science and the modern world (Lowell Lectures 1925)*. New York: The Free Press.
———. 1926. *Religion in the making. Lowell lectures*. New York: Fordham University Press.

———. 1929/1978. *Process and reality. An essay in cosmology. Gifford lectures delivered in the University of Edinburgh during the session 1927–28 (Corrected Edition, ed. by D. R. Griffin / D. W. Sherburne)*. New York/London: Free Press.

———. 1933. *Adventures of ideas*. New York/London/Toronto/Sydney/Singapore: The Free Press.

———. 1936. *Modes of thought*. New York: The Free Press.

———. 1941. Immortality. In *Essays in science and philosophy*, ed. Alfred N. Whitehead, 60–74. New York: Philosophical Library.

Wieland, Josef. 2014. *Governance ethics. Gobal value creation, economic organization and normativity*. Cham/Heidelberg/New York/Dordrecht/London: Springer.

Wittgenstein, Ludwig. 1953. *Philosophical investigations*. Malden/Oxford: Wiley-Blackwell.

Chapter 7
Creating Shared Value as Institutionalization of Ethical Responsibilities of the Business Corporation as a Good Corporate Citizen in Society

Jacob Dahl Rendtorff

Abstract This article discusses Michael Porter's paradigm of creating shared value (CSV) based on the criticism of corporate social responsibility by Milton Friedman in the perspective of contemporary debates on legitimacy and good corporate citizenship. This is a development of the argument presented by Jacob Dahl Rendtorff concerning the liberal property rights paradigm of business ethics in his book *Responsibility, Ethics and Legitimacy of Corporations* (Responsibility, ethics and legitimacy of corporations. Copenhagen Business School Press, 2009). This article discusses the work that Michael Porter has developed together with Mark Kramer, which can be presented as a strategic approach to business ethics and corporate social responsibility. This work began with Porter's concept of Strategic Philanthropy (The competitive advantage of corporate philanthropy. Reprinted In: Harvard Business School Press (ed) Harvard business review on corporate social responsibility, Harvard University Press, Cambridge, MA, 2003) which became Strategic Corporate Social Responsibility (Harv Bus Rev 84(12):78–92, 2006) and gradually developed into the concept of Creating Shared Value (Harv Bus Rev 89(1):62–77, 2011). We see how Michael Porter integrates the critical perspective on CSR from Friedman in a strategic concept of philanthropy, corporate social responsibility and creating shared value (CSV). Accordingly, the concept of creating shared value should be considered as a development of the ideas of strategic philanthropy and corporate social responsibility in the perspective of capitalism and freedom. At the same time, however, the concept of creating shared value is broader and more oriented towards society and towards the idea of profit-based CSR since it integrates the values of society and business in corporate legitimacy.

J.D. Rendtorff (✉)
Roskilde University, Roskilde, Denmark
e-mail: jacrendt@ruc.dk

J. Wieland (ed.), *Creating Shared Value – Concepts, Experience, Criticism*, Ethical Economy 52, DOI 10.1007/978-3-319-48802-8_7

7.1 Introduction

Socially responsible management concepts like values-driven management, stakeholder value and corporate social responsibility express new demands of legitimacy to businesses in the globalized world economy (cf. Jensen et al. 2013). There is an increased demand to businesses to be socially responsible and integrate values of ethics and responsibility in their businesses. There is an increased pressure for legitimate business in society in order to make social responsibility an increased part of good corporate citizenship in modern democracies (cf. Desjardin 2014). In particular, critical stakeholders are challenging the activities of businesses with their expectations that business corporations not only seek profits but also contribute to the good and well-being of society. Indeed, there has been several theories and understandings of this need of business to contribute to the good of society. In the following, I would like to discuss this approach to business and society with the concept of corporate social responsibility, corporate strategic philanthropy and creating shared value in the analysis of the approach suggested by Milton Friedman, Michael Porter and his colleague Mark Kramer. Here, I develop an argument that I have earlier proposed in my book Responsibility, Ethics and Legitimacy of Corporations (cf. Rendtorff 2009).[1]

I begin by discussing the framework for the economic understanding and approach for this idea of corporate social responsibility. Indeed, we can argue that there is a movement towards integrating ethics, values and social responsibility in the basic concepts of economics (cf. Rendtorff 2010). However, a more moderate suggestion is that this does include a transformation of our economic systems, but continues to be integrated in the neo-classical and transaction cost based concept of economics, including a strategic and economic view of the firm as an institutional arrangement for maximizing economic profits of the business corporation. In this context, we see how Friedman, Porter and Kramer are concerned with seeing the economic view of the firm as superior to any ethical and values-based conception that is external to the management roles, systems and market structures of the particular business corporation. It can be argued that Friedman's famous idea that the "Social Responsibility of Business is to Increase its profits", Porter and Kramer's arguments for strategic philanthropy and strategic social responsibility and the concept of shared value express an attempt to make a symbiosis between economic action and the good and welfare of society. The fundamental question is whether such a symbiosis is possible and how it emerges in terms of a fusion of business

[1] The sections in this article "Milton Friedman's concept of Corporate Social Responsibility" and "Michael Porter's interpretation of Friedman's concept of Corporate Social Responsibility as strategic philanthropy and creating shared value (CSV)" are partly slightly modified and updated versions of the pages on "the liberal property right of business" in the book *Responsibility, Ethics and Legitimacy of Corporations* (Rendtorff 2009: 91ff.). I am grateful to Copenhagen Business School Press for allowing me to use this material.

ethics and economic activity. Accordingly, on the economic basis Porter and Kramer contribute to the definition of corporate social responsibility in a way that expands the company's obligation to shareholders to involve a broader number of stakeholders, including shareholders.

When we talk about the social responsibility of businesses, it means that they have to take into account in business the relation between the corporation and society as a totality (cf. Ims and Pedersen 2015). The social responsibility of business includes its obligation to contribute to the welfare of society at the same time as it takes care of its own interests. It is the obligation of business to protect and improve the welfare of society in its totality. A business corporation does therefore not only have legal and economic obligations, but it has also obligations that go beyond these concerns. The social responsibility of business is to contribute to the improvement and development of society. This integration of corporate social responsibility in a concept of the firm begins with Milton Friedman's conception of the social responsibility of the business corporation as economic responsibility, but at the same time, it moves beyond this concept towards other concept of responsibility, including legal and ethical responsibility (Aras and Crowther 2009). As he defined economic responsibility Friedman emphasized that the social responsibility of business it to produce goods that can be sold on the market according to the principles of the free market. With this, there is the idea that real corporate social responsibility is to be a responsible corporation within the law and ethical custom of society (cf. Friedman 1996). With this idea of economic responsibility within the law and custom of society, we can define the idea of corporate social responsibility as based on the company's ethical responsibility that includes the company's economic responsibility and legal responsibility as the institutional basis for good business in the society. Accordingly, I would like to argue that we could only make sense of the developments of corporate social responsibility as strategic philanthropy and creating shared value as Ethical Responsibilities of the Business Corporation as a Good Corporate Citizen in Society. This means that creating shared value contributes to the institutional exercise of basic responsibilities of legitimacy of the business organization in society. In order to make sense of the concept of corporate social responsibility as creating shared value we therefore argue that it presupposes the ethical idea of respect for basic norms and customs of society including a concern for the common good and legitimacy of ethical business as good corporate citizenship. With this, we argue that idea of creating shared value in order to be meaningful and significant needs to imply a vision of the common good of society. The concept of creating shared value merges strategic philanthropy, corporate social responsibility and creating shared value in the vision of the common good for community. Accordingly, as a good corporate citizen the business contributes to the prosperous development of society for the best welfare for all.

7.2 Milton Friedman's Concept of Corporate Social Responsibility

I think that this ethical dimension can be demonstrated in Milton Friedman's argument if we look more closely into his discussions. Milton Friedman's position of the *Social Responsibility of Business is to Increase its Profits* (1996) is still very much discussed in business ethics and this position is even today understood as an important dimension of business ethics (cf. Rendtorff 2009). In most interpretations it is understood as a strong criticism of business ethics and this is also, what economists like Jensen and Meckling as well as Porter and Kramer continue to see as the most important case of this. I think it could be interesting to interpret this approach not as a refusal of business ethics, but after leaving economic dogmatics aside as kind of justification of an economic approach to business ethics and corporate social responsibility. The deep issue in the discussion of Friedman's position is the problem of whether corporate social responsibility and economic profit maximization represent an oxymoron, given Friedman's statement that the "social responsibility of business is to increase its profits" (Friedman 1996).

Friedman's point of view is a good expression of the neoclassical perception of corporate social responsibility that has long been dominating among the critics of values and ethics in business (Boatright 2003). The basic starting point is a criticism of the cultural and values-driven view of the company as an organic unity of meaning and culture, as Friedman assumes that the company is more than just a legal and economic construction to create economic and earnings and growth. Friedman's skeptical argument is therefore based on the premise that it is completely wrong to ascribe companies as such responsibility. The company is not anything else than a fictitious legal construction, due to different forms of ownership, e.g. sole ownership, partnership, or limited liability company. In the case of a limited liability company, the shareholders have limited liability, i.e. they are only liable for their contribution, while they have left to the practical management of the company to the board and management. Now Friedman emphasizes, that only those individuals who represent the company and not the company as such, may be responsible. It is therefore the board, management, and part owners of a limited liability company, who have overall responsibility. According to Friedman, it is the Executive's fiduciary duties, their important "moral" responsibility to enforce the rights of shareholders, ie to give them the greatest possible profit. If this does not happen, and, for instance, management uses all the money to charity, the company's management is according to Friedman's attitude bordering on the illegal, because it uses money for purposes other than intended. The result is that all talk about social responsibility can be considered a subversive doctrine, where the company is politicized in the direction of the "pure socialism".

Now you could argue that the money are used in the shareholders' long-term interest and thus appears as Long-term shareholder value because the socially responsible business is expected to achieve greater acceptance and trust of the community, ensuring the company's survival in the long term. In this Friedman so far agrees, but the argument according to him, adds nothing new in relation to the general economic understanding of the company, since it just expresses that social responsibility can be economically feasible.

Although such a strategic and economical approach to social responsibility can be seen as alluring, it is controversial whether profit maximization can be ethical. The argument for this is a utilitarian cost-benefit analysis in which it is argued that utility maximization ensures production of the best products at the cheapest price. Profit maximization occurs taking into account consumers and society and therefore it is ethically acceptable. Being socially responsible is simply an integral part of this profit maximization, and there is no economic news or theoretical innovation in the case of corporate social responsibility. The problem is that Friedman's defense of the relationship between social responsibility and the company's regular financial obligations is in danger of becoming meaningless. In a backward-looking perspective, the thesis of profit maximization is in danger of becoming a tautology when the profit and economic consequences only will be deduced later, since the most profitable per. definition also always is that which was found to be the most profitable according to the prediction. On the other hand, Friedman may be right that there are costs associated with social responsibility. Both administration and staff, reporting and auditing of financial statements and reports, development of codes of ethics and other matters can be quite expensive. It is therefore important to think through the economic consequences of work with programs of social responsibility.

Today, it is difficult not to be confronted with the seemingly oxymoronic relationship of social responsibility and profit maximization, which Friedman pointed out. It is, however, still possible to ask the critical question: What really is left when Friedman's position is examined more closely? Here, one interpretation is that Friedman makes a sharp division between economics and ethics and social responsibility. But another interpretation is that Friedman manages to integrate economics, ethics and social responsibility in his idea that the social responsibility of business is to increase profit maximization. Thomas Carson argues that Friedman's position is internally inconsistent when submitted to further scrutiny (cf. Carson 1993). Carson analyzes how the idea that the "obligation of business [is] to maximize its profits while engaging in open and free competition without deception or fraud" is cited differently in *Capitalism and Freedom* (Friedman 1962) than in "The Social Responsibility of Business is to Increase its Profits". In the latter publication, Friedman's position, according to Carson, is that "business executives are obligated to follow the wishes of shareholders (which will generally be to make as much money as possible) while obeying the laws and the 'ethical customs' of the society" (cf. Carson 1993: 3). In the former statement, emphasis is put on "open and free competition," while in the latter it is emphasized that the corporation should maximize profits following the laws and respecting the ethical customs of society. Carson argues that avoiding fraud and deception does not amount to the same thing as respecting ethical and legal norms.

In *Capitalism and Freedom*, Friedman does not integrate his concept of profit maximization (and creating shared value) into respect for ethics and law. In fact, this difference leads Carson to argue that Friedman's position in *Capitalism and*

Freedom is inconsistent with the position of the article, because the first statement says nothing about ethical custom while the second position integrates ethical custom in the limits of profit maximization, in a way that it explicitly states that profit maximization cannot happen contrary to ethical custom (Carson 1993: 11). The inconsistency in the second formulation, regarding the early libertarian position, implies an opening in Friedman's concept. It allows for some integration of ethics and economics, because Friedman says that legitimate profit maximization (as creating shared value) respects the laws and ethical custom of society. Consequently, it may be argued that the change in his position moves the liberal concept of business ethics away from a purely libertarian conception to one that implies an openness towards ethical and legal market constraints. From this point of view, Friedman can be seen as saying that after stockholders only corporations have obligations to their stockholders and that corporate social responsibility – if not conducted strategically for the benefit of the firm – may be considered to be illegitimate. This limitation on corporate social responsibility in the second formulation does not, however, exclude respect for business ethics and legal rules. In contrast to the libertarian position in *Capitalism and Freedom*, the idea that "the social responsibility of business is to increase its profits" (cf. Friedman 1996) is based on a fundamental ethical and moral conception of business, because open and free competition not only shall refrain from fraud and deception, but also always respect ethical custom and laws in society.

When Friedman argues that business executives should not give money to social objectives because it would violate the basic economic aim of the corporation, this is still respecting the laws and ethical custom of society. Seen from this angle, it becomes possible to argue that there is an ethical core in Friedman's article that is very close to the Protestant work ethic. Friedman can easily agree to basic ethical principles and duties while proposing the economic argument that the goal of corporate social responsibility is to increase profits (Carson 1993: 16). This ethical limitation of the economic activities of the firm does not support the argument that Friedman has his own position in business ethics; rather, he uses liberal and utilitarian arguments inspired by Adam Smith and neoclassical concepts of economic action (Carson 1993: 13). However, this is a shortcoming of the theory. By presupposing that the consequences of profit maximization are exclusively good, he neglects to discuss its negative potentiality. This premise of the argument requires further justification and a more developed ethical framework.

However, an ethical interpretation of Friedman's position may be a view that the honest businessperson is somebody who maximizes profits while at the same time respecting the ethical custom of society. Here we can talk about voluntary self-regulation of the responsible business as a good corporate citizen. The business as a good corporate citizen contributes to social responsibility by ensuring that profit maximization and the activities of the business respects the activities of society. In this way, a specific corporation contributes to the development of social and political responsibility at the general level of society. Accordingly, profit maximization is seen in close connection with the maximization of the good of society. This implies a broader concept of profit maximization that is put forward by most interpreters of Friedman's position in business and economics.

However, the obsession with profit maximization as the major economic responsibility of business haunts the followers of Friedman's conception of social or moral responsibility of business. More recently, authors like Michael Porter, Mike Kramer, Michael Jensen, and William Meckling have defended positions that are somewhat similar to the views of business ethics proposed by Friedman (cf. Friedman 1996). Jensen, for one, has persistently argued that corporate social responsibility is not compatible with the concept of the firm as an agent for the shareholders. He thinks that this idea destroys the original purpose of the firm and makes market economics inefficient (cf. Jensen and Meckling 1976).

7.3 Michael Porter's Interpretation of Friedman's Concept of Corporate Social Responsibility as Strategic Philanthropy and Creating Shared Value (CSV)

Michael Porter, the "grand old man" of strategy, tries for the last 10–15 years to use Friedman's approach to integrate corporate social responsibility and strategic management. Porter was in many years one of the most cited business economist on strategy and competitive advantage (Porter 1980). Porter saw it as essential for management to integrate competitive advantage in strategic planning (Porter 1987). Porter's theory of business is about the competitive forces that shape strategy (Porter 2008). Porter's approach to CSR and CSV emerges from this perspective. Porter started his approach to this debate with an argument about better economic use of corporate philanthropy (cf. Porter and Kramer 2003). With Kramer, his colleague, Porter argues that corporate philanthropy is in decline and that it is necessary to justify charitable expenditures in terms of bottom-line profits. As an example of this unreflective attitude to corporate philanthropy, the American tobacco company Philip Morris once used seventy-five million dollars on charitable contributions and hundreds of millions on an advertising campaign for their charitable contributions (cf. Porter and Kramer 2003: 29).

Quoting Friedman, Porter and Kramer argue that the corporation is an instrument of the stockholders who own it, and that its social responsibility is to increase profits. They discuss whether Friedman is right in saying that corporate philanthropy is a waste of money. They also argue that Friedman distinguishes between social and economic objectives and they assume that corporations are better than individual donors at addressing social objectives (cf. Porter and Kramer 2003: 31). They argue that corporations can use charitable giving to improve their competitive context and, contrary to Friedman, that charitable donations can improve long-term business prospects. This could be called *context-focused* philanthropy. Porter and Kramer attempt to abandon the separation between the company and society, which was still the point of view of Friedman, and consider companies to operate as a part of society. Competitiveness depends on productivity, which depends on good workers, good information and infrastructure, and the size of the local market (cf. Porter and Kramer 2003: 33).

Operating within Friedman's perspective of profit maximization but taking a critical stance against his separation of economics and society, Porter and Kramer argue that there may be a convergence of interest between pure business and pure philanthropy (cf. Porter and Kramer 2003, 33f). Competitive context has become more critical. Corporations are, therefore, dependent on local partnerships and more collaboration between suppliers and customers is needed.

Porter and Kramer refer to the four elements of the competitive context that is described in Porter's earlier work on competition and competitive strategy. According to the theory of competitive advantage, there is a cluster of elements that influences competitive advantage: local context of strategy and rivalry; demand conditions of customers and market segments; factor conditions of human resources, capital resources, and physical infrastructure; and related and supporting industries, local suppliers, and companies (cf. Porter and Kramer 2003: 36). Through corporate philanthropy, the company can purportedly improve its competitive context and long-term prospects by developing a better physical infrastructure, improving the sophistication of local customers, helping local societies with policies for more transparent and fair competition, and by helping suppliers perform better. In this context, Porter and Kramer emphasize that corporate philanthropy is more than public relations. In order to be efficient, corporate philanthropy should be much more focused on "the right causes in the right way." (cf. Porter and Kramer 2003: 52). Companies should adopt a context-focused approach of collaboration with local partners. Porter and Kramer argue for the need to focus strategies of giving based on an examination of the competitive context, and for the evaluation of philanthropic activities, potential new initiatives, partners, and results. Only in this way can companies, following Friedman, add significantly more value than individual donors (cf. Porter and Kramer 2003: 59).

In fact, this concept of philanthropy considers it from a purely economic and strategic perspective, which implies that Porter and Kramer do not really have a view on right and wrong in terms of principled business ethics. Along with Friedman, they are concerned with value creation and profit maximization; however, while Friedman remains within a somewhat skeptical liberal position regarding corporate social responsibility or corporate philanthropy as win-win situations for both business and society, the evocation of partnerships and mutual interdependence between business and society in corporate philanthropy prompts Porter and Kramer to consider this position with concern for welfare economics (i.e., common value creation of the greatest good to the greatest number).

Even though Porter and Kramer say that they do not agree with Friedman that corporate philanthropy is a waste of money, they rely on the strategic view of the firm combined with a utilitarian ethics based on the idea of profit maximization as the motive for corporate philanthropy. A fundamental problem with this position is that Porter and Kramer consider philanthropy and corporate social responsibility from a limited perspective of profit maximization. They, like Friedman, end up dismissing fundamental ethical problems with the aims of corporations in society. The question is whether Porter and Kramer refuse business ethics or simply do not see it as an important topic for this discussion. In fact, this view does not exclude a deeper foundation of corporate social responsibility in business ethics and the need for republican business ethics in order really to understand the role of corporations in society.

Porter and Kramer mention the donations of the Grand Circle travel company, which organizes cultural and historical travel for older American (Porter and Kramer 2002/2003: 44). This company has given generously to historical preservation projects, including protection of the State Museum of Auschwitz-Birkenau in Poland, so that the museum could be improved. This donation was a direct consequence of the interest of the travel company in having good sites for their customers to visit. Porter and Kramer mention this example as a kind of win-win situation of corporate philanthropy, because both company and museum get advantages out of the donations. This is, however, a perfect example of the limitations of crude utilitarianism because the ethically concerned Kantian may ask whether it is moral to be so focused on earning money from the Auschwitz tragedy. Accordingly, this example shows intuitively how the economic concept of corporate philanthropy cannot stand alone, but must be evaluated in terms of basic ethical principles in business ethics.

A further application of the concept of corporate social responsibility as strategic CSR renewing the concept of corporate philanthropy is found in another article by Porter and Kramer, in which the authors seem to be hostile to business ethics as the moralization of a firm's CSR activities (cf. Porter and Kramer 2006). The authors acknowledge that CSR has become an evitable element of business and that companies are pressured to think of CSR as a generic element of corporate strategy. However, the authors also argue that prevailing concepts of corporate social responsibility are fragmentary and not very strategy oriented. The authors want to conceive the relation between business and society in CSR as one of mutual benefit.

The authors acknowledge that CSR has moved into corporate boardrooms and that companies are compelled to make reports on ethical, social, and environmental risks (Porter and Kramer 2006: 80). Not many corporations seem, however, to have a focused CSR strategy, which necessitates re-evaluation of its prevailing justifications. They mention the *moral* appeal and imperative as something that is predominant in the CSR field. Moral calculus is considered as a method to weigh social and financial benefits (Porter and Kramer 2006: 82). According to Porter and Kramer this ends up at rendering many terms meaningless, for example, the term *sustainability*, this seems to lose its significance in this moral confusion of the CSR debate. Porter and Kramer recognize pragmatic elements in the concept of corporate citizenship as "license to operate." The stakeholder view is considered important, but also as a dangerous opening of the firm's interests to pressure groups. Finally, Porter and Kramer mention the *reputation school* as an approach to CSR that is also confusing. They go on to argue that it is a cliché that corporations should be integrated in society and that there is a close relation between good societies and successful corporations (Porter and Kramer 2006: 83).

What is needed, rather, is focus on creating shared value (CSV), which corporations are required to integrate into their core activities. This concept already emerges as a part of corporate social responsibility as strategic CSR. Porter and Kramer emphasize focus on generic social issues, value chain's social impacts, and interest in the social dimensions of competitive context (Porter and Kramer 2006: 85). CSR activities should be related to the value-chain creating economic value of the company as described with the concepts of strategy and competitive advantage. According to Kramer and Porter, effective corporate citizenship and responsive CSR should be integrated in the firm's value chain, for example by mitigating harm in this value chain (Porter and Kramer 2006: 88). Strategic CSR also moves beyond good corporate citizenship and mitigation of harm in the value chain, because it works for a symbiotic relation between strategy, social responsiveness, and creation of value by integrating inside and outside perspectives on strategy and CSR, and because it acknowledges that there is a social dimension to the value chain (Porter and Kramer 2006: 89). The authors end the article by saying that companies should stop thinking about corporate social responsibility, but rather focus on corporate social integration (Porter and Kramer 2006: 92).

What is the ethics in this conception of CSR? It seems confusing that somebody like Porter, who has been so focused on competitive strategy from the economic perspective, is so open to integration between business and society while being still very critical of moralization of the firm. In fact, this concept of strategic CSR is not so far from Friedman's position in the sense that Porter and Kramer now seem to agree that business – in order to be socially integrated – should operate within the legal and ethical customs of society. Nonetheless, this concept still combines self-interest and economic welfare arguments according to which CSR has mutual benefits for corporations and society. As the rhetorical criticism of corporate citizenship shows, Porter and Kramer still seem to work within a single objective conception of the firm, where profit maximization is the most fundamental aim of corporate activities. In this sense, they still represent liberal and utilitarian business ethics. Indeed, it is somewhat depressing that Porter and Kramer do not really recognize the great developments within the tradition of business ethics research of the recent years. In a sense the concept of strategic philanthropy and CSR is blind, deaf and mute in relation to ethical dilemmas and paradoxes of business strategy, and the strategic view of CSR does not move beyond the corporate-centered view of business. In the context of CSR, stakeholder theory and corporate citizenship the research on corporate social responsibility and business models combining strategy, business models and a broader view on corporate citizenship have been developed.

In the article about creating shared value Porter and Kramer go further with their perspective on corporate social responsibility and the relation between business and society (cf. Porter and Kramer 2011). In a sense, Porter and Kramer are far beyond Friedman because they emphasize the social role of business. In another sense, it can be argued that they still follow Friedman's framework because they argue that capitalism – even if transformed, is essential for value creation of shared value. And maybe, after all, Porter and Kramer end up with the same challenges and paradoxes as Friedman. So maybe the rupture with Friedman is only rhetoric or cosmetic; orienting business towards new profit possibilities in a goodwill industry of good intention for society and environment while doing business as usual behind the beautiful words. This may be the case when the authors argue that the problem of companies today is that they continue to understand profit maximization narrowly in the perspective of the firm without opening for a broader sustainable solution finding shared value for business and society.

Porter and Kramer argue that the principle of shared value implies a way to create economic value that connects the company with the needs and challenges of society (Porter and Kramer 2011: 64). There is a close connection between business and social progress in which shared value is currently argued to go beyond responsibility, philanthropy and sustainability. The paradigm of shared value is presented as a new paradigm of business that even "can give rise to the next major transformation of business thinking" (Porter and Kramer 2011: 66).

The concept of shared value can be defined as policies and operating practices that enhance the competitiveness of a company while simultaneously advancing the economic and social conditions in the communities in which it operates. Shared value creation focuses on identifying and expanding the connections between societal and economic progress. It is interesting that Porter and Kramer argue that the concept of creating shared value rests on "the premise that both economic and social progress must be addressed" (Porter and Kramer 2011). In this sense, companies must get a greater understanding of the basis of company productivity and they should also cross the profit/non-profit boundaries, according to Porter and Kramer. Moreover, this vision of a combination between company and social interests must be supported by government regulation (cf. Porter and Kramer 2011).

With the concept of creating shared value we may see a break with Friedman's economic theory while we still follow its basic intentions of free business in a free society. Society and business become closer connected and the purpose of the corporations is much more creating shared value than profit maximization. With creating shared value innovation and productivity we move towards social legitimacy as the aim of capitalism and business. In this context it is interesting that Porter and Kramer argue that the distinction between profit and non-profit must be blurred and externalities must be internalized. With the sentence "Societal needs, not just conventional economic needs, define markets, and social harms can create internal costs for firms" (Porter and Kramer 2011: 65) we see a redefinition of economic markets based on the needs and values of society and it is argued that business serves society. Accordingly, shared value is about contributing to society by the corporation and it is about how to create a common horizon and value that link together business and society.

Porter and Kramer describe how the creating shared value approach can be applied to different stakeholders and groups of stakeholders of the firm. In particular, there is a focus on redefining productivity in the value chain, involving procurement, energy use and logistics, resource use, procurement and distribution, local cluster development. Kramer and Porter mention companies like Walmart, Nespresso at Nestlé and other companies that contribute to creating shared value while at the same time improving their businesses (cf. Porter and Kramer 2011). Creating shared value means going beyond shareholder value towards improving community while at the same time making money for the business corporation. Indeed, social entrepreneurs, social activists and others contribute to this creation of value for civil society as a part of the strategy of creating shared value (cf. Porter and Kramer 2011).

Porter and Kramer emphasize that creating shared value represents "a broader conception of Adam Smith's invisible hand". This is a kind of self-interested behavior where capitalist companies contribute to the good of society in order to improve their own well-being and legitimacy in this society. With creating shared value, companies focus on social and environmental issues which represent a broader view of capitalism which contributes to the improvement of the social legitimacy of the business corporation. The concept of shared value in this sense implies an argument for a closer connection between corporate strategy and social goods in society, even though shared value is not defined as ultimate social goods but as "benefits relative to costs" (Crane et al. 2014). Creating shared value can be considered as a new way to legitimate business and reshape capitalism and its relation to society as it is presented as a transformational response to the crisis of capitalism. The strength of this idea of creating shared value is that it is easy for business people to understand the concept, just as it was the case with Friedman's concept of profit maximization. Creating shared value is considered as being good for practice and the strategic goals of business as conscious capitalist practice becomes clear. CSV has a potential for big business corporations and is already used by global businesses. However, the weaknesses of the concept of shared value imply that creating shared value ignores the tension between social and economic goals and the concept of creating shared value also seems to be naïve about business compliance and government regulation. And the role of business in society is not quite clear (Crane et al. 2014: 131). Moreover, the concept of CSV ignores much of the literature on business ethics, CSR and stakeholder theory and the achievements of this literature with regard to a business case of CSR and business ethics (Crane et al. 2014: 135). There is not really a kind of room for ethics in CSV because the concept ignores ethical dilemmas related to the tension between ethics and economic goals. The concept only looks at "low hanging fruits" and it ignores the other dimensions of the relation between these different kinds of goals (Crane et al. 2014: 136). Accordingly, it seems that CSV does not want to transform the economic market as such but only implies a kind of logic of business as usual with regard to the development of large international corporations. In this sense CSV becomes a parasitic concept that does not contributes to the transformation of capitalism itself. While looking closer on the concept of CSV and the analysis of the role of business in society related to the concept it can argued that the concept does not really respect the social embeddedness of business in society.

In this sense, the concept does not really break with a corporate centered conception of the economy and we can confirm that Porter's concept is very much an extension of Friedman's initial approach to business and society (Crane et al. 2014: 141). Accordingly, CSV is nothing more than an attempt to reformulate Porter's concept of strategy within the age of CSR, business ethics and political firm, while still insisting of the basic premises of this liberal property rights based view of the corporation while combining it with a utilitarian view of the role of business in society.

This view of business ethics can be put to a number of critical points (cf. Rendtorff 2009). One could argue that individual self-interest and profit maximization combined with reaching "low-hanging fruits" in the paradigm of creating shared value cannot be the ultimate aims of business. While free market theory relies on the assumption that individuals will respect the rules of the free market, in reality many violations of the principles of fair competition occur and government regulation and business compliance moving beyond shared value are needed. An ethics of the market is, therefore, needed to restrict egoistic action and CSV has to be combined with a political view of the firm insisting on the common good in relation to good corporate citizenship. Indeed, business ethics should fight against opportunism and discrimination, and ensure fair competition based on an integrative role of the relation between business and society. This should be a requirement of free market justice (cf. Velasquez 2002). As a social practice being integrated in society, business has definite internal and external boundaries.

Rights to profits are exclusively defined in terms of property rights, which, referring to Marxist criticism, are unequally distributed in a capitalist economy. Furthermore, though property right theory may define the firm in terms of formal and informal contracts; it does not overcome the difference between owners and employees. Profit maximization and creating shared value must be viewed from the perspective that business is a part of a social and cultural reality with specific norms in particular societies, because the view that "business is business", and that morality is internal to the market, is not aware of these structural conditions of legitimate business activities (cf. Rendtorff 2009). Indeed, it can be argued that no theory of profit maximization can escape external constraints, or that profit maximization is only meaningful as a moral duty within social legitimacy.

When we isolate the idea of profit maximization based on the idea of creating shared value, without content, the concept becomes empty. It is always important to ask the question about profit and shared value for what. And profit and shared value for whom? At what time? None of these questions can be answered within objective economic theory and a strategic view of the firm, but instead depend on definitions of human nature, society, and on values and ethical principles; thus, arguments for profit maximization as a metaphysical virtue and life form of Protestant "economic man" presuppose the external view of the common good. In this sense, behind shared value the strategic concept of business based on the concept of creating shared value remains empty and must be accomplished with a broader concept of business ethics and business and society. These external factors require that profit maximization must be justified from the perspective of general social welfare. Consequently, Pareto-optimality and utilitarian welfare policy might deliver the sufficient conditions for coherence of the doctrine of profit maximization. This approach to social welfare seems to undergird the arguments of Porter and Kramer.

It could be argued that concern for short-term shareholder profits should be replaced by long-term profits for the general welfare of consumers and community.

This is not, however, possible on a purely formal basis, or solely based on the conditions of the market. Principles for maximizing community welfare are dependent on social legitimation. Moreover, shareholder value can only be defined as a means of exposing the other stakeholders to long-term profit maximization. This is very far from the originally individualist definition of shareholder value, even though Porter and Kramer stay within the premises of this traditional economic theory of the corporation. Such external limitations of profit maximization signify that even if this principle is constitutive for the economic market, it should always be considered as integrated in other social life forms and practices. Real profit maximization can only be morally legitimate profit maximization and as such, it moves beyond creating shared value, because it requires legitimate social acceptance by participants in society (cf. Rendtorff 2009). It is dependent – from the perspective of the theory of corporate citizenship – on socially defined conceptions of the common good in a Republican state (cf. Rendtorff 2009). This view of business ethics should not be confused with an instrumental ethics or the tautological – some would say oxymoronic – reduction of business ethics to nothing other than a moral investment in good business, where "good ethics is good business" as creating shared value only in order to improve the company's strategic position, image, or public relations. The strategic improvement of external and internal relations might be an important consequence of ethical behavior, but is not the whole and exclusive meaning of the term "business ethics", which is further constituted by reference to external critical reflections on market conditions and conceptions of economic justice.

Business ethics must, therefore, go beyond the concept of strategic philanthropy and strategic CSR as well as creating shared value and be based on the assumption that ethical principles and theories regulating economic behavior cannot be found exclusively inside the rational choice and profit maximization conception. In order to justify a specific structure of economic markets, a broader discussion in the light of different theories of the aims, character, and functions of business as based on good corporate citizenship within political democracy is needed.

7.4 Creating Shared Value (CSV), Institutional Economics and Strategic Stakeholder Management

Accordingly, taking into account the severe criticism of the concept, we can argue that creating shared value is not possible without good corporate citizenship. Moreover, in order to develop this point we need to situate CSR and CSV within the framework of institutional economics. Even though they try to stay within the traditional economic paradigm, possible critical interpretation of Porter and Kramer's turn towards shared value could be that they cannot avoid becoming a part of the movement of institutionalization of business ethics in Europe and USA but also globally. Here we can mention the book *The Moral Dimension. Towards a New Economics* where Amatai Etzioni criticizes the neo-classical economic paradigm. (cf. Etzioni 1988). According to this point of view, profit-maximization and individual utility cannot be the only aim of the economic activity, but in really the economic system is based on a deontological economic paradigm where profit maximization of individuals is built on an illusion. Etzioni emphasizes that there is a social system behind the economics of profit-maximization. The market is a subsystem of the social system. Individuals act in a social system that is not different from the economic system. Human beings stand in a close relation with other human beings in me-though relations and they are at the same time embedded in a large number of social relations. According to Etzioni these social and moral bonds are not destructive fore economic competition but rather a presupposition for good economic interaction, because the economic system cannot be separated from the political and social relations in society (Etzioni 1988: 257).

This is an attempt to be more conscious about the embeddedness of the business in community and see its normative commitment in this light. This also concerns the structurally conditioned presuppositions for the business as a social agent. In order to create shared value we need to develop markets of social responsibility, where there both focus on individual ethics and institutional dimensions of economic interactions (cf. Rendtorff 2009). With this, we can argue that an important dimension of creating shared value is the possibility of introducing values-driven management with concern for both external and internal stakeholders of the business corporation. Accordingly, to create shared value means to go beyond the shareholders towards including a large number of stakeholders in the activities of the firm. To be aware of the concerns of stakeholders, including environmental concerns, social concerns and concern for local community must be an important dimension of creating shared value. Management needs to be responsible, not only to shareholders, but to a wide number of other stakeholders of the business corporation. Therefore, this approach is critical towards a restriction of the business activities only to serve a narrow group of shareholders.

We can say that the quest for creating shared values reminds us of changed conditions for business, which imply that businesses cannot any more be legitimate if they only serve narrow interests of stakeholders (cf. Rendtorff 2011a). As an organizational collective unity and as a legal subject the business firm takes part of a social system with a plurality of interests. Economic profits remains an important bottom-line and we cannot avoid taking into account the economic and legal reality of business when we define business strategy. However, at the same time there is a need to serve the general interest of society and business needs to create shared value. Again, we face the problem of the oxymoron i.e. whether it is possible to create shared value or whether we have to accept an insurmountable contradiction between business ethics and profits. Here we can argue that we only face an oxymoron if we focus too much on individual morality and do not look at the morality of the economic system. In fact, if we look at shared value, not from the point of view on individual morality, but rather from the point of view of social and institutional ethics it may be possible to overcome the oxymoron. Accordingly, by considering creating shared value not only of the perspective of the individual moral manager, but more broadly in relation to institutional roles and market organization, we can more easily give meaning to the idea of combining morals and profits (cf. Boatright 1999).

This institutional approach argues that we need to see creating shared value as a part of the function of the firm at the economic market (cf. Rendtorff 2013). The strategy of creating shared value is not about individual morality but it concerns the rationality of the economic system. We need to see creating shared value from the point of view of philosophy of management (cf. Rendtorff 2014). In such an institutional and structural model of the role of the business firm in society, ethics is not an external rationality of the market, but it integrates in the institutional self-regulation of the economic market. According to this view, creating shared value expresses the institutional responsibility of the business corporation. Social responsibilities of business corporations realize in their institutional actions in the global market system (cf. Rendtorff 2011a, b).

Accordingly, from the point of view of the institutional interpretation, the concept of creating shared value goes beyond the moral manager of individualist business ethics and at the same time, it follows Etzioni's criticism of the neo-classical market economy. Here we consider Porter and Kramer's concept of creating shared value in the perspective of institutional transaction cost economics (cf. Coase 1937) with its view of the firm as economic-legal unit and as a system of formal and informal nexus of contracts based on a complex interaction of bounded rationality, motivation and human dignity (cf. Williamson 1985). In contrast to the business ethics of idealistic moral managers, focusing on the ideal firm as based on a pluralist concept of a wide number of stakeholders, the concept of creating shared value implies a more monist concept of a close relation between ethics, law and economics.

According to the contract theory model of the business firm, the concept of profit maximization remains the basic aim of the firm understood as combination of formal and informal contracts (cf. Williamson 1985). Since a perfect market does not exist, we might refer to reasonable instead of maximal profits. Linking profits and creating shared value may related to the idea of long term value and sustainability so that the strategy of a business corporation does not directly follow the interests of the shareholders but instead searches to minimize risk by following the strategy of creating shared value (cf. Williamson 1975). In Coase's and Williamson's theory of the business firm as a nexus of formal and informal social and legal contracts the business firm is understood as an instrument at the disposal of the shareholders, if they want to be united in an organization with the aim of getting more profit and economic gain. As an organization, the firm is an instrument of the owners in order to act better on an economic market (cf. Williamson 1996).

However, we must admit that the shareholders only can ensure their interests with the best outcome by taking into account other stakeholders such as employees, consumers and local community. Moreover, bounded rationality in terms of motivation and dignity and creating shared value implies that the owners of the business act with other concerns than profit maximization. Therefore, we can integrate stakeholder theory into this combination of the contract view of the firm with the strategy of creating shared value (cf. Bonnafous-Boucher and Rendtorff 2014). The idea of creating shared value makes sense in the perspective of the contract theory since the owners include all stakeholders by minimizing risk, ensure more profit and create shared value for society and the different shareholders of the firm. In this perspective, the combination of creating shared value and institutional contract theory maintains the monistic perspective on the firm while integrating concerns for shareholders and stakeholders. With this ethics integrates with the inclusive concern for the stakeholders, while ensuring a broad dialogue about the future shared value for business and society. Creating shared value presents a kind of ethical reformulation of Adam Smith's invisible hand where the ethical self-regulation of the market contributes to the common good and welfare of community.

A further question in the discussion of CSR and CSV is whether the creating shared value approach fits with strategic stakeholder management. In fact, there is not necessarily an opposition between CSV and stakeholder management and it is possible to integrate the two perspectives on strategic management in common framework. We may argue that CSV is only possible by integrating stakeholder concerns in the strategic management of the firm. In contrast to shareholder management, stakeholder management includes not only shareholders but also all the important stakeholders of the company, including employees, customers, suppliers, local community etc. (cf. Phillips and Freeman 2010). An important founder of stakeholder theory R. Edward Freeman argues that business firms are social institutions who therefore have wider obligations and concerns than only to their shareholders and owners (cf. Freeman 1984/2010). In order to create shared value the manager needs to take into account a plurality of stakeholders. Accordingly, we can argue that the concept of CSV leading to good corporate citizenship based on corporate legitimacy needs to combine stakeholder management with the institutional conception of the firm including a broad variety of stakeholders with more or less formal contracts and conceptions of the business corporation. We can argue that stakeholder theory contributes to situating CSV management in a broader institutional context.

7.5 Creating Shared Value (CSV) in the Framework of Organizational Integrity and Corporate Legitimacy of the Good Corporate Citizen

We have placed the idea of creating shared value that Porter and Kramer have developed from their re-interpretation of corporate philanthropy, corporate social responsibility from the perspective of liberal property rights theory of business ethics, inspired by Friedman, in the perspective of institutional economics and stakeholder theory. On this basis, we will now try to build the bridge between the different perspectives on creating shared value by situating creating shared value in the perspective of the concept of organizational integrity (cf. Rendtorff 2015). In this context, we can define the institutional morality of the firm based on the concept of organizational integrity that we contribute to the business corporation as a responsible organization (cf. Paine 1994a). Lynn Sharp Paine has developed the concept of organizational integrity by emphasizing that integrity implies the wholeness, unity and honesty of commitment of the organization (cf. Paine 1994a). Integrity is important as a moral virtue of commitment and this implies the commitment of the organization to its basic values (cf. Rendtorff 2011b). Integrity means to do the right thing and to be committed with trust and respect. Integrity expresses a moral unity in individual and organizational action, but this is not only a moral notion, but also implies economic integrity committing the organization to its strategy and fundamental aims and goals, as suggested by Michael Jensen in his economic concept of integrity (cf. Rendtorff 2015). With this perspective, we can argue that creating shared value (CSV) as a strategic tool for the organization cannot stand alone, but must be managed with integrity and integrity includes not only moral integrity, but also economic and organizational integrity emphasizing unity, honesty and wholeness in economic and strategic action of the organization. To focus on integrity means that a business corporation is not only focused on rules and duties, but also integrates values and commitments to society in its strategic plans and aims.

In this context, we can emphasize the importance of strategic judgment for developing CSV in the framework of organizational integrity. Here we combine strategic and ethical judgment in developing organizational integrity. Lynn Sharp Paine has developed such a concept of managerial judgment in her work on the relation between law, ethics and managerial judgment (Paine 1994b). Here Paine proposes an ethical approach to management as superior to a pure compliance approach. This ethical approach is aware of the importance of ethical judgment moving beyond pure compliance to rules. We can say that exercise in managerial judgment combines decisions about economic organization, strategies for creating shared values and the ethical dimensions of development of individual and organizational integrity at the institutional framework and level of the organization. Such an awareness of the need for judgment and ethical formulation competency based on organizational integrity mediates between ethics and law without reducing or dissolving one discipline in the other. Managerial judgment aiming at creating shared value in the framework of good corporate citizenship focuses on an ability to understand the complex relation between economic value, societal value and ethics in relation to the respect for the values and interests of the implied stakeholders of the business corporation.

With this ethical interpretation of Porter and Kramer's concept creating shared value (CSV) we also move further to consider this strategic concept of business and society as a contribution to stabilization of the legitimacy of the business corporation in society. The proposed combination of stakeholder theory, institutional economics and the strategy for creating shared value with the idea of organizational integrity contributes to provide a solution to deal with the problems of the establishment of democratic legitimacy of the corporation in late modernity (cf. Habermas 1973/1975). As Habermas suggests we need to translate economic legitimacy into a broader democratic legitimacy in order to meet the demands of society. In this context, the problem of legitimacy becomes a problem of finding the right value foundation for business in order to give it a sustainable place in society. In relation to the business corporation, legitimacy implies both cognitive, normative and pragmatic legitimacy (cf. Suchman 1995). In this framework, creating shared value (CSV) contributes to the pragmatic legitimacy of the firm. Institutional theory and stakeholder theory provide the foundations for cognitive legitimacy and organizational integrity unites the three dimensions in normative legitimacy of the firm. In this sense, the vision of corporate legitimacy as a good citizen corporation complies with the institutional requirements of the market by integrating creating shared value (CSV) into the normative framework of good corporate citizenship.

7.6 Conclusion

This article developed an analysis Michael Porter's paradigm of *creating shared value (CSV)* based on the criticism of corporate social responsibility by Milton Friedman in the perspective of contemporary debates on legitimacy and good corporate citizenship. The idea was to consider Porter's approach as essential for developing corporate citizenship and integrate this approach in institutional economics and stakeholder theory. This was a development of the argument presented by Jacob Dahl Rendtorff as the liberal property rights paradigm of business ethics in his book *Responsibility, Ethics and Legitimacy of Corporations* (cf. Rendtorff 2009). We began by presenting Friedman's position saying that the social responsibility of a business corporation is to increase its profits in the perspective of Friedman's work on capitalism and freedom. On this basis, the article discussed the work that Michael Porter has developed together with Mark Kramer that implies a strategic approach to business ethics and corporate social responsibility. This work began with Porter's concept of Strategic Philanthropy (2003) which became Strategic Corporate Social Responsibility (2006) and gradually developed into the concept of Creating Shared Value (CSV) (2011). We see how Michael Porter integrates the critical perspective on CSR from Friedman in a strategic concept of philanthropy, corporate social responsibility and creating shared value (CSV). Accordingly, the concept of creating shared value is a development of the ideas of strategic philanthropy and corporate social responsibility in the perspective of capitalism and freedom. At the same time, however, the concept of creating shared value is broader and more oriented towards society that the idea of profit-based CSR since it integrates the values of society and business in corporate legitimacy. This was the basis for the analysis of the relation between creating shared value (CSV), institutional Economics and strategic stakeholder management where we have demonstrated how CSV is only efficient within transaction cost economics and stakeholder management. Finally, this lead to the demonstration of the possibility of considering creating shared value (CSV) in the framework of organizational integrity and corporate legitimacy of the good corporate citizen.

References

Aras, Güler, and David Crowther. 2009. *Global perspectives on corporate governance and CSR*. Farnham: Gower Publishing.

Boatright, J.R. 1999. Does business ethics rest on a mistake? *Business Ethics Quarterly* 9(4): 583–591.

———. 2003. *Ethics and the conduct of business*. New Jersey: Prentice Hall.

Bonnafous-Boucher, Maria, and Jacob D. Rendtorff. 2014. *La théorie des parties prenantes*. Paris: Editions La Découverte.

Carson, Thomas. 1993. Friedman's theory of corporate social responsibility. *Business and Professional Ethics Journal* 12(1): 3–32.

Coase, R.H. 1937. The nature of the firm. *Economica* 4(16): 386–405.

Crane, Andrew, Guido Palazzo, Laura J. Spence, and Dirk Matten. 2014. Contesting the value of creating shared value. *California Management Review* 56(2): 130–153.

Desjardins, Joseph R. 2014. *An introduction to business ethics*. New York: McGraw Hill.

Etzioni, Amatya. 1988. *The moral dimension. Towards a new economics*. New York: The Free Press.

Freeman, R.E. 1984/2010. *Strategic management. A stakeholder approach*. Cambridge: Cambridge University Press.

Friedman, Milton. 1962. *Capitalism and freedom*. Chicago: University of Chicago Press.

———. 1996. The social responsibility of business is to increase its profits. (1970) Reprinted In *Beyond integrity. A Judeo-Christian approach to business ethics*, ed. Scott B. Rae and Kenman L. Wong, 241–246. Michigan: Zondervan Publishing House.

Habermas, Jürgen. 1973. *Legitimation crisis*. Boston: Beacon Press.

Ims, K.J., and L.J.T. Pedersen. 2015. *Business and the greater good. Rethinking business ethics in the age of crisis. Studies in transatlantic business ethics*. Cheltenham/Northmaton: Edward Elgar Publishing.

Jensen, M.C., and W.H. Meckling. 1976. Theory of the firm: Managerial behavior, agency costs and ownership structure. *The Journal of Financial Economics* 3(4): 305–360.

Jensen, Inger, John D. Scheuer, and Jacob D. Rendtorff. 2013. *The balanced company: Organizing for the 21st century*. Farnham: Gower Publishing.

Paine, L.S. 1994a. Managing for organizational integrity. *Harvard Business Review* 72(2): 106–117.

———. 1994b. Law, ethics and managerial judgment. *The Journal of Legal Studies Education* 12(2): 153–169.

Porter, M.E. 1980. *Competitive strategy*. New York: Free Press.

———. 1987. From competitive advantage to corporate strategy. *Harvard Business Review* 65(3): 43–59.

———. 2008. The five competitive forces that shape strategy. *Harvard Business Review* 86(1): 79–93.

Porter M.E., and M.R. Kramer. 2003. The competitive advantage of corporate philanthropy. Reprinted In *Harvard business review on corporate social responsibility*, ed. Havard Business School Press. Cambridge, MA: Harvard University Press.

Porter, M.E., and M.R. Kramer. 2006. Strategy and society: The link between competitive Advantage and corporate social responsibility. *Harvard Business Review* 84(12): 78–92.

———. 2011. Creating shared value. How to reinvent Capitalism – And unleash a wave of innovation and growth. *Harvard Business Review* 89(1): 62–77.

Phillips, R.A., and R.E. Freeman. 2010. *Stakeholders*. Cheltenham: Edward Elgar Publishing.

Rendtorff, J.D. 2009. *Responsibility, ethics and legitimacy of corporations*. Koge/Portland/Abingdon: Copenhagen Business School Press.

———. 2010. *Power and principle in the market place, on ethics and economics*. London: Ashgate.

———. 2011a. Institutionalization of corporate ethics and social responsibility programs in firms. In *Corporate social and human rights responsibilities: Global, legal and management perspectives*, ed. Karin Buhmann, Lynn Roseberry, and Mette Morsing, 244–266. London: Palgrave Macmillan.

———. 2011b. Corporate citizenship as organizational integrity. In *Corporate citizenship and new governance: The political role of corporations*, ed. Ingo Pies, and Peter Koslowski, 59–91. Dordrecht/Heidelberg/London/New York: Springer.

———. 2013. Philosophical theories of management and corporations. In *Handbook of the philosophical foundations of business ethics*, ed. Christoph Luetge, 1409–1432. Dordrecht/Heidelberg/New York/London: Springer Science+Business Media.

———. 2014. *French philosophy and social theory: A perspective for ethics and philosophy of management*. Dordrecht/Heidelberg/New York/London: Springer Science+Business Media.

———. 2015. Business ethics, strategy, and organizational integrity: The importance of integrity as a basic principle of business ethics that contributes to better economic performance. In *Handbook of research on business ethics and corporate responsibilities*, ed. D.E. Palmer, 91–105. Herschey: IGI global.

Suchman, M.C. 1995. Managing legitimacy: Strategic and institutional approaches. *Academy of management review* 20(3): 571–610.

Velasquez, M.G. 2002. *Business ethics. Concepts and cases*. Prentice Hall: New Jersey.

Williamson, O.E. 1975. *Markets and hierarchies: Analysis and antitrust implications*. New York: The Free Press.

———. 1985. *The economic institutions of capitalism*. New York: Free Press.

———. 1996. *The mechanisms of governance*. Oxford: Oxford University Press.

Chapter 8
Creating Shared Value. Looking at Shared Value Through an Aristotelian Lens

Ford Shanahan and Peter Seele

Abstract While capitalism has proven to be one of the most efficient economic engines in modern history, the goal of simply pursuing profit has, according to many, left some of society's needs unmet if not further challenged. In 2006, Porter and Kramer developed the notion that corporations could and should pursue a higher goal of capitalism including "creating shared value" (CSV) as a means to improve performance and bridging the gap that developed between corporations and society (Porter and Kramer 2011). The concept was welcomed within both academia and the corporate world for the amount of energy it has generated, its potential to improve capitalism and repair what Brigley referred to as the "fractured contract" (Brigley 1995: 225). However, it is being equally critiqued for lacking in definitional clarity causing inconsistent strategy, and lacking in originality *vis-a-vis* existing concepts such as Corporate Social Responsibility (CSR). This paper proposes corporate virtue as a form of CSV, by identifying two theories which demonstrate how corporate virtue meets the definitional requirements of CSV and helps both the corporation and society fulfil unmet needs.

8.1 Introduction

While capitalism has proven to be one of the most efficient economic engines in modern history, the goal of simply pursuing profit has, according to many, left some of society's needs unmet if not further challenged. In 2006, Porter and Kramer developed the notion that corporations could and should pursue a higher goal of capitalism including "creating shared value" (CSV) as a means to improve performance and bridging the gap that developed between corporations and society (Porter and Kramer 2011). The concept was welcomed within both academia and the corporate world for the amount of energy it has generated, its potential to improve

F. Shanahan (✉)
Franklin University Switzerland, Lugano, Switzerland
e-mail: fshanahan@yahoo.com

P. Seele
Università della Svizzera italiana, Lugano, Switzerland
e-mail: peter.seele@usi.ch

J. Wieland (ed.), *Creating Shared Value – Concepts, Experience, Criticism*, Ethical Economy 52, DOI 10.1007/978-3-319-48802-8_8

capitalism and repair what Brigley referred to as the "fractured contract" (Brigley 1995: 225). However, it is being equally critiqued for lacking in definitional clarity causing inconsistent strategy, and lacking in originality *vis-a-vis* existing concepts such as Corporate Social Responsibility (CSR). This paper proposes corporate virtue as a form of CSV, by identifying two theories which demonstrate how corporate virtue meets the definitional requirements of CSV and helps both the corporation and society fulfil unmet needs.

8.2 Shared Value

8.2.1 The Promise

The concept of CSV grew out of Porter's initial contributions regarding business strategy and the perspective, that corporations were not being as effective as they could be in regard to societal obligations and opportunities (Porter and Kramer 2011). Citing the inherent interdependence of businesses and the surrounding society, they observed that in order to be successful, businesses need a healthy community and public policy which fosters growth (Porter and Kramer 2011). Conflicting views on the role of the modern corporation in society contributed to this problem: with some economists claiming that businesses should focus exclusively on profitability with little or no obligations to social or other community needs (Friedman 1970; Henderson 2001), and other economists claiming that businesses have a positive duty to society and should take an active role in addressing social needs. As to the latter, corporate social responsibility (CSR) became very popular and attempted to clarify this corporate role. CSR, characterized as a "duty," was often perceived as being antagonistic to other corporate mandates and therefore unable to systematically improve capitalism. As a result, CSR has been adopted by many corporations, but these efforts are inconsistent and often regarded as a part of self-serving defensive strategies, employed to limit reputational risk (cf. Beschorner 2013), rather than societal duty.

Porter and Kramer (2011) claimed that a more sustainable solution in the corporate world should focus on opportunity, as opposed to duty, and that there was ample potential to do so. They proposed that corporations should focus their energies on mutually beneficial opportunities which businesses could tap into and effect invaluable change through their "skills, resources and managerial capabilities" (Porter and Kramer 2011: 77). By reconceiving products and markets, redefining productivity in the value chain and enabling local cluster development, as outlined in Table 8.1, corporations could tap into a wealth of opportunity that would not only benefit the corporation, but society at the same time (Porter and Kramer 2011).

CSV has since been adopted as an economic theory and buzzword. It has been defined as policies and operating principles which enhance the competitiveness of a company while simultaneously advancing economic and social conditions of the

Table 8.1 Examples of shared value

Levels of shared value	Business results	Social results
Reconceiving product and markets:	Increased revenue	Improved patient care
How targeting unmet needs drives incremental revenue and profits	Increased market share	Reduced carbon footprint
	Increased market growth	Improved nutrition
	Improved profitability	Improved education
Redefining productivity in the value chain:	Improved productivity	Reduced energy use
How better management of internal operations increases productivity and reduces risks	Reduced logistical and operating costs	Reduced water use
	Secured supply	Reduced raw materials
	Improved quality	Improved job skills
	Improved profitability	Improved employee incomes
Enabling cluster development:	Reduced costs	Improved education
How changing societal conditions outside the company unleashes new growth and productivity gains	Secured supply	Increased job creation
	Improved distribution infrastructure	Improved health
	Improved workforce access	Improved incomes
	Improved profitability	

Source: Porter et al. (2012: 3)

communities in which it operates (Crane et al. 2013; Porter and Kramer 2011; Spitzeck and Chapman 2012).

CSV has also been adopted as a strategic goal by numerous multinational companies. Examples of reconceiving products and markets in a way that are consistent with societal needs include Intel's and IBM's innovations in digital intelligence as a means to achieve energy efficiency, and GE's ecomagination products (Porter and Kramer 2011). Examples of supply chain innovations include water reduction programs by Coca Cola and Dow Chemical, and procurement programs enabling direct local sourcing. Local cluster development enabled companies to operate more efficiently through proximity (Porter and Kramer 2011).

8.2.2 *The Critique*

Despite its popularity, CSV has also been criticized for lack of focus and originality. Having acknowledged the amount of positive energy that the concept had generated to reshape capitalism, Crane et al. (2014) criticized the theory for not being original vis-a-vis other existing theories such as CSR. According to Crane et al. (2014), CSV also underestimates the inherent tensions between social goals of society and economic goals of corporations. Lastly, they point out that its underlying presumptions and requirements e.g. that businesses always comply with regulatory and ethical standards (as a requirement for CSV to flourish) are naïve and unrealistic (Crane et al. 2014).

Similarly, Beschorner (2013) argued that CSV is a "one trick pony" incapable of addressing societal issues. Specifically, Beschorner (2013) challenged whether all of society's ills present proper business opportunities, and therein lies the failure of the theory.

In June 2014, Dembek et al. conducted an extensive literature review on CSV, attempting to describe the theory's current status nearly a decade after it was initially launched into the public domain. The review captured the amount of energy the theory had generated among both academia and the corporate world to revamp capitalism, but also revealed several critical flaws limiting its adoption and implementation. The authors noted the lack of a common definition across the various academic fields which is likely to affect successful implementation (Dembek et al. 2015). They identified three core characteristics of the definition of CSV which remained unsettled, relating to the means, outcomes and beneficiaries. In terms of "means" the authors point out that there is inconsistency whether CSV could just relate to a single project, or whether it requires the alignment of actions and behaviors within an organization (Dembek et al. 2015). For example, if a company adopts a program to reduce waste in a product line that would otherwise create unnecessary amounts of waste, the question is, whether this specific project would be considered as CSV.

From an organizational perspective, the outcomes include profits, access to resources and competitive positions (Dembek et al. 2015). On the societal side, the outcomes should focus on basic human needs (Doyal and Gough 1991), including environmental quality, health, water, education and income. Dembek et al. (2015) noted, however, that many of the examples of CSV cited in articles do not appear to cater to unmet needs, but rather convenience, such as faster shipping by Amazon for a fixed fee. While not questioning the intrinsic value of such programs, Dembek et al. (2015) point out that CSV would likely be diminished in value and remain only a buzz word if outcomes were defined so broadly that any corporate program could qualify.

Lastly, Dembek et al. (2015) noted the lack of consistency in the literature regarding the intended beneficiaries of CSV ranging from corporation and stakeholders (Maltz et al. 2011), the entire value chain and society (Fearne et al. 2012), or just the corporation and one social group (Porter and Kramer 2011). There were also discrepancies as to whether the environment itself could qualify as a beneficiary independently (Dubois and Dubois 2012), or if environmental affects should be linked to certain stakeholders. Lastly, Dembek et al. (2015) questioned whether the benefit of the social group should be of higher priority in shared value than the value to the corporate, or if the two should be considered equal in weight. This lack of unison on the definition and requirements of CSV has caused complications in how the concept was operationalized (Dembek et al. 2015). Hence, as a next step we propose to apply the criteria above to look at CSV from a corporate virtue perspective, providing more of a holistic approach to the positive and negative aspects illustrated above.

8.3 Corporate Virtue: A Holistic Approach

8.3.1 Corporate Virtue

While corporate virtue is not a traditional corporate program, product or service per se, the authors propose that it is beneficial to both corporation and society in a way that it qualifies under the definitions of CSV above. Virtue, or arête, refers to moral excellence. According to Aristotle in *Nichomachean Ethics*, a virtuous person is trained to recognize the balance between two vices, and choses the balanced and "virtuous" option in the middle between the two vices (Aristotle 1962). For example, on the subject of confidence: the two vices are cowardice at one end and recklessness on the other end. The virtuous person selects the balanced and virtuous option of courage in the middle. Similarly, in regards to material goods, the two vices are stinginess and extravagance, with the virtuous option at the balance point being generosity (Mintz 1996). Such virtuous behavior is developed through training, yielding a moral compass that can be employed in future decisions (Beauchamp and Bowie 2005). Virtue is then maintained by habituation, such that the virtuous decision becomes automatic, despite the allure of the vices.

While Aristotle's concepts were intended to be applied to individuals, the concepts today are applied in the corporate context as well. The concept of corporate virtue was initially coined by Solomon (1992), describing how corporations demonstrate virtue through stable decisions they make and actions they take as demonstrated over time, which impact other shareholders such as employees, customers, the environment, broader society. As stated by Aristotle,

> we become just be doing just acts, temperate by doing temperate acts, brave by doing brave acts (Aristotle EN 1103a)

Corporations therefore develop and display virtue via institutional craftsmanship (Moore 2005a, b).

8.3.2 Virtue in the Creation of Value

According to Aristotle, happiness is the ultimate goal. People live in a social world and rely on social relationships. The end goal or purpose relates to one's ability to achieve happiness in this environment. According to Aristotle, virtue is critical to this path. Virtue leads to happiness via social recognition by others which requires habituation of virtuous conduct through active self-management. This ultimate goal serves as a "telos", or inherent purpose for everything, providing a compass in moral decision-making. Pies et al. (2014) argue that this principle is equally applicable to corporations, which links virtue to the concept of creating value that benefits both corporation and society, or shared value.

Corporations principally seek to make a profit, but Pies et al. (2014) argue that profit is ultimately not an end goal for corporations, or corporate happiness. Like individuals, corporations operate in a social environment; profits are just an indicator that a corporation has performed well in this social environment. Corporations enter into business relationships with other companies if there is an element of trust and the other company is perceived to be reliable (Pies et al. 2014). Companies can only charge a profit if they are perceived to have added value. While profits are important, and often appear to be the end goal, creating value is in fact the most important goal which orients corporations, similar to a telos (Pies et al. 2014).

> "Just as Aristotle sees happiness as a signal that someone has perfected himself as a virtuous citizen, making a profit can be evidence that a company is giving more to society than it is taking from it." (Pies et al. 2014: 243)

"Creating value" within the social environment of global society is therefore the goal of corporate self-perfection, above the simple pursuit of profits, and this requires virtue.

Virtue, and its role in corporate moral decision-making, is a critical component of a corporation's capacity to achieve such happiness. Corporations are not individuals and therefore do not have the same singular capacity to demonstrate virtue, but they nonetheless demonstrate virtue via the patterns of decisions they make over time in the social environments or communities where they exist. Virtue can only be maintained through an active and healthy corporate culture that embraces virtuous conduct.

> "Not all habits are virtuous, but all virtues are habits" (Pies et al. 2014: 236)

However, virtue can only flourish in a society where there are collective self-commitments by other participants in the community (Pies et al. 2014). This need for a stable environment for business to operate in, with mutual commitments, motivates the corporation to participate as an active political member in the polis (Pies et al. 2014). While self-motivated, such participation also benefits society.

> "The ideas of self-perfection and potentiality of win-win cooperation are thus complementary; my own personal self-perfections is only possible if I interact with others, thus helping them realize their own self perfection: do ut des ("I give that you might give")." (Pies et al. 2014: 237)

Thus creating value in the community in which it operates is a higher goal for the corporation or eudaimonia. Eudaimonia can only be achieved through virtuous conduct maintained through habit and a healthy corporate environment. Because virtue can only survive in a society where there are active mutual commitments, companies are also required to play an active role in the governance of the com-munity, as well as in the management of its own corporate culture (Pies et al. 2014).

8.3.3 Virtue in Persuasion

Virtue also plays a more functional and direct role in the success of a company through Aristotle's concept of ethos, or moral character. Aristotle's theories on ethos were developed in part in his text *On Rhetoric*, which dissected the components of persuasion in the context of political dialogue and debate in ancient Greece, where they were critical to the function of the society.

According to Aristotle, ethos consists of three main components; arête (virtue), phronesis (practical wisdom) and eunoia (goodwill). Put another way, a person's ethos was sum of his or her virtue, caring for others and practical knowledge. Ethos is a critical component of persuasion along with pathos (emotion) and logos (logic). If a speaker in ancient Greece, for example, was successful in invoking all three of these components in a message, he or she would have been more effective in persuading the audience. If the speaker was able to effectively employ logic and emotion in his speech, but was perceived by the audience to be selfish (lacking eunoia as a component of virtue), he or she would be less persuasive. Similarly, if he or she was virtuous and employed logic, but was unable to effectively evoke any emotion among the audience, he or she would have been less effective as well. Putting all three together, as perceived by the audience, the speaker would have the best chance of persuading the audience. Thus, as can be seen in diagram 2 below, virtue plays a role in persuasion via Aristotle's concept of ethos. While this concept was developed for oral debate in ancient times, the principles in persuasion remain valid over 2000 years later, and have been adopted in the corporate context as well.

> "As persuasion itself enters into nearly every aspect of social life, rhetoric is omnipresent" (Robinson 2006: 7)

Whether convincing customers that their products are better than the competitors', asking shareholders to invest capital, or managing employees, corporations rely on their ability to be persuasive every day to all their stakeholders (Freeman 1984). In his article on this point, Conger identifies credibility as the "cornerstone of effective persuading [...]" (Conger 1998: 90) Credibility depends on "expertise and relationships", as evidenced by the ability to listen and work in the interest of others (Conger 1998: 88).

Corporate reputation itself has been identified as a valuable intangible asset, with up to 70% of a company's value being tied to the perception that stakeholders have (Eccles et al. 2007). Companies with good reputations benefit from more loyal customers who are in turn likely to purchase diverse products. Such companies are more likely to attract top talent. It is therefore in a corporation's vested interest to attend to its reputation (and the corporate actions which form it). From a reputation management perspective, persuasion is a critical tool, particularly in the case of a reputation-challenging crisis. The most common responses companies employ in the case of a reputational crisis are dialogue and advocacy (Heugens et al. 2004). Persuading the stakeholders to understand the company's position or facts is critical to this process. Thus, the following figure demonstrates how virtue plays a critical role in persuasion, through Aristotle's concept of ethos, and the role of ethos in the persuasive appeals (Fig. 8.1).

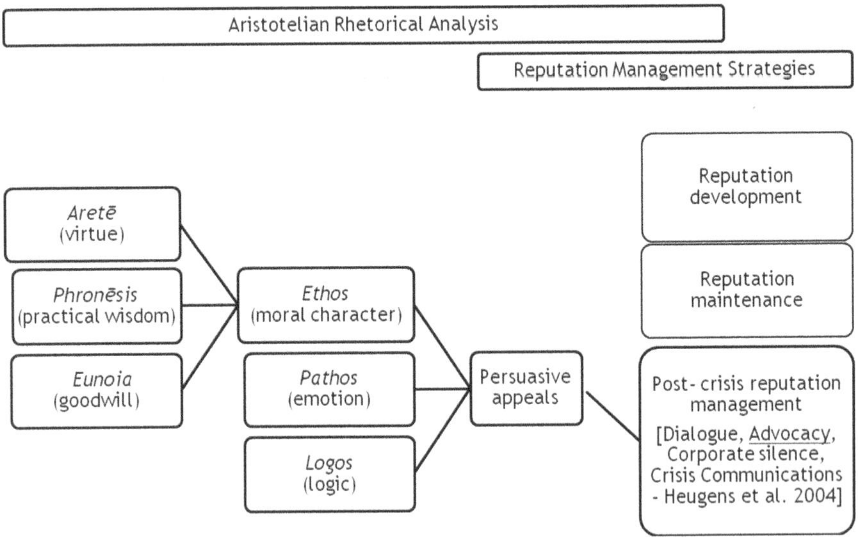

Fig. 8.1 Aristotelian rhetorical analysis (Source: Shanahan and Seele 2015)

8.3.4 Corporate Virtue as Shared Value

Corporate virtue is a critical component of value within the social economic system, and to the corporations end goal of eudaimonia. This requires that the corporation plays an active role in polis, so virtue can be sustained. Likewise corporate virtue plays a role in persuasion which is critical to corporate reputation management. Thus while being virtuous is beneficial to society, it is also self-serving to the corporation as a means to effectiveness and end-state happiness. In order to qualify as Shared Value, Dembek et al. (2015) suggest that prospective programs be clear and consisted with the definition and theory of Shared Value as proposed by Porter and Kramer (2011), particularly in terms of the means, outcomes and beneficiaries.

8.3.4.1 Means

Of the three means offered (reconceiving of products and markets, redefining productivity in the value chain and enabling cluster development), corporate virtue qualifies as redefining productivity in the value chain. While Porter and Kramer (2011) do not enumerate corporate virtue as an example of shared value, they do emphasize that this form of the means focuses on inventing new ways of operating. In the commercial process today, there are often situations where being virtuous is seen as being at odds with the need to either lower an expense or raise a revenue in the moment. Decisions in the corporate world today are often under immense pressure to meet financial goals (for example pressure in the commercial process to make a sale at any cost before the end of a quarter, to recognize revenue early, to not raise expenses that would ensure compliance, to not notify shareholders of a problem), which can be at odds with virtue as a mean between two vices. Courage, generosity, trustworthiness and friendliness can easily be perceived as a luxury that cannot be afforded at certain times in the corporate decision-making paradigm. However, if their value was reconceived and maintained through habit, it would not necessarily change any one of the value chain topics listed by Porter and Kramer (2011) such as resource use, energy use, employee productivity. It would change how decisions in those lanes were made, which would in turn improve the value chain offer and allow new economic value. According to Dembek et al. (2015), the impact should not be on just one country only, but rather be border-crossing, as effective corporate virtue would be. They also point out that it is unclear if shared value should be a single project or activity of an entire organization, but corporate virtue would be on the safe side as organization-wide habits.

8.3.4.2 Outcomes

In regards to outcomes, Dembek et al. (2015) point out the apparent lack of consistency across the literature on what types of outcomes meet the definition of CSV. On the corporate side, the outcomes focus on profits, access to resources and improved competitive position (Porter and Kramer 2011). Corporate virtue would have this outcome in view of the improved societal position raising profits, eudaimonia and persuasiveness. In regards to the outcome for society, Dembek et al. (2015) indicate there should be a clear focus on basic human needs, or the determinants of well-being and quality of life (Constanza et al. 2007). If corporations were to adopt and encourage a focus on virtue, the resulting increase in courage, truthfulness, generosity and friendliness would improve the well-being and quality of life for those directly affected. Virtue is critical to the polis (Pies et al. 2014). Courage and physical fitness allow individuals to defend the polis, and justice, temperance and generosity allow others in society to thrive (Pies et al. 2014).

8.3.4.3 Beneficiaries

In terms of proper beneficiaries of the outcomes of CSV, Dembek et al. (2015) again point out that there is inconsistency in the literature on this requirement, but their focus is on whether the beneficiary could be just one customer or broader society, whether certain stakeholders such as the environment itself qualify, and if there is a priority of society over the corporation. As an entity wide endeavour, corporate virtue likely meets the criteria for proper beneficiaries as it is not exclusive.

8.4 Conclusions

Corporate virtue is a proper example of CSV as proposed by Porter and Kramer (2011). It encourages corporations to develop habits that foster and maintain virtuous decision-making in leadership and the commercial process. It fosters the creation of value in society and the engagement of the corporation in the political process, and benefits the corporation not just as a result of increased persuasiveness and profits as a result of better positioning in the global social marketplace, but also through the attainment of corporate eudaimonia.

References

Aristotle, Oswald. M.. 1962. *Nicomachean Ethic*. Trans. New York: Macmillan Publishing Co.

Beauchamp, T.L., and N.E. Bowie. 2005. *Ethical theory and business*. Upper Saddle River: Pearson Custom Publishing.

Beschorner, Thomas. 2013. Creating shared value: The one-trick Pony approach. *Business Ethics Journal Review* 1(17): 106–112.

Brigley, Stephen. 1995. Business ethics in context, researching with case studies. *Journal of Business Ethics* 14: 219–226.

Conger, J.A. 1998. The necessary art of Persuasion. *Harvard Business Review*: 85–95.

Constanza, Robert, Brendan Fisher, et al. 2007. Quality of life: An approach opportunities, human needs and subjective well-being. *Ecological Economics* 61: 267–276.

Crane, A., D. Matten, G. Palazzo, and L. Spence. 2013. Contesting the value of the shared value concept. *California Management Review* 56(2): 130–153.

Crane, Andrew, Guido Palazzo, Laura J. Spence, and Dirk Matten. 2014. Contesting the value of creating shared value. *California Management Review* 56(2): 130–153.

Dembek, K., P. Singh, and T. Bhakhoo. 2015. Literature review of shared value: A theoretical concept or a management buzzword? *Journal of Business Ethics* 18(2): 153–190.

Doyal, L., and I. Gough. 1991. *A theory of human need*. New York: Guilford.

Dubois, Cathy L.Z., and David A. Dubois. 2012. Expanding the vision of industrial- organizational psychology contributions to environmental sustainability. *Industrial and Organizational Psychology* 5(4): 480–483.

Eccles, R.G., S.C. Newquist, and R. Schatz. 2007. Reputation and its risks. *Harvard Business Review* 85: 104–114.

Fearne, Andrew, Marian Garcia Martinez, and Benjamin Dent. 2012. Dimensions of sustainable value chains: Implications for value chain analysis. *Supply Chain Management: An International Journal* 17(6): 575–581.

Freeman, R.E. 1984. *Strategic management: A stakeholder approach*. Boston: Pitman.

Friedman, Milton. 1970. A Friedman doctrine – The social responsibility of business is to increase its profits. *The New York Times Magazine* 13:122–126.

Henderson, D. 2001. *Misguided virtue. False notions of corporate social responsibility*. London: Institute of Economic Affairs.

Heugens, P.M., C.B. van Riel, and F.A. van den Bosch. 2004. Reputation management capabilities as decision rules. *Journal of Management Studies* 41(8): 1349–1374.

Maltz, Elliot, Fred Thompson, and Debra Jones Ringold. 2011. Assessing and maximizing corporate social initiatives: A strategic view of corporate social responsibility. *Journal of Public Affairs* 11(4): 344–352.

Mintz, S.M. 1996. Aristotelian virtue and business ethics education. *Journal of Business Ethics* 15(8): 827–838.

Moore, Geoff. 2005a. Humanizing business: A modern virtue ethics approach. *Business Ethics Quarterly* 15(2): 237–255.

———. 2005b. Corporate character: Modern virtue ethics and the virtuous corporation. *Business Ethics Quarterly* 15(4): 659–685.

Pies, Ingo, Markus Beckman, and Stefan Hielscher. 2014. The political role of the business firm: An Odonomic concept of corporate citizenship developed in comparison with the Aristotelian idea of individual citizenship. *Business and Society* 52(3): 226–259.

Porter, M.E., and M.R. Kramer. 2011. Creating shared value. *Harvard Business Review* 89(1/2): 62–77.

Porter, M.E., Greg Hills, et al. 2012. Measuring shared value: How to unlock value by linking social and business results. FSG. http://www.fsg.org/tabid/191/ArticleId/740/Default.aspx?srpush=true. Accessed 20 Feb 2016.

Robinson, D.N. 2006. Rhetoric and character in aristotle. *The Review of Metaphysics* 60(1): 3–15.

Shanahan, M.F., and Peter Seele. 2015. Shorting Ethos: Exploring the relationship between Aristotle's ethos and reputation management. *Corporate Reputation Review* 18(1): 37–49.

Solomon, R.C. 1992. Corporate roles, personal virtues: An Aristotelian approach to business ethics. *Business Ethics Quarterly* 2(3): 317–339.

———. 2003. Victims of circumstance? A defense of virtue ethics in business. *Business Ethics Quarterly* 13(1): 43–62.

Spitzeck, Heiko, and Sonja Chapman. 2012. Creating shared value as a differentiation strategy—The example of BASF in Brazil. *Corporate Governance* 12(4): 499–513.

Chapter 9
Between Enthusiasm and Overkill. Assessing Michael Porter's Conceptual Management Frame of Creating Shared Value

Matthias Kettner

Abstract Michael E. Porter and Mark R. Kramer have been very successful, in terms of impact in the business community, in introducing a new management framework whose programmatic title points to the creation of shared value. However, their impact is due not to the scientific merit of their classic 2011 paper, which is indeed low, as many scholarly commentators have already pointed out. In my paper, I will explain the surprising discrepancy between impact and scientific quality and then draw a lesson from it that we as theoreticians of business ethics may find hard to swallow: modesty in the face of the real conditions of communicative propagation, uptake, and success of conceptual management frames. Alluding to Nelson Goodman, it seems that a good conceptual management frame should provide managers with a new way of symbolic worldmaking; it should help managers with their world disclosure; its bearing is primarily practical.

I explain the successful propagation of the CVS notion by reference to a number of factors: (1) a cultural dynamics of fame very similar to the contemporary pop star system, (2) a strategy of reducing complexity by deflecting attention from precursors, (3) entrepreneurial self-promotion, (4) club building mechanisms, (5) tactical devaluation of alternative management frames, (6) the creation of a peer group around a buzzword, (7) the attractiveness of the hip and the *en vogue*, and finally and most importantly, (8) the strength of a rhetoric that permits us (if we buy this rhetoric) to do two incongruous things at once: understand ourselves as change-agents contributing to nothing less than the glorious reinvention of capitalism, and stay firmly within today's capitalism's comfort zone without essentially changing anything. I go on to point out three massive shortcomings of the CSV framework: Its poor axiology, its inability to quantify polyvalues, and its conventional rationality assumptions. In the final part of my paper, I suggest a discourse ethical alternative concerning the really important issue that Porter and Kramer 2011 take as their

M. Kettner (✉)
Universität Witten/Herdecke, Witten, Germany
e-mail: Matthias.Kettner@uni-wh.de

J. Wieland (ed.), *Creating Shared Value – Concepts, Experience, Criticism*, Ethical Economy 52, DOI 10.1007/978-3-319-48802-8_9

starting point, namely the problem of a legitimation crisis of present-day capitalism.

> Shared Value Pioneers: Changing the World by Changing Business[1]
>
> No one should underestimate Mr Porter's intellectual energy or ambition. He has colonised entire fields of business theory. He has published 18 books to date. But for "shared value" to have the same impact that his earlier output undoubtedly had, he will need to do a lot more work on the idea.[2]

9.1 Introduction: Impact No Doubt

With round about 307.000 hits for <*Porter Shared Value*> on Google Scholar in the search interval form 2006 to 2016,[3] the impact of Michael E. Porter's and Mark R. Kramer's notion of creating shared value is truly massive beyond any bibliometric doubt. In their 2011 article that now counts as the birthplace of the Creating Shared Value framework, Michael E. Porter and Mark R. Kramer acknowledge widespread interest in mainstream notions of CSR at the time. They observe, however, that companies' efforts to improve their social and environmental impact have not been as productive as they could have been. They argue that mainstream CSR thinking pits business against society and is often not tailored to a company's strategic needs. Porter and Kramer then go on to propose that CSR should be grounded in the *interdependence* that exists between corporation and society, thus recognizing that businesses can create shared value by strategically investing in areas where both business and society gain. Already in their 2006 article, they refer to the idea of a two-sided win-win-strategy as "strategic" CSR that is achieved through product and value chain innovation. They illustrate this idea with some case study examples of multinational corporations that adopt this strategy. However, in their later article of 2011 that has now acquired the status of the locus classicus, they endulge in heavy (and mindless, cf. the exchange in Crane et al. 2014; Porter and Kramer 2014) CSR-bashing. I will explain this surprising and at first sight whimsical turn below in the section on rhetorics.

Not only in terms of clicks in the cloud though, but also on the tangible ground of management practices and the entire educational, promotional and consulting industry that supports them, Porter and Kramer must be credited with having founded a momentous new strand that in the meantime amounts to something like a new establishment. To illustrate: The *Shared Value Initiative*, according to its self-description on its website has cascaded into a powerful mainstream management movement:

---

[1] From the Agenda of the Shared Value Leadership Summit 2016, May 10-11, 2016, N.Y., "Shape the strategies that will change the world", http://sharedvalue.org/agenda-shared-value-leadership-summit-2016 (accessed 10.03.2016).

[2] Schumpeter-Blog (2011).

[3] Count as of March 30 2016.

> "In 2012, the Shared Value Initiative was launched as a Clinton Global Initiative Commitment to Action with the support of Mark Kramer, Harvard Business School Professor Michael Porter, and the new executive director of the initiative, Justin Bakule, formerly a managing director at FSG. With shared value embedded in its corporate history and a strong consulting relationship with FSG, Nestlé signed on as the inaugural partner to fund the Initiative with Verizon, Mercy Corps, and the Rockefeller Foundation. Today, 35 cross-sector organizations comprise the leadership group for the initiative. (...) How is the Shared Value Initiative making a difference? 25 innovative partners from leading Fortune 500 companies. 8,000 shared value practitioners across all sectors learn by accessing community resources.70 practitioners certified in 30 countries on nearly every continent. 450 of the most advanced shared value leaders gather each year at the Shared Value Leadership Summit." [4]

The chosen maxime that provides an incentive for peer group identity of the Shared Value Initiative is gloriously laconic: "We are a global community of leaders who find business opportunities in addressing societal challenges."[5]

So, like it or not, Porter and Kramer have stirred up a lot of thinking and have created a tremendous impact so far, the end of which is not yet in sight. In the rest of my paper, I explain this fact and try to draw a lesson from it that we as theoreticians of business ethics may find hard to swallow. But we should, because the lesson is valuable, or so I argue. In the final section of my paper, I summarize a number of criticisms, mine and that of others, that point to irremediable deficits in the Creating Shared Value conceptual management frame. I end by suggesting a discourse ethical alternative to the issue that Porter and Kramer 2011 take as the starting point of their reflections, the problem of a legitimation crisis of present-day capitalism, or in the lurid opening words of their paper: "The capitalist system is under siege". I think they are completely right in their choice of a starting point. Unfortunately, their operative main intention is to launch their conceptual management framework, not to address in any but superficial ways the deep issue that they concoct in order to add drama to the launch.

9.2 Similar Ideas, Similar Problems

I do not summarize the conceptual Creating Shared Value management frame here. Porter and Kramer have kept their main points short and simple enough. And all the critical papers that I have listed contain summaries and overviews of Porter's and Kramer's main points.[6] Nor do I attempt to give a comprehensive overview of all the

[4] http://www.sharedvalue.org/about-initiative (accessed 10.03.2016).

[5] For a list of shared value case examples, see http://sharedvalue.org/example-listing (accessed 10.03.2016).

[6] Cf. Aakhus and Michael (2012); Beschorner (2013); Beschorner and Hajduk (2015); Crane et al. (2014); Hübscher (2015); Liel and Lütge (2015); Scholz and de los Reyes (2015); Williams and Hayes (2013).

critical arguments that were levelled against Porter's and Kramer's approach.[7] Again, this work has already been done up to the point of exhaustion. Indeed, due to its serious underarticulation, misleadingness, hyperbole, unfair and/or distorting representations of alternative approaches, heavy ideological burdens and lack of self-critique, Porter's and Kramer's approach is vulnerable to so many and so different massive objections that one may speak with only slight exaggeration of an overkill of criticism.

Instead, in this section I want to redirect our attention to two positions that were relegated to oblivion by the triumphal procession of Porter's and Kramer's formulations. Before Porter and Kramer effectively usurped the entrepreneurial conversation about reshaping capitalism from within business, Jed Emerson's and Sheila Bonini's (2005) concept of "blended value" already pointed very much in the direction that Porter and Kramer were later to mark out as their proper turf. In the section entitled "concluding thoughts" in their landmark paper, Bonini and Emerson already clearly acknowledge the desideratum of robust measurement and performance metrics for polyvalues, i.e. for values of more than one single evaluational kind: "In the area of performance measurement and metrics for the non-financial aspects of organizations and funds we believe that the focus should be on: (1) Supporting the creation of greater capacity for measurement on the part of organizations attempting to document the full breadth of their value creation efforts. (2) Investment of philanthropic funds in a more deliberate testing of assumptions underlying the theory of change being pursued by organizations—a process of testing that is often beyond the capacity of individual managers within organizations. (3) Supporting the exploration of how best to create standardized frameworks for measurement and performance metrics, such as the emerging work on Social Return on Investment."

One critical reviewer of Porter's and Kramer's 2011 paper (Schumpeter-Blog 2011) hints at yet another forerunner, namely Stuart L. Hart, an American academic, writer and theorist and the founder of *Enterprise for a Sustainable World*.[8] In his 2005 book on capitalism, Hart wrote: "Sustainable global enterprise thus represents the potential for a new private sector-based approach to development that creates profitable businesses that simultaneously raise the quality of life for the world's poor, respect cultural diversity, and conserve the ecological integrity of the planet for future generations. Making such a societal contribution while simultaneously creating shareholder value will take real imagination and a fresh approach to business strategy" (Hart 2005: xi).

I want to draw a simple conclusion from this finding: It has become too easy to take Porter and Kramer to task for the many flaws in the exposition of their ideas in their seminal texts. One should not forget that the real bone of contention, and the touchstone for any serious ethical and otherwise philosophical thinking about the commercial society in which we live, is the justificatory standing which all the dif-

[7] A superb overview is Crane et al. (2014). For another decent overview, see Williams and Hayes 2013.

[8] For more on Hart's background see the article on https://en.wikipedia.org/wiki/Stuart_L._Hart (accessed 10.03.2016).

ferent concrete elements that together comprise commercial society either have or lack ("legitimation crisis"). So we should not dismiss Porter and Kramer too quickly. If we do so, we must register and discuss similar and perhaps more interesting, though perhaps inchoate positions, such as those of Bonini and Emerson, and Hart.

9.3 A Cultural Explanation of the Success of Porterian Rhetorics

Aakhus and Bzdak, looking at cases of implementation and alternative perspectives on innovation, come to the conclusion that

> "despite its appeal and uptake in corporate and philanthropic circles, shared value merely advances the conventional rhetoric that what is good for business is good for society. The shared value approach narrows what counts as social value and avoids the friction between business and society. The consequence is that the approach is problematic as a framework for addressing sustainability and development, and an insufficient basis for decision-making about philanthropy and CSR" (Aakhus and Bzdak 2012: 231)

When we consider how much impact Porter's and Kramer's central publications on the concept of shared value have had and continue to have, then we cannot help noting that the concept's effective history – *Wirkungsgeschichte* – has an air of paradox. On the one hand, we witness the impressive orchestration of a CSV-movement of international dimension. We witness a lot of euphoric resonance across managerial boards of many prestigious business enterprizes, and the concept has been fondly accommodated on the part of many academic business schools in order to refurbish their curricula that are always threatened by turning stale and unfashionable. On the other hand, the critical attention focused on the CSV-framework in debates within economic, philosophical, and ethical discourse has revealed the theoretical looseness of the CSV-framework, as far as Porter and Kramer have articulated this framework till today. With only a bit of exaggeration, we can say that there is a clash of two perspectives here: Looked at as a new proposition in scientific discourse, CSV (from 2006 until 2016) is thin gruel;[9] however, looked at as an innovative managerial movement and practice, CSV is as popular and as much in demand as snake-oil ever was in the Wild West.

I think that there is something quite disturbing in this discrepancy and that we should take its annoying ambivalence seriously. By "we" I refer to us as members of communities of investigators who work on problems in theoretical economics, in ethics, and in philosophy of economics. We should admit that the observed discrepancy is painfully disappointing for us. If we face our disappointment, I concur, we might be able to turn frustration into creative energy. As a theoretician, my impulse is to turn polemical or cynical when I see how patently simplistic concepts (such as CSV) displace beautifully elaborated and complex concepts (such as CSR).

[9] For a scathing critique of new wave management thinking, cf. Stewart (2009).

Something analogous to Gresham's law that bad money drives out good appears to be at work here. However, I also have to bring myself to understand the disappointment on the side of many people that we want, and imagine, to be our audiences and addressees but that we (very?) often fail to address and reach with any noticeable impact. The wide acclaim and considerable success that the CSV-frame has undoubtedly had could hold for us a productive lesson in modesty in the face of the real conditions of communicative propagation, uptake, and success of conceptual management frames.

By "conceptual management frame" I mean more than a conceptual model that would help researchers to understand and explain certain phenomena in some target domain. A great part of the theorizing in economics proceeds with the help of conceptual models (Morgan 2012) and, to a lesser extent, the same holds for normative ethics and metaethics (Svensson and Wood 2008). A conceptual management frame, such as CVS, helps managers to make better sense of their decisional behavior and brings a sense of counterfactual relevance into the potentially infinite (and therefore meaningless) space of factual challenges and responses by increasing the saliency of some challenges and responses and reducing the saliency of others. A conceptual management frame is tailored to the "world" of managers and has a practical bearing on being, i.e. understanding oneself, in such a world. Alluding to Nelson Goodman's classic, one may say that a good conceptual management frame should provide managers with a new way of symbolic world-making or, paraphrasing this in a Heideggerian jargon, it should help managers with their world disclosure. Its bearing is practical and theoretical, to be sure, but primarily practical. So what would be on a list of real conditions of communicative propagation, uptake, and success of conceptual management frames?

First, certainly, and probably on top of the list in terms of causal impact, there is a cultural dynamics of fame very similar to the contemporary pop star system, though in the pertinent vernacular Michel E. Porter would be called a *guru* ("the doyen of living management gurus, a professor at Harvard Business School", The Economist 2008) rather than a star.[10]

Second, there is at work a strategy of reducing complexity by deflecting attention from precursors and forebears. Novelty and originality go hand in hand.

Third, there is the factor of entrepreneurial self-promotion: Porter's own Institute for Strategy and Competitiveness, Porter's Monitor Consulting Group[11], Porter's and Kaplan's "Value Based Health Care Delivery Initiative" (VBHCD).

Fourth, club building mechanisms: Porter's Shared Value Initiative that touts itself as a global community of leaders who find business opportunities in societal challenges.

Fifth, we have to reckon with coarsening and tactical devaluation of alternative management frames that compete with one's own. Concerning Porter's and Kramer's CSV-frame, critics (notably Crane et al. 2014; Beschorner and Hajduk 2015) have

[10] Cf. Liel and Lütge (2012) for an analysis of the importance of this strategy within the success story of the CSV-frame.

[11] The Monitor Group went bancrupt in 2012. For a scathing explanation, cf. Denning (2012).

documented how distorting, biased and misleading Porter and Kramer present CSR approaches.

Sixth, the power of familiarity that comes with the establishment of one's own peer group. CSV has become a buzzword, and by CSV related jargon its proponents recognize each other readily as like-minded members of a peer group of avantgard entrepreneurs and managers.

Last, but probably not least, a relevant factor is the attractiveness of hip and *en vogue* stuff as such.[12] In the case of CSV, there is a close connection with the fifth factor mentioned above: There is mounting evidence that CSR-thinking is in the process of being widely perceived as somewhat dated, as old school, or at least as overly familiar and no longer thrilling.[13] This is so despite the fact, or perhaps because of the fact, that discourses on CSR have been going on for a long time, with a plentitude of progress, ramifications and differentiations achieved. For us, philosophers and other theoreticians, it is distressing to ascertain that all this progress is pleasing and laudable from a scientific point of view but at the same time is tiresome from the point of view of what is fashionable. Owing to this slackness, Porter and friends could tout their concept of CSV as *dernier cri* and as a superior preferable alternative to CSR with its – purportedly exhausted and old-fashioned – semantics of responsibility.

I find it expedient to add yet another factor to the provisory list of factors that help explain the success of conceptual management frames no matter how good or poor their theoretical credentials are. The eighth factor is of an exquisitely cultural nature. This highlights particularly well the perceived rhetorical strength of the CSV-frame. I find it plausible to think that a specific strength of "creating shared value" is the strength of a rhetoric that permits us (if we buy this rhetoric) to do two incongruous things at once: to understand ourselves as change-agents contributing to nothing less than the glorious reinvention of capitalism, and to stay firmly within today's capitalism's comfort zone without essentially changing anything.[14]

---

[12] For an analysis of this factor with regard to the CSV-frame, see Hübscher (2015).

[13] "Few people outside the public-relations industry can listen to the CSR man-tras of "win-win" and "doing well by doing good" without grimacing" (Schumpeter-Blog 2011).

[14] Cf. Hübscher (2015) for comments on Porter's merely apparent emancipation from the neoliberal paradigm of capitalism. Also compart this ironical comment: For "the sake of Mr Porter's brand a good deal depends on the reception of his latest big idea. He claims to have found nothing less than a formula for reinventing capitalism: "shared value". Old-fashioned capitalists focus too narrowly on profits, he argues. Newfangled corporate social responsibility (CSR) types are bewitched by the idea that there is a tension between business and society. But shared value offers companies a way to pursue their self-interest while also acting in the common good. It will unleash a cascade of innovation and productivity gains. And provide capitalism with the popular legitimacy it clearly needs" (Schumpeter-Blog 2011).

9.4 The Poverty of Porterian Axiology

How much value theory do we find in the conceptual management framework of CSV, and what is its theoretical merit? As I already mentioned, in the very opening lines of their paper, Porter and Kramer (2011) promise nothing less than the solution to the legitimation crisis into which the capitalist economic system has plunged. In the light of CSV, the solution is to be expected from (1) strategically disposing creative energies of entrepreneurship to the discovery specifically of "society´s needs and challenges" which are susceptible to being turned into profitable business models that do not already exist, plus (2) consolidating to the maximum all suitable already existing entrepreneurial chains of value creation. When both the innovative and the consolidative impulses converge (as, e.g., in the invention of micro-crediting as a business model in economically undeveloped countries – one of Porter's favorite examples), *economic value* is created in the standard sense of profits that business enterprises doing business under the general imperatives of highly competitive markets are able to realize. Yet at the same time, Porterians suppose, *another kind of surplus value* is created, something valuable "for society", namely "the satisfaction of societal needs". Moreover, still another kind of value is created. Call it the value of *systemic trust* in the capitalist economy: "learning how to create shared value is our best chance to legitimize business again" (Porter and Kramer 2011: 4). If this trifold distinction appears exciting, Porter and Kramer have done a good job in curbing the excitement by failing to elaborate this distinction.

Neglect in elaborating distinctions in talk of values is not incidental. Rather, it is symptomatic for a certain decline in expectations concerning rigorous conceptual elaboration. Business ethicists with long-term memory will not fail to notice an interesting sequence of attenuations in key concepts that each set the tone for some time in the mainstream discourses on ethics. A first wave of business ethics discourse revolved around concepts that were close to common sense morality, such as moral rights, moral obligations, moral ideals and moral rules.[15] Conceptual work of elucidation and elaboration was generally expected from anyone with a claim to expertise in the field of business ethics. And it was fairly easy to deliver.

A second wave shifted emphasis away from clear cut moral concepts to a variegated lot of concepts of responsibility. Note that responsibility tends to have less clear cut normative implications than notions of rights and obligations usually have. Especially theoretical debates about problems of attributions of responsibility that come to nothing (e.g., attributing responsibility for untoward invisible-hand effects of decentralized governance-structures like complex competitive markets, to those structures themselves, or to some actors in particular whose activity contributes to the operation of those structures) attest to a struggle for removing the vagueness that apparently besets attributions of responsibility much more than attributions of normative contents like obligations and rights.

[15] For the best philosophical analysis of common morality, cf. Gert (2005).

At present, we witness a transition to normatively even further diluted and more inscrutable concepts, i.e. concepts of values. When Porterians talk of "shared values" they create an impression as if CSV would open windows in the hard and drab shells of business enterprises so that the rich colors of life-worldly value-orientations could be let in like sunshine and could be absorbed into strategy. However, the only thing happening is a reduction of the richness of life-worldly value-orientations to the hackneyed monotonic calculus of utility, since Porter and Kramer (2011: 6) define their key concept of value narrowly as "benefits relative to costs". CSV, we learn, "is about expanding the total pool of economic and social value" (Porter and Kramer 2011: 5). This may sound like a conception of value with a promising wide range of different relevant values to be taken into account. The just quoted central value-proposition about the axiological import of CSV makes it sound as if business enterprises, by adopting the CSV-frame, will pay much attention to whatever it is that makes their profit-driven business activities more valuable or less valuable to everyone concerned by those business activities. To wit: valuable according to a diversity of value-standards that inhere in all the substantial interests of people across all the different social contexts in which the respective business enterprises pursue their proper business interests and activities.

However, a closer inspection of the CSV-frame reveals that this intention, which we have culled from CSV's central value-proposition by charitable interpretation, is not at all meant to be part of the frame. Within the CSV-frame, all diversity of value is meant to boil down to the conventionally narrow space of value of monetarily measurable business success and growth of productivity.

Let us look into another axiological plunder of the CSV-frame. Consider the term "social value". Taking the notion of social value seriously, one would expect its reference to be to a plethora of values that many people think are important values for many people (e.g. health, wealth, education, good governance, friendship, parenthood, love, peace, harmony). Yet, when Porterians speak of "social value", the term is nothing but an umbrella term for values that fulfill two conditions: Such values do not as yet exist as the value of profit for business (Profitwert), and entrepreneurs should probe their potential to transform these values via suitable business activities into the value of profit for business.

Let me make my objection of axiological reductionism in a slightly different way once again: The plethora of social value becomes entrepreneurially relevant to the extent, and only to the extent, that social values can be transformed into the value of profit for business. This is the unequivocal message of Porter's statement that CSV "is integral to profit maximization" (ibid: 16). That CSV is integral to profit maximization is a claim that may be very reassuring for managers and shareholders alike who, much in the spirit of Milton Friedman's notorious quip about corporate social responsibility, would be loath to hear of management strategies that might go astray from profit-maximization. On the other hand, the claim that CSV is integral to profit maximization reveals a fatal structural conservatism from the point of view of reasonable people who think that profit maximization is a part of many problems in capitalism and not necessarily a part of their solution. Moreover, the claim that CSV is integral to profit maximization flies in the face of the flamboyant rhetoric of *renewing capitalism* that is so dear to Porterians. *Giving profit-maximizing capitalism a new dress* would perhaps be a more appropriate parlance. I think that the observations in this section clearly establish the axiological poverty of "value" within the CSV-frame. In comparison, advanced CSR-discourse is axiologically incomparably richer. For reasons of space, I cannot go into this comparison here.

9.5 The Axiological Achilles' Heel: Quantifying Polyvalues

To be fair to Porter, I hasten to add that he is aware of some of the axiological problems that were pointed out in the previous section. In a collaborated paper "Measuring shared value; how to unlock value by linking social and Business Results", Porter et al (2016) recognize that until there is clear evidence of the impact of the SV proposition (and tools to measure its value) it will be difficult to attract investors.

A recent review of seminar papers on the CSV-frame concludes:

> "There has been little rigorous analysis into the impact of CSV mechanisms, with the majority of evidence existing as standalone case studies of mixed analytical rigor. (…) [M] any of these are highly positive stories combining evidence of increased revenue growth with first hand stories of social impact. However, at least in the course of this research, it was difficult to find a comprehensive and rigorous study into their overall impact." (William and Hayes 2013: 11)

Feel-good stories aside, when it comes to facts and numbers, mere enthusiasm for the CSV-frame does not win the day. Attempts to measure and operationalize value-concepts such as "social impact" frequently boil down to a narrow focus on raise in income, missing wider social dimensions and ignoring potential negatives such as undesirable products becoming more accessible. In the gamut of workshops announced for the 2016 Shared Value Summit, one of the workshops at least registers a certain awareness of the fact that lack of measurement pertaining to value-concepts is a serious deficiency in the SV framework.[16]

If this line of probing (and perhaps remedying) axiological deficits of the CSV-frame were to be pursued further, I think that some comparative analysis would be helpful. After all, similar problems crop up wherever attempts are made to quantify value-concepts, for instance value-concepts such as "social return on investment".

Compare the following typical description of an instrument developed for measuring social return on investment (SROI): An SROI analysis is

---

[16]The respective workshop is entitled "Creating New Measurement Models to Capture Shared Value". Here is how the organizers describe its agenda: "The shared value field is rapidly evolving, and new measurement tools are needed to capture the intersection between shared value strategy, business returns, and social outcomes. Practitioners will share their new measurement models, and participants will explore applications to their own shared value work." http://sharedvalue.org/breakout-labs-shared-value-leadership-summit-2016 (accessed 10.03.2016).

"a participative approach that is able to capture in monetised form the value of a wide range of outcomes, whether these already have a financial value or not. An SROI analysis produces a narrative of how an organisation creates and destroys value in the course of making change in the world, and a ratio that states how much social value (in £) is created for every £1 of investment."[17]

In the stepwise description of the procedure, at step 3 it becomes painfully clear to the philosophical observer that the assignment of monetary value to chosen data is largely arbitrary: Step 3 of the procedure consists in "evidencing outcomes and giving them a value. This stage involves finding data to show whether outcomes have happened and then giving them a monetary value". What, if any, are robust rational constraints on "giving them" a monetary value? One more illustration of the axiological Achilles' heel of conceptual management frames in which value concepts play a crucial role but value theory does not get a hearing: Porter (2011) sets out to answer the intriguing question of what value could mean in the context of health-care but ends up with lamentably lame answers:

"Since value depends on results, not inputs, value in health care is measured by the outcomes achieved, not the volume of services delivered, and shifting focus from volume to value is a central challenge. Nor is value measured by the process of care used; process measurement and improvement are important tactics but are no substitutes for measuring outcomes and costs" (op. cit. 2477)

The take home message of Porter on CSV in the health-care sector is the banal one that measurement is badly needed. But Porter is tellingly silent on the crucial problem of adequate metrics and standards.

9.6 The Conventionality of Porterian Rationality

Beschorner and Hajduk (2015), in Sect. 9.4 of their paper, recover an important point that Lee Preston clear-sightedly made already a long time ago (1975).[18] Preston saw that it is essential for any viable normative and descriptively adequate framework of business ethics that we need a robust theoretical elaboration of the distinction, both descriptive as well as normative, between what counts as (good) business in a society and everything else, i.e. the rest of society.[19]

In the preceding section, we have observed that invested into the CSV-frame is a reductionist business-centric axiological perspective. When we now focus on the business-to-the-rest-of-society-relation as construed within the CSV-frame, we reg-

[17] Cf. http://www.proveandimprove.org/tools/sroi.php (accessed 10.03.2016).

[18] Preston (1975: 446) wrote that "serious analysis of the corporation-society relationship requires rigorous and comprehensive conceptions of both the corporation and society; and these conceptions must be articulated in comparable, or at least translatable, terms". Society "at large might be interested in performance features of the economic system other than the amount of total current output and its distribution" Beschorner (2013).

[19] Authors own wording.

ister a certain *déjà vu*. Focusing on Porter's and Kramer's flimsy characterizations of how business organizations and the rest of society are related, what recurs is a business-centric point of view. Quoting their earlier analysis, Beschorner and Hajduk conclude that Porter and Kramer basically

> "tell the old story of economic rationality as the one and only tool of smart management, with faith in innovation and growth, and they celebrate a capitalism that now needs to adjust a little bit. But there is little chance that an increasingly critical civil society will buy into such a story" (Beschorner and Hajduk 2015: 226).

The way I understand their estimate, the point is that civil society will not buy into such a story because of the cognitive dissonance in the following triple of beliefs contained in the CSV's story of the business-to-the-rest-of-society-relation:

(1) Business organizations are loci of economic rationality.
(2) Renewing capitalism requires the CSV-frame as an enhancer of economic rationality.
(3) Economic rationality has been a major source of capitalism's present legitimation crisis.

Why expect solutions to problems that a certain mode of thinking about rationality has engendered by more of the same mode of thinking?

9.7 A Bit More on Reasons

In an insightful formulation, Scholz and de los Reyes (2015: 195) capture a lot of the factors that are explanatorily relevant for the career of conceptual management frames no matter their theoretical merits. They summarily locate the high attractiveness of the CSV-frame in the "Mantra der grundsätzlichen Vereinbarkeit von gesellschaftlichen und unternehmerischen Interessen".[20] As a matter of fact, cases where societal and entrepreneurial interests *are* successfully reconciled do exist, namely all cases in which interests of both kinds, if one wants to distinguish them in this way at all, do not clash anyway. Any case where business enterprises market truly useful commodities and services at reasonable prices is a case in point. And in the enchanting sense of a "mantra", such "A-cases" (as Porterians call them) can certainly become a source of good reasons that can be publicly shared and thus provide common ground for (re)affirming systemic trust in the capitalist economy. Such reasons for (re)affirming systemic trust in the capitalist economy *can* present commercial society with its competitive market economy as an object that *merits* positive evaluative attitudes, some well-grounded criticisms on balance notwithstanding. Carefully showcasing type A successes may even yield justificatory pro-reasons that are quite convincing for many people if these people should ever happen to come

[20] "Mantra of a fundamental compatibility of societal and entrepreneurial interests" (own translation).

into a position to reflect on capitalism, its content and discontent. Normally, most people are not able or willing or both to engage in this kind of reflection. Normally, capitalism does not encourage the formation of an examined understanding of itself on the part of the majority of the people who stand to inhabit the capitalist form of life. This is an unfortunate fact from the point of view of business ethicists like us, but a fact nonetheless. Recently though, for many people the point of having to reconsider merits and demerits of capitalism was driven home by force in the unfolding of the global financial crisis from 2007 on.

Yet such sceptical reasons can hardly be expected to run up to the strength of pro capitalism reasons that Porterians and kindred unwavering and unflinching zealots of commercial society appear to have when they pronounce as dogma that "capitalism is an unparalleled vehicle for meeting human needs, improving efficiency, creating jobs, and building wealth" (Porter and Kramer 2011: 4). Here, dogmatism replaces reasonable doubt.

I want to conclude this quick dive into the waters of rationality theory with a constructive suggestion. We have seen that for a conceptual management frame that would come even close to addressing at least some of the worries that capitalism's legitimation crisis signifies, it is necessary to underpin such a frame by a both *factually* ("descriptively") adequate and *normatively* significant theoretical framework for making sense of business-to-the-rest-of-society relations without business-centrism. For business-centrism, the rest of society "outside" of the business enterprise is but its environment. In other typical approaches, on the other side of the business enterprise proper we find a variegated lot of stakeholders. On the contrary, for a decentered view, business enterprises are not simply organized *homines economici* but corporate agents that maintain a wealth of non-economic and not strictly economic relations with agents of other kinds within the overall cultural landscape of a society, e.g. political relations. This, by the way, is the main reason why economics properly understood is political economics down to the bottom. And this is of course the point where discourse about corporate citizenship gets a grip on the matter. Porter and Kramer eschew this discourse.

The task of making sense of business in society, and of making sense of the ethics of business within the political ethics of a political community, cannot be bypassed, if capitalism's discontent is to be properly addressed. Nor can this task be shortcut by inserting some scant sentences about business versus society and government into a visionary conceptual management frame, as Porter and Kramer do.

If really "capitalism is under siege" (as Porter/Kramer would have it) and if we really want to (re)open serious thinking about the possibilities, prospects and normative qualifications of "value creation" within the global economic system (as business ethicists should) then the Esperanto of conventional economic rationality and of profit maximization will soon give out. Obviously we need more expressive vocabularies and axiologically richer evaluative discourse, as for instance Elizabeth Anderson has argued already a long time ago (1993). Only if such richer conceptual resources are in place can we begin to clarify in practical and in the end political discourse the complex justificatory question, who (=which actor) can, should, or must connect which determinate normative requirements with which social values (e.g., in the form of CSR requirements). And only along this route can we hope to deepen a warranted, trustworthy and generally acceptable understanding – call it an overlapping rational consensus – about the forms of the social within the forms of the business enterprise and vice versa.

9.8 A Bit More on Discourse

Let me at finally add a more specific remark that, unlike my previous observations, presupposes a background of discourse ethics.[21] The expressively most powerful medium of communication that we have for articulating how we conceive of relations between facts, values, and norms, is the dialogical practice of rational argumentative discourse.[22] In argumentative discourse, we can ask for reasons, can give and explain our reasons, try to understand, endorse or reject, criticize or revise others' reasons and vice versa. Everything that we can express in terms of values, norms, interests, needs, purposes, means and ends, we can also express in terms of better or worse reasons (Kettner 2012). The converse does not hold.

I would be prepared to defend the following position: A discourse about present shortcomings and desirable futures of capitalism, a discourse that would wholeheartedly, unconditionally and without dogmatic centrisms embrace issues of criticism and justification, is what would be required in order to respond meaningfully to "capitalism under siege", i.e. to problems of legitimation and delegitimation within today's forms of capitalism.

My more specific and arguably stronger thesis is, that a good deal of this kind of radical discourse about capitalism would follow lines, and reconsider positions, that have already been helpfully elaborated within the field of CSR discourse.

As to Porterian CSV discourse, I estimate that it would contribute many points to consider. However, it would certainly not provide the contours of the discourse we need.

References

Aakhus, Mark, and Michael Bzdak. 2012. Revisiting the role of "shared value" in the business-society relationship. Business and Professional Ethics Journal 31(2): 231–246.

Anderson, Elizabeth. 1993. *Value in ethics and economics*. Cambridge: Harvard University Press.

[21] I cannot here argue for the plausibility and the advantages of the discourse ethics approach. Cf. Kettner (2003, 2004, 2006, 2011).

[22] The term *"discourse"* has many different meanings. To clarify: I speak of discourse in the context of a philosophical theory of rationality, ethics, and communication. Argumentative discourse, in my sense of the term, "is a social practice, open to all persons in their capacity as reasonable evaluators, which has as its aim the communicatively rational revision of conflicting reasons with (apparently less conflicting) reasons" Kettner 2016).

Beschorner, Thomas. 2013. Creating shared value: The one-trick Pony approach – A comment on Michael Porter and Mark Kramer. *Business Ethics Journal Review* 17(1): 106–112.

Beschorner, Thomas, and Thomas Hajduk. 2015. Creating shared value: Eine Grundsatzkritik. *Zeitschrift für Wirtschafts- und Unternehmensethik (zfwu)* 16(2): 219–230.

Bonini, Sheila, and Jed Emerson. 2005. Maximizing blended value – Building beyond the blended value map to sustainable investing, philanthropy and organizations. Working paper. http://www.blendedvalue.org/wp-content/uploads/2004/02/pdf-max-blendedvalue.pdf. Accessed 01 Feb 2016.

Crane, Andrew, Guido Palazzo, Laura J. Spence, and Dirk Matten. 2014. Contesting the value of 'creating shared value'. *California Management Review* 56(2): 130–149.

Denning, Steve. 2012. What killed Michael Porter's monitor group? The one force that really matters. *Forbes*. http://www.forbes.com/search/post/Porter,%20Monitor/15/All-time/0/. Accessed 01 Jan 2016.

Gert, Bernard. 2005. The definition of morality. *The Stanford Encyclopedia of Philosophy*. http://plato.stanford.edu/entries/morality-definition. Accessed 01 Mar 2016.

Goodman, Nelson. 1978. *Ways of worldmaking*. Indianapolis: Hackett.

Hart, Stuart L. 2005. *Capitalism at the crossroads*. New Jersey: Prentice Hall.

Hübscher, Marc C. 2015. Understanding CSV: Ein neues Narrativ des Kapitalismus? Zur Geschichte der scheinbaren Emanzipation vom neoliberalen Paradigma Milton Friedmans. *Zeitschrift für Wirtschafts- und Unternehmensethik (zfwu)* 16(2): 203–218.

Kettner, Matthias. 2003. Gert's moral theory and discourse ethics. In *Rationality, rules, and ideals. Critical essays on Bernard Gert's moral theory*, ed. Walter Sinnott-Armstrong, and Robert Audi, 31–50. Lanham: Rowman/Littlefield.

———. 2004. Das Spezifikum der Diskursethik ist die vernunftmoralischc Normicrung diskursiver Macht. In *Wirtschaftsethik im philosophischen Diskurs. Begründung und "Anwendung" praktischen Orientierungswissens*, ed. Peter Ulrich, and Markus Breuer, 45–64. Würzburg: Königshausen + Neumann.

———. 2006. Discourse ethics. Apel, Habermas, and beyond. In *Bioethics in cultural contexts. Reflections on methods and finitude*, ed. Christoph Rehmann-Sutter, Marcus Düwell, and Dietmar Mieth, 299–318. Berlin: Springer.

———. 2011. Discourse ethics beyond Apel and Habermas. A realistic relaunch. *Nordicum-Mediteraneum* 6(1). http://hdl.handle.net/1946/14254. Accessed 08 Sept 2016.

———. 2012. Gute Gründe für und in Konzeptionen ökonomischer Rationalität. In *Welt der Gründe. Deutsches Jahrbuch Philosophie*, ed. Julian Nida-Rümelin, and Elif Özmen, 231–245. Hamburg: Felix Meiner.

———. 2015. Creating shared reasons: Von CSV zu CSR+. *Zeitschrift für Wirtschafts- und Unternehmensethik (zfwu)* 16(2): 235–238.

———. 2016. Raising validity claims for reasons. Transcendental reflection in Apel's argumentative discourse. In *Transcendental inquiry: Its history, methods and critiques*, ed. Halla Kim and Steven Hoeltzel. Basingstoke: Palgrave Macmillan (in print).

Liel, Benedikt von, and Christoph Lütge. 2015. Creating Shared Value und seine Erfolgsfaktoren – ein Vergleich mit CSR. *Zeitschrift für Wirtschafts- und Unternehmensethik (zfwu)* 16(2): 182–191.

Morgan, Mary S. 2012. *The world in the model: How economists work and think*. Cambridge: CUP.

Porter, M.E., and M.R. Kramer. 2006. Strategy and society: The link between competitive advantage and corporate social responsibility. *Harvard Business Review* 84(12): 76–89.

———. 2011. Creating shared value. *Harvard Business Review* 89(1/2): 62–77.

Porter, Michael E. 2011. What is value in health care? *New England Journal of Medicine* 363(26): 2477–2481.

Porter, Michael E., Greg Hills, Marc Pfitzer, Sonja Patscheke, and Elisabeth Hawkins. 2016. Measuring shared value. How to unlock value by linking social and business results. FSG Consulting Services. http://sharedvalue.org/sites/default/files/resource-files/Measuring_Shared_Value.pdf. Accessed 10 Mar 2016.

Porter, M.E., and M.R. Kramer. 2014. A response to Andrew Crane et al.'s article. *California Management Review* 56(2): 149–151.
Preston, Lee E. 1975. Corporation and society: The search for a paradigm. *Journal of Economic Literature* 13(2): 434–453.
Scholz, Markus, and Gaston de los Reyes. 2015. Creating shared value – Grenzen und Vorschläge für eine Weiterentwicklung. *Zeitschrift für Wirtschafts- und Unternehmensethik (zfwu)* 16(2): 192–201.
Schumpeter-Blog. 2011. Oh, Mr Porter. The new big idea from business's greatest living guru seems a bit undercooked. *The Economist*. http://www.economist.com/node/18330445. Accessed 10 Mar 2016.
Stewart, Matthew. 2009. *The management myth. Debunking modern business philosophy*. New York: Norton Publishers.
Svensson, Göran, and Greg Wood. 2008. A model of business ethics. *Journal of Business Ethics* 77(3): 303–322.
The Economist. 2008. Guru Michael Porter. http://www.economist.com/node/11848432. Accessed 10 Mar 2016.
Williams, Richard, and Janet Hayes. 2013. Literature review: Seminal papers on 'shared value'. http://partnerplatform.org/?5mar03m5. Accessed 10 Mar 2016.

The manufacturer's authorised representative in the EU is Springer Nature Customer Service Centre GmbH, Europaplatz 3, 69115 Heidelberg, Germany. If you have any concerns regarding our products, please contact ProductSafety@springernature.com

Printed and bound by CPI Group (UK) Ltd, Croydon, CR0 4YY
25/09/2026
02222869-0020